THE
RUSSIAN
WAR
MACHINE
1917-1945

THE
RUSSIAN
WAR
MACHINE
1917-1945

EDITED BY S. L. MAYER

CHARTWELL BOOKS INC.

Published by Chartwell Books Inc., A
Division of Book Sales Inc., 110 Enterprise
Avenue, Secaucus, New Jersey 07094

Copyright © 1977 by Bison Books, London, England

Printed in Japan

ISBN 0–89009–082–3

Library of Congress Catalog
Card Number: 77-71724

JOHN BRADLEY was educated at the
University of Cambridge and is a
specialist in Eastern European affairs.
Author of numerous books, including
*Lidice, La Legion Tschecoslovaque en
Russie, Allied Intervention in Russia,
Czechoslovakia: A History*, and his recent
and much acclaimed *Civil War in
Russia: 1917-20*, Dr. Bradley is Reader
in Government at the University of
Manchester and Visiting Professor in
International Relations at the Uni-
versity of Southern California.

Chapters 1 and 2.

CONTENTS

IAN V. HOGG served in the British Army for 27 years, completing his career with the rank of Master Gunner. Among his many works are *Armies of the American Revolution, The Guns: 1939-45, German Secret Weapons, The Guns of World War II, Artillery, The Guns: 1914-18, German Pistols and Revolvers* and his forthcoming *Infantry Weapons of World War II.* He is one of the world's leading specialists in the study of artillery and small arms.

Chapters 3, 4, 8, 9 and 12.

ANTONY PRESTON was educated at the University of Witwatersrand, South Africa and served on the staff of the National Maritime Museum, Greenwich. Among his many works are *Navies of the American Revolution, Battleships of World War I, Submarines, V and W Destroyers* and his most recent work, *Navies of World War II.* An editor of *Navy International* he is one of the world's foremost specialists in modern naval history.

Chapter 7.

DOUGLAS LEE WELSH was educated at the University of Maryland. He joined US Army Intelligence in 1970 and served in the northern provinces of Vietnam as an adviser with XXIV Corps. He received numerous decorations, including the Bronze Star, Army Air and Commendation medals, and several Vietnamese awards including the Cross of Gallantry. He is now serving with NATO in the 2nd Military Intelligence Battalion, and is working in the Army Reconnaissance Liaison Section between the Army and the USAF.

Chapters 5, 6, 10, 11 and Conclusion.

INTRODUCTION BY S.L. MAYER

It is often said that pride comes before a fall. Those who have challenged the autonomy of the Russian people have fallen hard. Charles XII of Sweden tried to conquer them in the Great Northern War and failed. Napoleon, master of Europe, could not master Kutuzov and his armies or the strength of the Russian will to resist the foreign conqueror. Within two years of his attack on Russia in 1812, Napoleon was in exile and Tsar Alexander I marched with his armies down the boulevards of Paris. The challenge of the 20th century was two-fold. First the Kaiser's armies marched through Russian Poland and by 1917 were penetrating the Baltic provinces and the Ukraine. The government of Tsar Nicholas II, unstable at best, fell around him, and the Russian Revolution began. Its purpose was to drive out the foreign invader and to institute long-needed reforms. In the chaos of German invasion and internal collapse the Bolshevik Party attempted to unite the peoples of Russia once more under their red banner. In the death throes of the Romanov Empire and the birth pangs of Communism arose the weapon which was to strike fear in the hearts of all Europeans: the Russian War Machine.

Facing the dual threat of collapse of their nascent regime and further German penetration, the Bolsheviks under Lenin chose to make peace with the foreigner first in order to create internal stability out of the confusion which swept Russia in the wake of the fall of Tsarism. As the Germans departed after their defeat at the hands of the Western Allies, and the Poles, for a time, replaced them as the Soviets' principal foreign challenger, the new Red Army divided its enemies at home

BELOW: Soviet wartime poster urges the Soviet Army and people to stand firm in defense of their cities and fatherland. Stalin was forced to appeal to nationalism rather than Communism when the Nazis invaded Russia.

BELOW RIGHT: This Soviet cartoon shows Hitler and Mussolini cowering with fear now that the US has joined Britain and Russia in the fight against Fascism. The caption reads: '1942 must become the year of the enemy's final rout'.

BELOW: A crushed Soviet soldier whose body has been run over innumerable times by a column of tanks.

BOTTOM: Horse drawn sleds in the pale dawn of a Russian winter.

LEFT: Leon Trotsky, who organized the Red Army in the Russian Civil War. He was later purged and exiled by Joseph Stalin.

BELOW: An order (and its English translation) issued by Trotsky at the outbreak of fighting in the Civil War after the Bolsheviks seized power in Petrograd and Moscow.

inherited this ramshackle but temporarily effective structure, was determined to eliminate dissidents and build a modern industrialized society whatever the cost. The cost was high and the time was short, for with the onset of the economic Depression in the 1930s the second and most powerful challenge to the autonomy of Russia was taking shape in the West: Nazi Germany.

If the horrific purges of the 1930s, which followed logically on the purge of the Party of Trotskyite heretics, had any justification, it was this: the 'disappearance' of millions of *kulaks* (independent peasant farmers), the terror of midnight confessions through torture, the incarceration of millions more in labor camps, most of whom never returned to their homes—all of these brought an enforced unity to the Russian people when they needed it most. Hitler hoped to make Russia into a giant colony for the Germanic peoples, with the Slavs reduced to servitude or robot-like obedience to his racist will. Stalin knew that only

through total unity could the Russian people survive total war. Only through the omnipotence of the State and his dominance over it could Russia be industrialized quickly enough to withstand its greatest foreign challenger. The cost in human dignity was high, but the Nazi menace was greater. But with all these sacrifices the Soviet Union stood unready to meet the Nazi challenge when it came all too quickly. Japan and Finland proved that Stalin was right in making his 'deal' with Hitler in August 1939. The Russian Army, purged of its experience and leadership, was weak, but it was united. The time had come for Stalin to rapidly create the greatest weapon ever placed in the hands of a totalitarian dictator: the Russian War Machine.

Its exploits were monumental; its heroism unquestioned; its weapons, like the T-34 tank, modern and formidable; the unity of the people behind it hard as steel; and the determination of those people to undergo suffering almost beyond endurance was undaunted and

and overwhelmed them one by one. The Allied intervention to help anti-Bolshevik forces dropped its clients as the Red Army established control throughout the Soviet Union. The Soviet state survived, and the Army and the Party were the state.

Despite ideological absurdities and harmful, though brief innovations which weakened Party and Army discipline, Trotsky and Lenin created a powerful party structure behind the guns of the Red Army. Stalin, who

---

РАЙОННЫМЪ
Совѣтамъ Рабочихъ Депутатовъ
Фабрично-Заводскимъ Комитетамъ

ПРИКАЗЪ.

Корниловскія банды Керенскаго угрожаютъ подступамъ къ столицѣ. Отданы всѣ необходимыя распоряженія для того, чтобы безпощадно раздавить контръ-революціонное покушеніе противъ народа и его завоеваній.

Армія и Красная Гвардія революціи нуждаются въ немедленной поддержкѣ рабочихъ.

Приказываемъ районнымъ Совѣтамъ и фабр.зав. комитетамъ:

1) выдвинуть наибольшее количество рабочихъ для рытья окоповъ, воздвиганія баррикадъ и укрѣпленія проволочныхъ загражденій;

2) гдѣ для этого потребуется прекращеніе работъ на фабрикахъ и заводахъ, немедленно исполнить;

3) собрать всю имѣющуюся въ запасѣ колючую и простую проволоку, а равно всѣ орудія, необходимыя для рытья окоповъ и возведенія баррикадъ;

4) все имѣющееся оружіе имѣть при себѣ;

5) соблюдать строжайшую дисциплину и быть готовыми поддержать армію революціи всѣми средствами.

Предсѣдатель Петроградскаго Совѣта Раб. и Солд. Депутатовъ
Народный Комиссаръ ЛЕВЪ ТРОЦКІЙ.

Предсѣдатель Военно-Революціоннаго Комитета
Главнокомандующій ПОДВОЙСКІЙ.

TO THE DISTRICT
SOVIETS OF WORKER'S DEPUTIES AND SHOP-FACTORY COMMITTEES

ORDER

THE KORNILOV BANDS OF KERENSKY ARE THREATENING THE OUTSKIRTS OF OUR CAPITAL. ALL NECESSARY ORDERS HAVE BEEN GIVEN TO CRUSH MERCILESSLY EVERY COUNTER-REVOLUTIONARY ATTEMPT AGAINST THE PEOPLE AND ITS CONQUESTS.

THE ARMY AND THE RED GUARD OF THE REVOLUTION ARE IN NEED OF IMMEDIATE SUPPORT OF THE WORKERS.

THE DISTRICT SOVIETS AND SHOP-FACTORY COMMITTEES ARE ORDERED:

1) To bring forward the largest possible number of workers to dig trenches, erect barricades and set up wire defenses;

2) Wherever necessary for this purpose to SUSPEND WORK in shops and factories, it must be done IMMEDIATELY.

3) To collect all available plain and barbed wire, as well as all tools FOR DIGGING TRENCHES AND ERECTING BARRICADES;

4) ALL AVAILABLE ARMS TO BE CARRIED ON PERSONS;

5) Strictest discipline must be preserved and all must be ready to support the Army of the Revolution to the utmost.

President of the Petrograd Soviet of Workers & Soldiers Deputies
People's Commissar LEV TROTSKY.

President of the Military-Revolutionary Committee
Chief Commander PODVOISKY.

BELOW: Soviet troops in winter gear move through a Moscow suburb on the way to the front a few miles distant in December 1941.

steadfast. This is the story of the Russian War Machine, in all its terror and magnificence, which in the hands of an utterly cold and heartless tyrant became more than a defender of the soil of Russia in the tradition of earlier despots. The war machine which he created became the dominant power on the Continent of Europe and the spearhead of modern Russian imperialism carrying the hammer and sickle as its icon.

Today, more than three decades after its magnificent victory over Germany, the Russian War Machine is a dominant force in the world. Its ships ply the waters of every ocean; its planes and missiles hold the world to ransom; its troops stand in Central Europe, the Pacific, in the Middle East, southern Africa and the Americas. A great defensive weapon has gone on the march.

How this weapon was forged, how the Russian War Machine was built, is discussed here by four noted historians and students of military and naval affairs. Each has seen the danger of Russian weaponry and imperial power first hand. The birth and development of the greatest military power in Europe is the story of the 20th century. Those who tend to belittle Russian strength and to vainly over-estimate their own power in comparison with this military colossus will suffer the same fate as Hitler and Napoleon. The 25 millions of Russians who died in the Second World War, and the nameless tens of millions who died forgotten in Soviet concentration camps bear silent testimony to the struggle for autonomy of the Russian people, a dream which has become an unending nightmare for those whose lives have been touched by the terror of the Russian War Machine.

THE FIRST RED ARMY

The Bolsheviks inherited the old Imperial Army when they seized power on 7 November 1917 in Petrograd. Since they controlled the administrative center of the country and claimed to be the central government, their claim extended to the army in the field for Russia was still at war. They claimed all its reserves and administrative regions as well. In fact, at least to start with, the Bolsheviks controlled only a few units of the Imperial Army and their own militia forces, the Red Guards.

The army units which did acknowledge Bolshevik authority were so little trusted that Lenin personally insisted on the formation of shock units consisting mainly of Baltic sailors who had proved themselves in the Petrograd coup. These shock units, and not the useless Red Guards, were sent out into provinces either to take them over militarily, or help the local Bolsheviks in their attempts at taking power. Thus in Moscow, the arrival of these shock units tilted the balance of power in favor of the local Bolsheviks, who had to fight hard with the loyalists for power. This story was repeated in many provinces and cities all over Russia; the demoralized units of the Imperial Army led by their officers wanted to prevent the Bolsheviks from seizing power, but were beaten to it by the local Bolshevik forces and the shock troops sent from the center.

In these initial days of Bolshevik rule it is difficult to define the Red Army. To all practical purposes it consisted of the Red Guards, any army units which professed their loyalty to the Bolshevik government, and the shock troops which did the actual fighting on behalf of the Bolsheviks. Despite this lack of cohesion, command and organization Bolshevik power gradually spread. By March 1918 Lenin and the Bolshevik Party through this incredible army controlled the greater part of what used to be the Russian Empire. Lenin and the Bolsheviks quite rightly concentrated on this political-military takeover; others immediately began to plan a new army.

As soon as it became clear that the Russian armies in the field were neutralized and ceased to constitute a danger to the new regime, the Bolsheviks found it necessary to reconstruct the armed forces. They had two basic reasons for doing so: the Great War continued and another German offensive seemed pos-

sible; and anti-Bolshevik forces began to get organized and the Bolsheviks felt compelled to defend their revolution. At first, after Ensign Krylenko, (C-in-C appointed by Lenin) had taken over the Stavka (General HQ of the field armies) in November 1917, the Bolsheviks thought that they could salvage the old Imperial Army and make good use of it. Colonel Daller proposed to split the army into the border guards and internal militia forces. However, Bolshevik politicians had other ideas. Kedrov wanted to form 'Socialist guards', based on industrial districts from which peasants would be excluded. On 16 December 1917 Krylenko, the Generalissimo, produced his own ideas on the subject in a memorandum to the Bolshevik leaders, and they subsequently became the basis of Bolshevik military policies.

On 28 December 1917 Lenin attended the congress of demobilization to clear up his own mind, but while various plans were discussed and a complete demobilization urged, mass desertions from the front made the discussions superfluous. In the end the demobilization congress voted overwhelmingly for the dissolution of the old army, and Lenin requested 'revolutionary' units and the sailors, his shock units, to hold the front line wherever possible, while organized demobilization was completed. On 29 December 1917 all the ranks of the old army were abolished, and a decision in principle was made to organize a new Red Army through the Stavka and the All-Russian College for the Formation of the Red Army. At the same time Lenin set up the Supreme Military Soviet which helped with the organization of the Red Army in the rear, while the Stavka organized units on the fronts. The Soviet also took over some of the functions of the former, now dissolved War Ministry. Thus early in 1918 the Bolsheviks had all the administrative machinery ready for the re-formation of their armed forces.

Early in January 1918 various city Soviets, such as Petrograd, Moscow, Ivanovo, Kazan and Saratov, discussed the problem of the new armed forces and urged Lenin and the Bolshevik leadership to re-establish them. Lenin could see their point and the need, but still continued to discuss the new army, especially at the Congress of Soldiers' Soviets on 28 January 1918. These

discussions probably finally helped him to make up his mind, and immediately after the congress he personally drafted a decree establishing the Red Army. On 14 February 1918 it was approved by the Central Soviet Executive Committee and became effective immediately.

As if in anticipation of the decree, on 1 February 1918. K. S. Yeremeyev, member of the College of the Red Army, began to organize his 1st Army Corps in Petrograd; some 10,000 men of this Corps were subsequently sent to the front. After the decree had become law army corps were organized all over the territory controlled by the Bolsheviks. Many old units were incorporated in the Red Army *en masse*, as for example, the 5th Zaamur Division, the 12th Finnish Rifle Division, the Latvian Rifle Division and the 45th Infantry Division. The organization of the Red Army proceeded most energetically, although the recruitment for it was on a voluntary basis. Another member of the Military College, T. I. Ulyantsov, began to reorganize the fleet.

It is obvious that the organization of the Red Army was not sufficiently advanced when, on 20 February 1918, the Germans renewed their offensive on the Eastern Front in retaliation for the Bolshevik refusal to sign the peace treaty at Brest-Litovsk. The young Red Army completely collapsed in face of the disciplined enemy armies and Red units imitated the 'irregulars' (Russia was honeycombed with 'private' armies)

and dissolved themselves. On 21 February 1918 Lenin asked Sverdlov to form yet another military organ, the Committee of Revolutionary Defense, to speed up the formation of efficient army units capable of resistance to the advancing Germans. But this supplementary call-up, though stiffened with party members, proved disappointing, and with all the enthusiasm in the world it failed completely even to slow down the German advance.

The Bolsheviks certainly learned from this early experience. On 28 March 1918 Lenin personally made sure that the Red Army came under central command without elective officers: former Tsarist officers were recruited and employed as military specialists. To make sure of their loyalty and also in order to keep political control Lenin imposed dual command on the Red Army: military specialists were checked by and could do nothing without the *politruks*, their political counterparts. Political control was applied at all levels in the Red Army from the Stavka to the smallest unit in the field, and at the top it was exercised by Lenin, Sverdlov, Trotsky, Stalin or Ordjonikidze; and on the battlefield by the local political commissars. Bolshevik political leadership reserved all the important decisions for itself, especially during the frequent crises, and remained in effective control of the Red Army throughout the Civil War. It became therefore, in contradistinction to the Whites (anti-Bolshe-

FAR LEFT: The center of Kronstadt, where the sailors rebelled in support of the Bolsheviks in 1917.

CENTER LEFT: The Nevsky Prospect, a principal boulevard in Petrograd, on the second day of the March coup. Sniper fire from a nearby window scattered people in all directions.

LEFT: The public reads news sheets issued by the Duma after the March Revolution in Petrograd

BELOW: Bolsheviks address a throng of soldiers and workers gathered in Petrograd's Palace Square after the November coup d'état.

BELOW: The public runs
from machine gun fire on
the Nevsky Prospect in
Petrograd during the
Bolshevik take-over in
November 1917. A
number of people did not
escape.

viks), the real organizer of victory in the Civil War.

After the conclusion of the Peace of Brest-Litovsk many military organizations, including Svedlov's committee, were dissolved, and on 8 May 1918 Soviet Russia had re-established the Army General Staff, though at this stage it only had partisan units under its 'command', which, of course, was a purely formal notion. In the Ukraine these partisan units were led by Kikvidze, Voroshilov, Rudnak, Sivers, Kotovsky and Primakov. Reorganization of the Red Army was resumed only after the German advance had stopped. Trotsky became War Minister (People's Commissar of War Affairs); Major-General Bonch-Bruyevich, Lenin's friend, was the new COS, and General Suleyma QMG. Five fronts were established: the Northern, Western, Ukrainian, Southern (Don) and Eastern, and front HQs were also set up. Although some armies had only 3000 men the organizational machine was ready and the Bolsheviks were therefore able to

fight a civil war when it broke out in earnest late in May 1918.

When we deal with the Civil War 1918–1920, it would be easy, though inaccurate, to say that the Bolsheviks and the Red Army were superior to their White opponents and therefore won the war. The Red Army was obviously better prepared, more organized and better led politically: still none of these factors fully substantiates the assumption of Red superiority. An attempt will be made to isolate a few of the more decisive factors which operated in favor of the Bolsheviks and enabled them to emerge victorious from the struggle.

From the very beginning, November 1917, the Bolsheviks had one significant factor favoring them: they seized power by design in the Imperial capital, Petrograd, and succeeded in consolidating their power in the central regions of Russia. It is equally significant to note that in practically all the border areas, Bolshevik attempts at imposing their power had collapsed

under the slightest show of opposition. Moreover, these border areas were largely inhabited by dissident nationalities, which instead of being interested in retaking power in Russia, preferred to leave the Russian Empire and become independent states. Thus because of the victory by the Bolsheviks in the central Russian regions, all the opposing Russians, the Whites, had to build up their bases of resistance to the Bolsheviks in these largely non-Russian territories.

Therefore politically and demographically the Bolshevik central position was undoubtedly of tremendous importance, and it was meant to be so. The two capitals, Petrograd and Moscow, and the regions between them, practically dominated the whole of Russia. What was even more important, the Bolsheviks had time to establish themselves firmly in these central regions before the Civil War started, and consequently fought the Civil War from well-prepared defense positions, which made their tasks much easier

compared to the Whites, who invariably had to attack.

Thus the Reds controlled the central mass of Russia which was thickly populated and contained most of the large cities and industry as well as fertile agricultural land, while the Whites were invariably perched in non-Russian regions with local separatist element operating strongly against them. In the South the Caucasian peoples—the Georgians, Armenians, and others—aimed at achieving independence and as a consequence damaged the White cause. Apart from these independent nationalities, the Whites had also the problem of the autonomists, that is, people who were either ethnically Russian or not, who for various reasons desired greater autonomy. They also weakened the White movement, and perhaps even more fatally than the independent nationalities who never fought in the ranks of the Whites: the autonomists' morale tended to collapse during the decisive battles of the Civil War.

The Bolsheviks benefited from certain economic advantages as well. The Petrograd and Moscow regions were also the most heavily industrialized, which made the Bolsheviks less vitally dependent on foreign aid, which in any case no one offered them. It is true that the Whites conquered the Donets and Ekaterinburg (Urals) industrial regions, but they found them devastated and disorganized. They failed to reorganize them and controlled them for too short a time to gain any appreciable advantage. Tactically it was probably easier to defend central Russia, although the Bolsheviks had to face problems similar to the Whites, except perhaps on a smaller scale: local nationalities in revolt, peasant uprisings and conspiracies. In contrast to the Whites the Red Bolsheviks could afford to treat these problems differently. From the beginning Lenin and the Bolsheviks rejected Russian Imperialism and preached federalism in the future, never mentioning the reconstitution of Imperial Russia. They never

employed national forces of their allies in battles and operations which could have resulted in decisive Red defeat and would have brought about their allies' autonomy or independence. Nationalities fought in the Red Army as auxiliaries who, as a result of Red victories, came to power in their regions and provinces within the future Federal Union of the Soviets. With the exception of Red Ukrainians and Red Don Cossacks who also fought at home, the Bolsheviks preferred their Kirghiz cavalry to fight in the Ukraine and Poland, the Chinese units as security forces in predominantly Russian units, the Latvians in the Volga region, the dissident Caucasians in the South against Denikin etc. Hence the Bolsheviks had much less trouble with nationalist dissidents and made better use of them militarily. Though various peasant rebellions and revolts caused the Bolsheviks considerable headaches and tactical defeats, they never allowed them to spread and disrupt their rear; when negotiations failed, sharp, de-

Ко всѣмъ рабочимъ
ПЕТРОГРАДА!

Товарищи! Революція побѣждаетъ—революція побѣдила. Вся власть перешла къ нашимъ Совѣтамъ. Первыя недѣли самыя трудныя. Надо раздавить до конца сломленную уже реакцію, надо обезпечить полное торжество нашимъ стремленіямъ. Рабочій классъ долженъ, обязанъ проявить въ эти дни **величайшую выдержку и выносливость,** чтобы облегчить Новому Народному Правительству Совѣтовъ выполненіе всѣхъ задачъ. На этихъ же дняхъ будутъ изданы новые законы по рабочему вопросу и въ томъ числѣ одинъ изъ самыхъ первыхъ законъ о рабочемъ контролѣ надъ производствомъ и объ регулированіи промышленности.

Забастовки и выступленія рабочихъ массъ въ Петроградѣ теперь только вредятъ.

Мы просимъ васъ немедленно прекратить всѣ экономическія и политическія забастовки, всѣмъ стать на работу и производить ее въ полномъ порядкѣ. Работа на заводахъ и во всѣхъ предпріятіяхъ необходима новому правительству Совѣтовъ, потому что всякое разстройство работы создаетъ для васъ новыя затрудненія, которыхъ и безъ того довольно. Всѣ къ своему мѣсту.

Лучшее средство поддержать новое правительство Совѣтовъ въ эти дни—исполнять свое дѣло.

Да здравствуетъ твердыя выдержки пролетаріата! Да здравствуетъ революція!

Петроградскій Совѣтъ Р. и С. Д.
Петроградскій Совѣтъ Профессіональныхъ Союзовъ.
Центральный Совѣтъ Фабрично-Заводскихъ Комитетовъ.

302

TO ALL WORKERS
OF PETROGRAD!

Comrades! The Revolution is winning, the Revolution has won. All the power has passed over to our Soviets. The first weeks are the most difficult ones. The broken reaction must be finally crushed, a full triumph must be secured for our endeavors. The working-class ought to —must—show in these days

THE GREATEST FIRMNESS AND ENDURANCE

in order to facilitate the execution of all the aims of the new People's Government of Soviets. In the next few days, decrees on the Labor question will be issued. Among the very first will be the decree on Worker's Control over the production and regulation of industry.

STRIKES AND DEMONSTRATIONS OF THE WORKER MASSES IN PETROGRAD NOW CAN ONLY DO HARM.

We ask you to stop immediately all economic and political strikes, to take up your work, and do it in perfect order. The work in factories and all industries is necessary for the new Government of Soviets, because any interruption of this work will only create new difficulties, and we have enough as it is. All to your places.

The best way to support the new Government of Soviets in these days—is by doing your job.

LONG LIVE THE IRON TENACITY OF THE PROLETARIAT!
LONG LIVE THE REVOLUTION!

Petrograd Soviet of W. & S. D.
Petrograd Council of Trade Unions.
Central Council of Factory-Shop Committees.

303

BELOW: Meeting in the grenadiers' barracks in Petrograd in November 1917. Gaining control of at least significant portions of the military was a primary aim of the Bolsheviks.

BELOW RIGHT: A crowd assembles outside the Duma during the November Revolution.

BOTTOM RIGHT: Alexander Kerensky (left) takes the salute during his brief period of power in the summer of 1917. Kerensky was unable to create sufficient stability of government nor victories against the Kaiser's armies to remain in power long.

RIGHT: A tram is taken over by Communist supporters in Moscow and is used as a barricade during street fighting in November 1917.

OVERLEAF: Recruits for the Red Guard to defend the Bolshevik coup are assembled in a Petrograd factory.

cisive counter-measures, usually carried by para-military Cheka detachments or Chinese units, proved extremely efficient.

Thus tactically and strategically the Red Armies had certain advantages before the outset of the Civil War; organizationally, however, the Reds were considered inferior. It is argued that the Imperial officers backed the Whites so overwhelmingly that they must have created a superior White Army in terms of organization, training and supplies. The Red Army certainly did not lag far behind. Perhaps paradoxically, the Reds developed and retained the best aspects of the defunct Imperial Army. Thus the Red Army, created by political amateurs, inherited the Imperial Army's administration, barracks and depots. The Red Army also proved itself most methodical and strictly enforced mobilization orders and thereby appeared invariably more successful than their opponents in this respect. In May 1918 the Red Army consisted of some 306,000 men, while in December 1920, at the end of the Civil War, the command and administrative staff alone amounted to 446,729. In fact between May 1918 and October 1920 the Bolsheviks succeeded in mobilizing some 5,498,000 men. Naturally most of the Bolshevik recruits never saw active service: 2,587,000 served in reserve armies and 391,000 in labor units. However, 1,780,000 men were drawing military rations in the Red Army and at least 800,000 of them were actual combatants. This tremend-

ous achievement was due to the closest organizations and without this the Bolsheviks would have lapsed into the same chaos as the Whites, with their recruits turning instantly into deserters, and subsequently into dangerous partisans.

Leon D. Trotsky, as Commissar for War, was primarily responsible for the organization of the Red Army, and to make his army really effective he was forced to discard many of the revolutionary innovations dating back to March 1917, which he had then approved with so much enthusiasm. His Red Army officers were no longer elected by their men, but appointed by himself: their authority was largely restored. Necessarily Trotsky had to appoint a large number of former Imperial officers to command his army, and to control them politically of 1917, the duality of command. A Bolshevik political commissar (*politruk*) was attached to all Red Army units, from company to regiment, division to corps and army level, up to the field command, the last being the replacement for the old general staff. Thus the Red Army not only had the ordinary structure of command, but was also subject to control by the Bolshevik (Communist) Party. To make this control real the Communist Party stiffened all units with its own members. This stiffening of the army by Bolshevik cadres and the efficient use of security forces, the Cheka, was largely responsible for keeping the Red Army together, at least until the end of the Civil

War. Moreover, to retain the loyalty of the former Imperial officers Trotsky instituted a system of hostages, which might have been barbarous, but was nevertheless effective: for treason or desertion an officer's family was executed instead. Thus the Reds did on the whole succeed in forcing Imperial officers, called specialists (*spets*), to fight for their cause. However, despite these draconian measures many an officer did desert and betray the Bolsheviks; men also mutinied, some newly-formed units refused to go into battles, and others left the front without permission. Still the scale of desertions and betrayal was not comparable to that of the Whites. In any case in such occurrences of indiscipline Trotsky did not hesitate to apply the supreme punishment to all and sundry. Summary courts martial were kept busy and the Chinese internationalist units, reserved for security tasks, carried out executions by firing squad continuously. At least once Trotsky himself took part in a summary execution; on 19 August 1918, in order to stop the Red Army's precipitate retreat from Kazan, he ordered executions of every twelfth man in a regiment which was running away from the battlefield. In this instance the executions included regimental commissars — Bolshevik Party members, which raised quite a lot of eyebrows within the Communist Party. In contrast, there were very few instances of such determination and ruthlessness within the White armies, but it was this merciless terror as well as

intelligent organization that had kept the Red Army in the field fighting under Trotsky and the field command.

Although the Communist Party disliked the idea of reconstituting the general staff and general headquarters (Stavka), [or field command], it was forced into setting up one, as the fighting on the various Civil War fronts had to be coordinated. At the early stage of the Civil War the Supreme Military Soviet, whose chairman was Trotsky, and whose deputies were Podvoysky, Sklyansky and Danishevsky, all experienced soldiers, had acted as a command center. However, in April 1918 the All-Russian Supreme Staff had to be set up to deal with the worsening military situation. Still later the Republican Revolutionary Military Soviet was formed and became the top political council of war with Trotsky as chairman, and Sklyansky, I. N. Smirnov, Rosengolts, Raskolnikov, Muralov and Yurenev as leading members. This body then appointed the ex-Imperial Colonel, Vatsetis, then commander of the Latvian Rifle Division, as Commander-in-Chief of the Red Army, and Vatsetis collected his field staff which became the nucleus of the general staff. He selected other Imperial Colonels, B. Shaposhnikov and P. P. Lebediev, for his Stavka, and they became responsible for operations, planning and coordination of the five Red Armies and five fronts then in existence.

After the formation of the field staff, when real military operations were re-established, Trotsky, a political

amateur himself, had to dismiss most of the self-appointed Bolshevik commanders, who proved unable to carry out military orders or conduct military operations. Their places were taken up by the spets-Imperial officers, and the Red Army's generalship began to measure up to the Whites. On the Eastern Front, where five Red Armies were concentrated, the overall command fell to the former Imperial colonel, S. S. Kamenev, who proved himself so effective that he subsequently replaced Colonel Vatsetis as C-in-C, a post which was clearly above the intellectual capacity of the latter. Of the five armies fighting in the East, [that is in the Volga and Urals regions] and subsequently in Siberia and Turkestan, three were commanded by ex-Imperial officers: 1st by Lieutenant Tukhachevsky, 2nd by Colonel Shorin and 4th by General Baltiysky and later Colonel Khvesin; one by an ex-Imperial NCO (3rd, by Lashevich); only Blyumberg, in command of the 5th Red Army, was a Bolshevik commander without a background in the Imperial Army. Although 'wild' Bolshevik commanders (called partisans) had been eliminated, the operational performance of the Red commanders varied widely. In December 1918 Admiral Kolchak's conquest of Perm proved to be one of the greatest disasters suffered by the Red Army, despite Commissar Gusev, who had kept a close eye on this front. The 4th Red Army had to be re-organized altogether and Gusev proposed for its new commander not a professional soldier, but a Bolshevik intellectual, M. V. Frunze, which turned out to be an excellent choice, and the 4th Army soon redeemed its tarnished reputation. Still it was Admiral Kolchak's White Armies which struck first in the spring of 1919; initially they again split the Red fronts wide open, forcing the Red Armies to retreat. In these conditions the relations between the field command and the Eastern Front became strained and the Red Army lived through the first crisis of command.

Trotsky left Moscow to supervise operations on the Eastern Front in person. Inevitably command reshuffle followed: Frunze took over the command of the Turkestan Army, but also retained the 4th: G. D. Gai became the commander of the 1st, Shorin of the 2nd, Mezheninov of the 3rd and Tukhachevsky of the 5th. Frunze also formed a separate Revvoyensoviet for his southern group of armies and placed V. V. Kuybyshev on it as his commissar. On 28 April 1919 the re-organized Red armies went into action and completely out-fought and out-generalled the White armies.

Even while victorious and advancing the Red Army went through a series of crises, which invariably resulted in changes in operations and personnel. Vatsetis, who insisted on directing the operations on the Eastern Front, transferred Colonel Kamenev, who persistently opposed him, to the Northern Front, and put the Northern Front commander, General A. A. Samoilo, in his place. The new commander, however, hesitated too long, changed his orders for a general offensive several times, and after objections from army and political leaders he was sent back North and Kamenev was restored to his previous command. All these moves and power struggles went on while the Red Army was fighting one of its most important battles and success came despite the trouble. This was mainly due to the excellent performance of the Red Army on the divisional level: hard fighting continued unabated with capable commanders and commissars, such as Kashirin, Mamontov, Zhigalin, I. N. Smirnov and others, scoring great victories.

As a result of the political struggle on the Eastern Front Trotsky registered the first political defeat in his career as Commissar for War. Through his nominee, Vatsetis, he was in fact responsible for all the changes in the East, and since they all proved rather unfortunate Trotsky's political opponents had a pretext for censoring the arrogant commissar. Stalin, Gusev, Kuy-

byshev and others finally persuaded Lenin that Trotsky had to be checked, and their proposals were accepted and implemented. These proposals entailed the sacking of the Commander-in-Chief, Vatsetis, and his replacement by Kamenev; they also contained the continuation of offensive activity on the Eastern Front, while the old command favored a halt to operations and concentration in the South against General Denikin and his White Armies. By July 1919 Trotsky had to yield on all points and even saw his Republican Revvoensoviet reorganized and his personal enemies, Gusev, Smilga, Rykov and Kamenev, added to it. Still the Eastern Front gamble came off and Western Siberia was overrun. By then, however, Trotsky and the new high command had to concentrate their attention on the Southern Front, where the military situation deteriorated with incredible rapidity late in 1919.

While early in 1919 the Bolsheviks concentrated all their military power in the East, they only really had the 10th Red Army in the south facing the Don Cossacks and General Denikin. The men who led this army were quite bizarre characters and it was with them that the Caucasian Bolshevik, Stalin, struck up a friendship, after interrupting his original mission of procuring food supplies for his native Caucasus. The local commander was the ex-Imperial NCO, Voroshilov, with ex-tailor Shchadenko as commissar and local orator Minin thrown in. It quickly became obvious that instead of conducting military operations, this new-style leadership of the Red Army at Tsaritsyn (later called Stalingrad, and still later Volgograd) indulged in card playing and vituperative denunciations of Trotsky and the field command. They certainly aroused antagonism and in the end Trotsky succeeded in dispersing them: Stalin was transferred elsewhere and even Voroshilov had to leave the Tsaritsyn army for the Ukraine. But even then Trotsky's problems in the South were not solved,

FAR LEFT: Podvoysky addressing Red officer trainees in 1918. He was one of the leaders of the Bolshevik coup in Petrograd.

CENTER LEFT: Podvoysky speaking to a Red regiment near Kazan on the Volga in 1918. At this stage of the Civil War the Bolsheviks were fighting for their very existence.

LEFT: Podvoysky with a group of Red commanders at Tver in 1918. Note that some of them are still in Tsarist uniforms.

RIGHT: Podvoysky parades through Kursk in the summer of 1918. The Czech legions came through the area subsequently.

for suddenly General Denikin struck against the 9th Red Army in May 1919 and scattered it: Vsevolod, the commander, preferred to join the Whites, and Trotsky once again found himself in disagreement with Kamenev as to how the Southern crisis should be tackled. Kamenev favored a drive into the Don region and another drive along the Volga to prevent a Denikin-Kolchak junction. He hoped that this dual maneuver against the Whites would destroy their bases in the Don and the Kuban and thus knock them out of the conflict. However, the Kamenev plan meant that the 10th Red Army would be given top operational tasks and Trotsky had not yet forgotten his quarrels with Stalin and Voroshilov about this army. He was reluctant to favor such a troublesome army with such important operations and also objected to the proposals coming from Kamenev, with whom he was not on the best of terms although he was the C-in-C. In the end he had to compromise: he appointed V. N. Yegorov, his man to command in the South and carry out the Kamenev plan. The result was not brilliant. The 9th and 10th Red Army Commander, Shorin and Selivachev, failed to achieve the objectives of the Kamenev plan, and both Trotsky and Kamenev had grounds to complain about each other. When in turn the Whites struck back and their cavalry tactics proved particularly effective in the struggle, it became clear that Trotsky and Kamenev would have to settle their differences, re-organize the Red Armies and employ the same army to check the Whites. Despite this dire necessity Trotsky continued to oppose the development of Red cavalry, for once again the two Don Cossacks, Dumenko and Budyonny, who had initially organized it, were friends of Stalin and Voroshilov, and Trotsky was prepared to forego this significant innovation in the Civil War.

It is curious to see that the organization of the Red cavalry, whose significance vastly increased with Denikin's

breakthrough, was hindered because of bad personal relations. Budyonny, ex-Imperial NCO who took over the Red cavalry corps from Dumenko after he had fallen ill, was Voroshilov's friend and was therefore detested and underestimated by Trotsky who continued to oppose it even when it became clear that it was a tactical weapon of immense importance.

After November 1918 the Red cavalry was re-equipped and began to be used against the Cossack cavalry of the Whites. Ultimately, the 'professional' soldiers came from this arm and a little paradoxically, it produced practically all the outstanding future military leaders: Marshals Timoshenko, Zhukov and Rokossovsky. More immediately it became a counter to the White cavalry forces led by Generals Mamontov and Shkuro, who, with their raids into the Red rear, were creating a particularly heavy havoc there. Although the deployment of the Red cavalry meant the complete abandonment of the Kamenev plan and the re-adoption of Trotsky's original proposal, both Kamenev and Trotsky were now ready to compromise. The Whites were at Oryol and Voronezh, in dangerous proximity to Moscow, and another cavalry raid could have caused a complete collapse of the Red Army. The Southern Front was therefore split into two groups of armies placed under Yegorov and Shorin: they were to strike simultaneously to the northwest of Oryol and east of Voronezh. Budyonny and his cavalry had to defeat Mamontov's cavalry and then drive a wedge between Denikin's Volunteers and the Don Cossack armies. In November 1919, when this offensive was finally launched, it was carried out with dispatch, the cavalry deciding most of the battles. With Mamontov's defeat Budyonny's raids caused in turn panic in the White rear and the White armies fell rapidly back to Rostov, their original base. In December 1919 Budyonny's cavalry corps became the 1st Red Cavalry Army with a separate

Revvoysoviet, which comprised not only of Voroshilov and Shchadenko but also Stalin. The Red Cavalry continued its triumphant advance leaving the 8th, 9th and 10th Red Armies behind, until it reached the Bataisk Heights south of Rostov, which were heavily invested with Don Cossack cavalry and the rest of Denikin's artillery. This was the Whites' last stand to protect their Kuban base and bar the Reds from the northern Caucasus. Shorin, the new commander in the South, ordered Budyonny to attack these prepared positions frontally and the Red cavalry experienced its first defeat in battle. Still Shorin persisted and refused Budyonny to take the heights from behind: this was another military-political deadlock. In the end a political intervention and command reshuffle resolved it. Tukhachevsky, recently transferred south from Siberia, assumed command, and with his Commissar S. Ordjonikidze, finally permitted Budyonny to take the heights his way: the fate of the Whites was sealed. They withdrew to the Crimea while the Red Armies conquered the Kuban and North Caucasus.

It was logical for the Reds to turn onto the Crimea and liquidate this last remaining base of the Whites in European Russia. However the Red politicians suddenly became involved with Poland and the Red Armies were forced to deal with this 'external' enemy first. Strictly speaking a greater part of Poland was part of Imperial Russia, and the Reds were arguing that they were still fighting a civil war and bringing aid to their Polish allies, the Communists. It should be pointed out that quite a number of Poles were Bolshevik leaders in Moscow who had to wait for a long time for a plausible pretext to strike against their internal Polish enemies, the bourgeois puppets of the West who were in power in independent Poland. In May 1920 the Poles who seemed unconcerned about civil war in the Ukraine suddenly affected a *volte face*, concluded an alliance with

В. И. Ленин, И. В. Сталин, М. И. Калинин на VIII съезде РКП(б). Март 1919 г. (Фото)

В. И. ЛЕНИН. Вставка к политической части программы РКП(б). (Рукопись)

the defeated Ukrainian nationalists and invaded the Ukraine, driving the Reds out. The Bolshevik Poles had a pretext and quickly gathered in the proximity of the front to form a Polish government as soon as the Red Army launched a counter-attack and drove the Poles out of the Ukraine.

Both sides seemed to have prepared for the final clash, the Bolsheviks as early as February 1920. The Red Army's plan envisaged the conquest of the Minsk area: from there a classic pincer operation by the Southern and Northern groups of armies would destroy Poland. First, the Poles were forced to withdraw precipitately from the Ukraine when the Ukrainian nationalist armies failed to materialize. Next the Northern Red Armies (now renamed Western) under Tukha-

chevsky launched their pincer attack against Warsaw in the North. But the Southern (now renamed South Western) Armies were not ready: Yegorov had to wait for Budyonny's Cavalry Armies and other reinforcements. Also the new White leader in the Crimea, General Baron Wrangel, launched a diversionary attack against the Red Army and recorded some success. This further delayed the offensive preparations. In the end the South Western armies failed to deliver the southern blow against Warsaw; instead the Polish C-in-C., Josef Pilsudski, noticed this divergence between the Red Armies and decided to counter-attack on this spot. On 16 August 1920, with the Reds quarreling about orders, subordination and coordination, the Poles struck, and within two days

Tukhachevsky's group lost its left wing. In subsequent operations the Poles cut the Red Army to pieces and even the élite Red cavalry had to extricate itself from encirclement and retreat into the Ukraine without achieving anything.

After this bloody rebuff the Red Armies regrouped and were successfully used against the Crimea to complete the victory in the civil war in Russia. In mid-September 1920 the Red Army massed two armies the 6th (Commander Uborovich—Commissar Mezhin) and the 13th (Commander Gorodovikov—Commissar Shchadenko) against the Crimea with Frunze taking over the front command. He launched the final offensive on 28 October 1920 and drove the Whites back into the peninsula. On 8 November Blyukher's 51st Division, brought there from Siberia, broke

FAR LEFT: Stalin, Lenin and Kalinin during the Party Congress in 1919. The draft of Lenin's report on the Civil War to the Congress appears below.

LEFT: Russian commanders on the Polish Front in 1920, from left to right: Poletiyev, Kotovsky and Zhestokanov.

OPPOSITE LEFT: Kalinin and Budyonny on the Southern Front in 1920. Kalinin had recently been elevated to the Presidency of Soviet Russia after the death of Jakov Sverdlov.

OPPOSITE RIGHT: Kotovsky (with moustache) and the 2nd Cavalry Corps Band in 1923.

BELOW: Kotovsky surrounded by members of the 2nd Cavalry Corps in their reunion in 1924.

BOTTOM LEFT: Kotovsky on maneuvers with the 2nd Cavalry Corps in 1923.

BOTTOM RIGHT: Kotovsky during a Soviet Congress in Kiev in 1924.

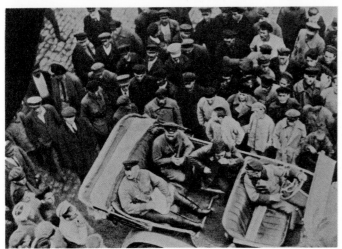

26

RIGHT Scene from Lenin's funeral. His coffin is carried from the Paveletsky Station by Kalinin and Bukharin, followed by Tomsky, head of the Labor Unions, Kamenev and Stalin. Zinoviev is at the back of the coffin, and Molotov is at the right. The pall bearers all went bareheaded despite a temperature of 14 degrees below freezing.

through the White defenses and the civil war in European Russia was over. After dealing with the Green partisan units as well, Frunze dissolved the front armies and reported complete victory to Moscow.

Although revolts and partisan fighting continued throughout Bolshevik-controlled Russia, the organized, large-scale civil war came to an end. That the Bolsheviks emerged as victors was largely due to the political leadership of Lenin, military leadership of Trotsky and security of Dzerzhinsky. Politically Lenin led the Bolshevik Party to victory because of his skill in internal and external policies: he never lost control over the military situation and never allowed an external coalition to form itself against his Russia. But in all his political maneuvers he had to rely on the Red Armies which were

organized and led by his fellow politician, Trotsky. From the Polish defeat they both learned that their armies could only be used with success internally and they certainly used them to this effect. even after the civil war against the rebels at Kronstadt, in the Tambov province, Turkestan and the Far East. (This is not to count the re-conquest of the Caucasus, Adzerbeijan, Georgia and Armenia, which were former provinces of Imperial Russia.) However, the civil war engendered political conflicts in the Bolshevik leadership, which were only resolved in the 1930s.

It is obvious that the Red Army which emerged victorious from the civil war was a peculiar army, *sui generis*, dominated by politicians. As soon as Lenin died in 1924 the factional struggles among the Communist leaders became apparent, and the hardest battle was fought for the control of this internal power instrument. Stalin succeeded in ousting Trotsky as War

Minister in 1924: he was replaced by Frunze who died shortly afterward as a result of a surgical operation ordered by the political leadership. Thus in 1925 Voroshilov took over on Stalin's behalf. However, the final takeover by Stalin took place in 1938, when all old scores were settled and blame apportioned. Up to that moment the Red Army settled down to peacetime existence, learning to be a real army for both internal and external purposes. The other defeated nation of World War I, Germany, did help the Soviet Russians; however, the progress was slow and unspectacular.

THE GREAT PURGE

We can only speculate as to why Stalin suddenly decided on destroying the Red Army in 1937, for that is what the great purge amounted to. He certainly had enough reasons for feeling hostile towards that body of men in 1920 when he terminated his army involvement after its defeat by Poland. But since he had left the Red Army to occupy himself with the Communist Party, Trotsky and the group of army leaders who were the followers of the War Commissar must have heaved a sigh of relief when the tough Georgian finally left them to their own devices.

Stalin seemed busy with establishing a different power base for himself. He was gradually transforming the Communist Party into his own instrument of power and as soon as Lenin died in 1924, Stalin began to broaden this power base. The army had to be neutralized and then put under his political control, and he achieved all that within a year, which showed how immensely dependent all power institutions were on the party. Trotsky was forced to leave the Commissariat of Defense shortly after Lenin's death, and after his successor Frunze's untimely death, Stalin then had his old crony Voroshilov appointed as Commissar for Defense who held the appointment until 1940. Many followers of Trotsky left the Commissariat and the Army with their patron, but even more of them stayed on without the slightest indication of disfavor by Voroshilov and, of course, Stalin.

However, just as with the Communist Party, Stalin never forgot the frustration and anger that the Red Army caused him in the 1920s. It was logical for him to purge any power instrument that he wanted to use for his purposes, and by 1936 Stalin must have thought of the Red Army as an internal and external means for his policies. Internally he wanted to be sure that the Army would not oppose his party purges; and externally he began to be interested in policies which would involve the Red Army abroad. Once Stalin made up his mind he acted swiftly, although he was not yet quite sure of the pretext under which the Red Army should be purged. His original idea was to purge it within the campaign against Trotsky and Trotskyism, that is, on political grounds. It was a fact that many of the appointments made by Trotsky survived the master and they were now in key positions. Thus Voroshilov's first deputy, Jan Gamarnik, now in charge of the political administration and also a full member of the Communist Party's central committee, had Trotskyite antecedents and would have to be dealt with if Stalin wanted absolute control of the Red Army. Then there was Tukhachevsky, Voroshilov's deputy and generally acknowledged as the best brain that the Army had. Yakir and Uborovich, both in command of two vital military districts, the Kiev and the Belorussian, appeared equally dangerous because of their past associations

BELOW FAR LEFT: Budyonny surrounded by commanders during the 1920s. Sun Yat-sen, leader of the Chinese Nationalist Party, is seated next to Budyonny on the far right.

BELOW CENTER LEFT: Budyonny talks to delegates to the Party Congress from Central Asia in 1930.

BELOW LEFT: Budyonny now in the role of the good civil servant, in 1931. His secret of survival seems obvious. He did what was required.

BELOW RIGHT: Budyonny, Frunze and Voroshilov on the Crimean Front in 1920 plan the final victory against Wrangel's forces in the Crimea.

RIGHT: The cavalry commander Budyonny hands over the regimental colors during the Civil War.

and present power. In any case they were the first who had to go unconditionally, if Stalin was to achieve his aims within the Red Army.

As was usual with Stalin he disguised his intention extremely well. In 1935 he restored all the military ranks (with the exception of general) and named the first five Marshals of the Soviet Union: Voroshilov and Budyonny were his nominees, but Tukhachevsky, Blyukher and Yegorov were not. It seemed impossible that he was plotting the downfall of the latter since he had only just conferred on them such signal distinction. However, throughout 1936 Stalin watched these 'military' men closely and in the end became convinced that they were his political enemies. While in the Central Committee Voroshilov and Budyonny invariably supported Stalin, the 'military' acted otherwise. Both Gamarnik and Yakir were full members, while Tukhachevsky, Blyukher, Yegorov, Uborovich and Bulin, who was Gamarnik's deputy in the political administration, were candidate members and they all were said to be against the arrest of Bukharin, an erstwhile party leader, now completely outmaneuvered and humiliated by Stalin. Such behavior must have been the final stimulus for Stalin's pathologically suspicious mind.

On 5 July 1936 the NKVD, Stalin's secret police, arrested a commander of a tank division in the Kiev Military District, Yakir's domain. Yakir was not even told of the arrest, which was obviously aimed at himself. The arrested commander, Dmitry Shmidt, was a Ukrainian Jew, who during the civil war became an outstanding cavalry leader; politically he always backed Trotsky and was in opposition to Stalin. In 1927 this same Shmidt, after he had been defeated at the party congress, is said to have come up to Stalin and threatened to cut his ears off one day in the future. This was certainly a bad joke, and Stalin who took things seriously allowed him to serve in the Army for some nine more years before taking his revenge. Shmidt was the first arrested, and when Yakir hurried off to Moscow to intervene on his behalf, Yezhov, then chief of the NKVD, showed him the evidence for the arrest. It was based on confessions by Mrachkovsky and other Trotskyites and was said to have implicated Shmidt in the projected assassination of Voroshilov. Subsequently Mrachkovsky spoke of a military terrorist group which wanted to assassinate both Voroshilov and Stalin.

It became quickly evident that Shmidt and Kuzmichev, another air force officer, arrested simultaneously, were just the tip of the iceberg and that the whole 'military terrorist group' would be dealt with as soon as they confessed or further evidence was uncovered. However, in the Ukraine no one believed that the two arrested officers were guilty and everyone, especially Yakir, thought they would soon be released. Then in September 1936 Sablin, commander of a division in Yakir's district, was arrested: this time Yakir was told by an NKVD officer that evidence against Sablin was forged. By now Yakir must have become suspicious, especially since Sablin committed suicide shortly after his arrest. Still Shmidt under interrogation denied any knowledge of the assassination plans and Yakir continued to hope for the best.

The NKVD was by then given firm directives from Stalin to deal resolutely with military conspirators, and they began to arrest people right and left to implicate the bigger fish in this political-military plot. In connection with the Zinoviev trial an officer from Tukhachevsky's immediate circle, Dreitzer, accused the military attaché in London, Putna, of maintaining secret contacts with Trotsky. Putna was recalled from London and placed under arrest; he and another arrested officer, Corps Commander Primakov, began to

BELOW: Red Army
training of civilians was
part of an ongoing
program to prepare the
Soviet Union for war
during the 1930s.

RIGHT: The five original
Marshals of the Soviet
Union in the 1930s.
From left to right:
Tukhachevsky, Voroshilov
and Yegorov; top row:
Budyonny and Blyukher.
Only Voroshilov and
Budyonny survived the
purges.

FAR RIGHT: Budyonny
enjoying his new role as
the first deputy Defense
Commissar in the
Caucasus in 1940. By this
time his other rivals had
been eliminated.

implicate Yakir and Tukhachevsky in Trotskyite plots and assassinations. Putna even went as far as to accuse Tukhachevsky of being a British spy. Still no action was taken against Yakir or Tukhachevsky, and both in fact scored an obscure and shortlived triumph. During the Pyatakov trial Radek, one of the accused, emphatically denied Putna's charges against Tukhachevsky. On the other hand Yakir was allowed to visit Shmidt in jail to ascertain his guilt or innocence.

Shmidt, as everyone else, was finally broken by interrogation and confessed. Yakir wanted to verify the confessions and during his visit in jail Shmidt repudiated them. Triumphant, Yakir was able to take a signed statement to this effect from jail to Voroshilov and then left for Kiev. It seems incredible how naively both Tukhachevsky and Yakir acted thinking themselves exonerated. Shortly afterward Voroshilov telephoned Yakir in Kiev telling him that Shmidt signed another confession: what he did not tell him was that this time Shmidt declared that he wanted to start a tank revolt at the instigation of Yakir himself. As for Tukhachevsky events now took quite a different turn and he was to emerge not as a Trotskyite or British spy, but a German agent.

32

BELOW: Marshal Budyonny in Berlin in 1945. Few Stalinist officers of the 1930s lived to celebrate the Soviet victory.

BELOW RIGHT: Marshal Malinovsky, who survived the purges by a minor miracle, lived to become Minister of Defense under Khrushchev. He escaped the purges largely because of his lowly position in the Soviet Army in the 1930s.

It is clear that Stalin began to dislike the idea of linking the military with the political, probably to avoid disturbing the soldiers who might not have approved the liquidation of their officers on pure political charges without resistance. In any case such political charges were much more difficult to 'prove' with the military, especially the professional ones like Tukhachevsky, Yegorov, Blyukher and others. It was therefore considered a godsend when evidence of high treason was uncovered, or better, when Stalin received such evidence from an innocuous source like Czechoslovakia. Though it was an obvious plant by the German *Sicherheitsdienst* and its chief, Reinhard Heydrich, it did not disturb Stalin in the slightest; he seems to have originated the whole conspiracy anyway. Heydrich and the German leaders were told of Stalin's 'suspicions' that Tukhachevsky and Red Army generals were conspiring with the German General Staff, probably by General Skoblin, young hero of the civil war on the White side, who was also a double agent of the NKVD and SD. Heydrich immediately seized on the idea and set to work: he compiled a whole file on this conspiracy containing Tukhachevsky's signatures (taken from the agreement that Tukhachevsky signed with the Germans in 1926) and those of the German generals (from their bank cheques). Heydrich loved the idea which enabled him to discredit both his own high command with whom he

quarreled continuously, and the Soviet one as well. His forgeries were works of art. The story of Tukhachevsky's German contacts were skillfully leaked through Sudeten Germans to Czechoslovakia, where President Benes decided to discreetly inform both the Deuxième Bureau in Paris and Stalin in Moscow. In May 1937 Heydrich showed the forgeries to Hitler and Himmler who approved the operation: Heydrich then sent the file directly to Yezhov and therefore to Stalin.

Throughout the early months of 1937 the military knew full well that they were in trouble. Stalin began to reshuffle them. Tukhachevsky was demoted and sent to the obscure Volga district, while Yakir was kicked upstairs and transferred from Kiev to Leningrad. Uborevich was also going to move from Minsk, and so were many other subordinate officers. Then suddenly between 28 and 31 May 1937 they were all called to Moscow for urgent talks, and one by one were arrested by the NKVD and taken to the Lyublyanka prison. They were all totally surprised and proclaimed their innocence, Yakir writing a personal letter to Stalin on which the papers commented obscenely. Between 1 and 4 June the Supreme Military Soviet dealt with the 'military conspiracy' and a special military tribunal was set up to judge the conspirators. The tribunal consisted of a lawyer, Ulrikh, who was its chairman, and Marshals Budyonny and Blyukher, and General-Commanders Shaposhni-

kov, Alksnis, Belov, Dybenko, Kashirin and Goryachov, most of whom perished in a subsequent purge. On 11 June 1937 they tried and sentenced the following military leaders to death by shooting: Marshal Tukhachevsky, Deputy Minister of Defense, lately commander of the Volga Military District; Army Commander Yakir, of the Kiev Military District; Army Commander Uborevich, Commanding the Belorussian Military District; Corps Commander Eideman, head of OSOAVIAKHIM (Civil Defense); Army Commander Kork, Commandant of the Frunze Military Academy; Corps Commander Putna, formerly Military Attaché in London; Corps Commander Feldman, Chief Administrator of the Red Army; Corps Commander Primakov, Deputy Commander of the Leningrad Military District. Jan Gamarnik, head of the political administration, who was undoubtedly implicated in the 'conspiracy', committed suicide and thus cheated Soviet justice and its executioners.

This was the way Stalin finally decided to tackle the Army and its purge. The military themselves judged their peers and sentenced them to the ultimate penalty for such terrible crimes as high treason. All this was done without a single shot being fired on behalf of the condemned by either officers or men, although they all felt that the purge would not stop there. In fact Stalin contemplated and then carried out two more waves of purges which

BELOW: Marshal
Rokossovsky, who was
tortured during the
purges, was subsequently
released without any
explanation and lived to
play a major role in
World War II.

would ultimately leave the Red Army to all intents and purposes 'headless': three out of the five Marshals were purged; 14 out of 16 Army Commanders; 8 of the 8 Admirals; 60 out of 67 Corps Commanders; 136 out of 199 Divisional Commanders; 221 out of 397 Brigade Commanders; all 11 Deputy Commissars of Defense and 75 out of 80 members of the Supreme Military Soviet; some 35,000 officers were purged and killed in this and subsequent waves of terror.

Immediately after these spectacular trials and executions Stalin gave instructions to the NKVD to continue the purge of the Army, but also investigate (in other words prepare the purge) of the other arms: the Navy, Air Force, artillery and armor, and finally of the political administration itself, which was also compromised by Gamarnik's death. In the Navy Stalin made a clean sweep of it, although it is quite difficult to see his reasons. He never quarreled with the admirals but killed them all nonetheless. Admiral Muklevich, who rebuilt the Red Fleet, and had associations with the Tukhachevsky group, disappeared in 1937, but they were all, including the C-in-C Admiral Orlov, liquidated in 1938 and never tried publicly. Perhaps this was not Stalin's purge at all, but the squaring of the account by Tevosyan, Commissar for Ship Building, who had had disputes with the naval command all along. Still Stalin must have given the final yes! However, Tevosyan could not have quarreled with everybody, especially with Admirals serving away from Moscow. Admiral Sivkov of the Baltic Fleet, Admiral Koshchanov of the Black Sea Fleet and Admiral Viktorov of the Pacific Fleet, were all arrested and executed. By 1941 Muklevich's views of a small defensive force in each naval area were vindicated, but he was not even rehabilitated.

In the Air Force Army Commander Alksnis was member of the military tribunal which sentenced the Tukhachevsky group. He was himself a Tukhachevsky man and the death sentence of his friend did not save him. His deputy, Khripin, and the sponsor of all of them, Corps Commander Todorsky, head of the Air Force Academy, were also arrested and of the many air force officers liquidated at this stage, only Todorsky survived to tell the tale. Khalepsky, the creator of Soviet armor,

was also executed and there seems no apparent reason for his liquidation, for he was a real expert and prepared the Red Army for the future armored combat. Rogovsky, who commanded Soviet artillery, went the same way, and his successor Marshal Kulik, a grotesque Stalinist, was sacked in 1941, when he had to admit that he had neglected the development of this arm and especially ammunition.

The political administration, in Stalin's eyes, was obviously guilty of something, since its head, Gamarnik, committed suicide. On the whole they were criticized and purged on political grounds rather than military. Gamarnik's two deputies, A. S. Bulin and G. A. Osepyan, followed the old commander almost immediately as well as all the departmental heads in Moscow HQ. All 17 Army commissars were purged; 25 out of 28 Corps Commissars disappeared as well as 34 of 36 Brigade Commissars. Mekhlis, who had succeeded Gamarnik, argued that the political commissars were politically responsible for the military conspiracies, and purged them mercilessly: at least 20,000 politruks were purged, some two-thirds of that élite establishment. In the Belorussian and Kiev

34

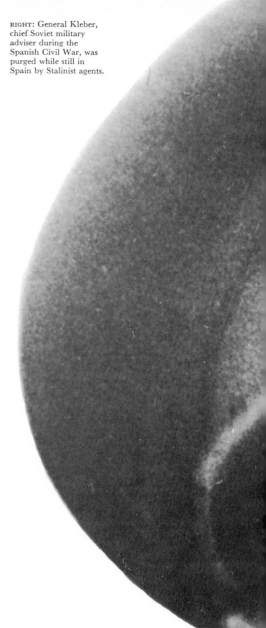

Military Districts the purge went as deep as regiments and battalions, and the politruks were replaced by their butchers, mainly minor NKVD officials, who subsequently, became responsible for the massacres and atrocities, when the Red Army found itself at war.

In the meantime the Red Army became unofficially involved in the civil war in Spain, which proved an excellent opportunity for some officers to escape the purge. The future Minister of Defense, Marshal Malinovsky, served in Spain at this time and disobeyed two orders to return, until threatened with being posted as deserter. When he finally got back the wave of terror had subsided and he survived. Others were not so fortunate. Berzin, hero of the civil war, and virtual C-in-C of the Spanish Republican forces, where he served under the name of Grishin, returned and was shot together with his successor as Chief of Military Intelligence, S. P. Uritsky. The Soviet commander of the International Brigade, 'General Kleber', was executed in Spain itself. The hero of the battle of Madrid, Brigade Commander Skoblevsky, was executed two days after he had received the Order of Lenin for his military prowess and merit. 'Douglas', the leading Soviet airman in Spain, returned home, but in 1941 was executed as Lieutenant-General Smushkevich. Even the civilians in the Spanish war fared badly. The old politruk Antonov-

Ovseyenko, who had been Trotsky's follower, was Consul-General in Barcelona. When he returned together with the Soviet Ambassador Rosenberg, they were both arrested and executed.

The second wave of terror in the Army was launched early in 1938 and it completed the liquidation of the high command so successfully started with the Tukhachevsky group. Stalin decided to root out not only the 'enemies' but also the 'silent ones', i.e. other officers who in any way disagreed with the army purge and the purges in general. Uborevich's judge and successor in Belorussia, Belov, was recalled to Moscow where he was arrested and later perished. Yakir's successor in Kiev, Fed'ko, was called to Moscow to become Deputy Commissar of Defense. However, he was arrested almost immediately afterwards and also perished. The neighboring Kharkov Military District, commanded by Dubovoy, must have contained a lot of spies and enemies, and its commanding officer and most of the staff were executed.

This time Stalin was proving quite merciless even to his 'friends'. Yegorov, an old Tsarist officer, who had been Stalin's companion during and after the civil war, had only recently been promoted to the rank of Marshal of the Soviet Union. After Tukhachevsky's execution Stalin, in a friendly gesture, offered Yegorov Tukhachevsky's villa, which he refused. Perhaps that was the sign of treason that Stalin was looking

FAR LEFT: Marshal S. M. Budyonny, founder of the Red cavalry, the only survivor of the purges of the 1930s other than Voroshilov.

LEFT: Marshal Timoshenko, commander of the Red cavalry, was Stalin's protégé during the period of the purges.

for. Yegorov also disappeared and was executed. Similarly, Army Commander Dybenko, who was Stalin's creature since the Bolshevik Revolution in 1917. Dybenko was then a sailor and as such he committed many an atrocity to further the cause of the Bolsheviks. In the '30s he was in command of the Volga Military District and was relieved of this command by Tukhachevsky, who had been transferred there shortly before his execution. Dybenko in fact witnessed the arrest of Tukhachevsky at the HQ in Kuybyshev. This was a terrible shock to the old sailor. But Stalin, who moved him to command the Leningrad Military District, a clear promotion, did not like his servants to be shocked by anything he did. Dybenko was arrested in the Urals where he was on a mission, and was executed shortly afterwards. Kuybyshev's brother, Commander of the Caucasian Military District, was also shocked by the purges and said so openly: his dead brother's political reputation did not save him either. The Baikal and Central Asian Military District commanders, Velikanov and Gryaznov, disappeared as a matter of course, while the first C-in-C of the Red Army in the civil war, Vatsetis, was arrested during a lecture he gave at the military academy. The future Marshals Rokossovsky and Meretskov were both arrested, treated most inhumanely, but were not shot: instead they were sent to concentration camps, from which they emerged in 1941 to become Army Commander and Chief of Staff of the Soviet armed forces respectively. Rokossovsky probably saved his life by confessing to some peculiar crimes during the civil war. During his trial the judge commented that a witness confirmed Rokossovsky's crimes. It was then pointed out that the alleged witness was dead for some 25 years, and Rokossovsky was not shot. This second wave of terror destroyed the officer corps completely. When the future Marshal Biryuzov arrived at his posting at the 30th Division as Chief of Staff, he noticed that the most senior officer was a captain.

So far Stalin concentrated on purging the Moscow HQ and the European Military Districts where the purge was carried on real depth. However, the Far Eastern District, led by another hero of the civil war, Marshal Blyukher, had been left untouched. At the time it was

thought that this was because of Blyukher's resistance to the NKVD and Stalin. It now seems clear that Stalin did not want to disturb the army in the Far East because of the danger from Japan, but certainly not on Blyukher's account. It is not certain whether Bluykher (Blücher) was his name or pseudonym, but this worker and strike organizer, distinguished himself in the civil war in Siberia and Turkestan. In the 1920s under another pseudonym, Galen, he served in China as Chiang Kai-shek's military adviser and later, after the Japanese invasion of Manchuria, he was put in charge of the Red Armies facing Japan. It was in Stalin's interest to keep these armies as undisturbed as possible. Nonetheless he decided to strike while Blyukher was in Moscow judging his fellow soldier Tukhachevsky. Blyukher's Chief of Staff, Sangursky, was involved in an obscure local political intrigue and the NKVD decided to use him as a pretext for a purge. He was arrested, tortured and confessed. He implicated in his 'plotting' practically the whole command in the Far East.

But then, as suddenly as it started, the purge was halted, and Blyukher was allowed to go back to the Far East to resume his command. The Japanese were making probing attacks in the region, and a real battle was in the offing. Blyukher set about consolidating his cadres and he happened to have some outstanding officers left commanding his forces. The future Marshal Koniev was there as well as Corps Commander Shtern, recently back from Spain, where he had distinguished himself. However, Japanese danger or not, for Stalin the purge was a question of logistics: his chief purger, Mekhlis, in charge of the political administration of the Red Army, only managed to arrive at Khabarovsk in May 1938. The chief of the NKVD forces detailed to the Far East, Frinovsky, was arriving hot on Mekhlis's heels. The NKVD Commander of the Far Eastern Frontier Guards, Lyushkov, an experienced secret policeman, read the signs on the wall. On 13 June 1938 he slipped across the border and joined the Japanese forces. This was a sign for another purge.

The NKVD struck first against Blyukher's new staff: his deputy commander, Chief of Staff, Air Commander and Army Commander Levandovsky, all disappeared. Some 40

per cent of the regimental commanders, 70 per cent of the divisional and corps commanders as well as 80 per cent of the front commanders followed suit. It was now Blyukher's turn, but at that stage the Japanese Army launched another probe on Lake Hassan and the purge was temporarily halted.

The exact origin of this incident is still obscure: Lake Hassan is close to the Soviet-Manchurian border, and the Japanese and Soviets had been facing each other in this area since 1934. On 6 July 1938 a Soviet patrol moved up a deserted ridge and shortly afterwards Soviet troops began to fortify the place in order to establish a permanent post there. On 15 July the Japanese Ambassador in Moscow demanded Soviet withdrawal from the territory, but the Soviets refused to do so. Diplomatic exchanges followed, but the Soviets also mobilized their 40th Division which was stationed in the vicinity of Lake Hassan. Then on 29 July the 19th Japanese Division attacked and dislodged the Russians from the disputed ridge. Perhaps Lyushkov told the Japanese that the Red Army was demoralized by the purges; perhaps the Japanese just wanted to test Soviet war preparedness. Voroshilov mobilized the whole Far Eastern Military District, including the Maritime group of armies, as well as the Pacific Fleet on 1 August 1938. The 39th Corps under the command of Shtern concentrated on the lake and launched its counter-attack on 6 August. Soviet bombers hit Japanese positions and tank and infantry stormed the ridge which they held against Japanese counter-attacks. After a few days of further fighting the Japanese offered a cease-fire which was accepted by the Soviets. The battle was over and the purge could be resumed. Blyukher was called to Moscow on 18 August, immediately after the battle had ended. He was not yet arrested and in fact reported on the Lake Hassan battle to the Supreme Military Soviet, but instead of congratulations Voroshilov criticized him sharply. He was told that he would not be going back to his command and would stay in Moscow until a job was found for him.

Blyukher certainly felt that his arrest was coming, but he did nothing and just waited. On 22 October, on personal orders from Stalin, he was arrested and within a month he was dead. It was rumored that he was killed by Yezhov

BELOW: Podvoysky at a meeting of Komsomol recruits in Moscow during the Civil War. During the purges of the 1930s he disappeared without trace, but escaped formal execution.

personally, but we cannot be sure of that nor of the reason for his arrest. It may be that he was dragged down by his former associates, Fed'ko, Kashirin and Postyshev, 2nd Secretary in the Ukraine, previously Blyukher's Commissar in Siberia. Or was it Lyushkov's reports to the Japanese about groups of opposition in the Far East that brought his downfall? It should not be forgotten that the Soviets had an efficient spy in Tokyo, Richard Sorge, and he must have reported something on Lyushkov's desertion. As it was, on 28 October 1938 the Supreme Soviet awarded medals to those who distinguished themselves in the recent fighting. Among those who were awarded a medal was Shtern, also to be liquidated shortly afterwards. Blyukher, already under interrogation, did not receive any military reward.

After this bloodletting the great purge of the armed forces came to an end, but officers continued to disappear throughout 1939–1941. Those who survived in concentration camps were either released in 1941 to fight the Germans or had to wait for Stalin's death in 1953. By 1939 Stalin had the following as his military leaders: Voroshilov, who was to survive his master and die peacefully full of years and honor; Budyonny, the cavalry sergeant, who would survive even the aged Voroshilov; Shchadenko, the old tailor of Stalingrad-Tsaritsyn-Volgograd; Mekhlis, the bloodthirsty journalist; Kulik, the inefficent artilleryman; Timoshenko, the cavalry NCO and former Tsarist colonel; and Boris Shaposhnikov, who became the Chief of General Staff. There was no one to lead the Navy, so Frinovsky, the NKVD liquidator, soon to be liquidated, was appointed to the post.

Many of the younger officers and future leaders, such as Koniev and Zhukov, were far away from Moscow and therefore relatively safe. However, in Moscow itself only military mediocrity survived. Stalin who had no illusions about his cronies was, nevertheless, shocked when the testing time came in 1940. As a result of the failure of the Red Army against Finland he neutralized and dismissed practically the whole of the remaining command. However, capable young military men were only allowed back to Moscow and to the high command when Hitler struck in 1941. Even then the consequences of the political purge of the Red Army were incalculable. However, the Red Army would have fought better in the initial phase of the war with trained and experienced officers rather than with untested political appointees, none of whom had made the slightest mark in the Red Army.

WEAPONS OF THE RED ARMY

The Red Army emerged from the Revolution and subsequent Civil War as little more than an armed mob; discipline, except for a few remarkable units, was non-existent, and indeed some units appear to have been operating on the borderline of brigandage. The existence of this vast body-in-arms was an embarrassment and a danger to the Soviet authorities, who therefore bent their energy to demobilizing the vast bulk of the troops and exhorting them to get back to their farms and workbenches. Most did, but some had become so enamored of the wild and free life that they lapsed into outright banditry, to be hunted down and exterminated throughout the 1920s. On 1 October 1920 there were almost 5½ million men in arms; by the end of 1924 the strength was down to 1½ million and still being reduced.

The principal problem confronting the Soviet leaders was that of the constitution of the future Red Army. The immediate task confronting the Army, as the leaders saw it, was to secure the country against the possibility of counter-revolution, and secondarily to prepare for the eventual class war in which the workers would assume control throughout the world, and for which struggle the Red Army would form the vanguard. There were two schools of thought on how best to organize the Army to discharge these functions. The first group, led by Trotsky and supported by many generals, wanted a Regular Army which would act as a counter-revolutionary force and as a cadre in the event of an external war; if such a war came, this cadre would form the nucleus about which the mass of workers and peasants could be formed

RIGHT: Russian soldier wears his fur coat on patrol. Although too scantily dressed for the Finnish war, the Russians had proper clothing by 1941.
BELOW: Czech troops in German service manning a 2-cm light flak gun on the Eastern Front.

into an organized force, their 'revolutionary zeal' more than compensating for their lack of formal military training.

The second group, led by Frunze and most of the men who had held command appointments during the Civil War, argued for a small Regular Army and cadre and a large, trained, territorial militia. They considered the danger of counter-revolution to be less than assumed by Trotsky, and, as practical soldiers, they had little faith in the ability of 'revolutionary zeal' to turn peasants into soldiers overnight.

Similar argument raged about the method of training. Voroshilov and Budyonny, for example, argued for a 'revolutionary theory' of warfare, implying that Marxist theory had suspended to normal theories of warfare, tactics and strategy. Trotsky and the more

intelligent generals such as Frunze and Tukhachevsky derided this notion, pointing out that the principles of war were not amenable to party dialectics.

As is usual with policy questions in Russia, the actual parameters of the arguments tended to get lost under layers of political argument and dogmatization. Eventually a compromise form of organization was evolved, a Regular Army of 600,000 men backed up by a trained territorial Militia force. The shifting winds of politics had removed Trotsky from the scene, and Frunze, Voroshilov and Tukhachevsky were in control of the setting up of the new Red Army. There were to be 29 regular Infantry Divisions, 42 Militia infantry divisions, 12 regular Cavalry divisions and four militia cavalry divisions; military districts were drawn up on demarcation lines which differed from

national and provincial boundaries, so that there could be no danger of a provincial autonomy arising; and political commissars were appointed throughout the army, given equal status with unit commanders and with the power to change military orders on political grounds. Conscription was re-organized, with call-up at 21 years of age, followed by two to four years of regular service, depending upon the arm of service, after which the soldier served a further period in the reserve army.

Frunze, the architect of the Red Army, the man who gave it discipline, organization and a sense of purpose, died while undergoing an operation, and he was replaced as People's Commissar of the Army and Navy by Voroshilov. He headed the Revolutionary Military Council, a 'collective' body set up in order to prevent any possibility of a coup and to instil the necessary political weighting factor into the High Command. The Council, in turn, controlled the People's Commissariat for Military Affairs, beneath which came the various Administrations — Ordnance, Supply, Planning and so on — and the Military Districts. By 1928 this machinery of command was functioning smoothly, the Army was in existence as planned — indeed, some elements of it were in combat, mopping up the last of the bandits left over from the revolution and forcing the Soviet collectivization policies on the unwilling peasantry of the more remote areas — but for all the impressive numbers and paper structures it was still a long way from being the Red Army that its leaders wanted, since it was gravely deficient in equipment. Even such basic items as uniforms, boots, trucks and barrack accommodation were scarce, let alone such things as tanks and guns.

This shortage had, of course, been apparent since the earliest days, and by 1928 there had been sufficient rebuilding of industry to permit a start on alleviating the worst deficiencies. Moreover the 1920s had not been wasted, since there had been room for planning and basic research ready for the day when the country could afford to actually begin producing weapons in quantity. And so in 1928 the First Five-Year Plan was announced, the principal accent of which was the modernization of the armaments industry and the mechanization of the army.

The first priority was the formation of an armored force; the groundwork for this had been laid a long time before. In 1922 the secret agreement signed at Rapallo between Germany and Russia had provided for the setting up of a variety of cooperative military research establishments. Krupp set up an experimental tractor factory at Rostov-on-Don which, in fact, was more concerned with tank design than with agricultural endeavor, while an 'Armaments Development Company' was financed by the German government and set up offices in Moscow to control the provision of German technicians to Russian research stations which were investigating tank and aircraft design and chemical warfare. In 1927 a combined German-Russian tank testing and training facility was built at Kazan, to which various German and Russian experimental vehicles were sent for testing, and to which German and Russian officers were sent to be trained in the tactics and technicalities of the tank.

The target of the First Five Year Plan was that by 1934 the Red Army should have three mechanized brigades, 30 mixed tank battalions, four reserve heavy tank battalions, 13 mechanized cavalry regiments with tanks and armored cars, and an armored car company in each infantry division, a total of something in the region of 3500 combat vehicles. In 1928 the tank strength of the army was about 100, with about 50 armored cars, almost all of which had been left over from the war or purchased from abroad in subsequent years, the majority being either French Renault or locally-built copies. Now the designers began to look at what was new in the tank world and to draw up some designs of their own. Various German tank prototypes had appeared at Kazan, but by 1930 the Russians began to suspect that they were not getting the full value out of the set-up there; they were right, too, for the Germans were careful not to send anything really important into Russia. For example they did not allow any vehicles with the experimental Maybach tank transmission to leave Germany, as a result of which the Russians were to have a long and hard time developing a transmission of their own, and they never succeeded in developing anything as technically advanced as the Maybach. As a result of their suspicions, the Russians set up, secretly, another test facility at Voronezh, in which the majority of their own experimental work was carried out.

As an interim measure, a number of tanks were bought from abroad, and licenses obtained to build some of these foreign designs in Russia. Some of the tanks were purchased singly, simply for evaluation, but a quantity of Vicker-Armstrong tanks were bought from Britain, sufficient to equip one or two tank battalions.

In order to provide the manufacturing basis for the Plan, the heavy industry was revitalized. The Putilov Works in Leningrad was expanded to give a capacity of 10,000 tractors a year; a new tractor plant at Stalingrad was scheduled to produce 40,000 a year; with the assistance of the Ford Motor Company a huge truck plant was built at Nizhni-Novgorod, renamed Gorki, and this began production in 1932. All these expansions were ostensibly for the economic good of the country, and there was great propaganda play with the statistics of tractors produced. But in fact every one of them had a place in the armored vehicle production plan; the tractor assembly plants were the future tank production facilities, while

the car and truck factories were earmarked for the production of staff cars and soft-skinned vehicles.

Once the manufacturing plant was organized, the Army could submit its demands for tanks, and by 1931 they had sufficient experience, gained at Kazan and Voronezh, to be fairly confident of what they needed, and their requirements were enshrined in the '1931 Tank Program Schedule' as:

1. Reconnaissance Tanks. Light, fast, lightly armored and armed, difficult to detect, amphibious if possible.

2. Pursuit tanks. Of 12 to 15 tons, these were to be the weapons to deal with enemy tanks, machine guns and so forth on the battlefield. They were to be well armored and carry powerful guns.

3. Breakthrough Tanks. Heavy tanks, well protected and powerfully armed, for forcing a way through prepared defences and fortifications.

4. Special Purpose Tanks. These included flame-throwers, bridge-layers, smoke-screen layers, gas dischargers, self-propelled guns, mine-laying tanks and so forth.

5. Armored Cars. Of medium and heavy classes, these were to be based on commercial truck chassis.

Beginning in 1931, vehicles to these specifications began to appear in growing numbers, and by 1933 the Red Army had almost 7000 tanks ranging

RIGHT: Dawn breaks early for two Russian soldiers, near Kursk, in 1943.

BELOW CENTER: Students of a teachers college learn how to operate a Maxim machine gun in Krementschug in 1939.

BOTTOM: Students of the Kharkov Technical College receive instruction on the Maxim machine gun in 1938. Students like these fought as partisans after the Nazi invasion in 1941.

LEFT: The Mosin-Nagant 7.62 mm carbine, Model of 1910, a shortened version of the Russian service rifle.

BELOW: The Soviet 12.7 mm DShK machine gun, which was developed to replace the Maxim gun since it was easier and quicker to manufacture.

BELOW CENTER: The Maxim Model 1910 heavy water-cooled machine gun on the Sokolov wheeled mounting. This was the standard heavy machine gun from the days the Tsar until the end of World War II.

BOTTOM: Red Army recruits undergo training with the Maxim heavy machine gun. Notice the gun in the background has a small shield.

LEFT: A woman sniper outside Sebastopol using the Tokarev automatic rifle with telescopic sight.

from the 2.8 ton T-27 'Tankette' to the 50-ton T-35. The T-27 was a two-man vehicle armed with a machine gun and based on the British Carden-Lloyd design. Next in order of size came the T-26, a design based on the British Vickers 6-ton tank; this was a three-man, twin-turretted model with a machine gun in each turret.

The 'pursuit' tank class was represented by the BT-2, which had been derived from the American Christie design, two specimens of which had

ABOVE LEFT: Mosin-Nagant Model 1891/30 rifle with Model PE telescope,

LEFT: The short carbine version of the Tokarev automatic rifle SVT-40. While most Tokarev rifles were used for sniping, numbers were issued to NCOs.

LEFT: German soldiers examine a number of captured Soviet Mosin-Nagant rifles Model 1891.

ABOVE RIGHT: The Tokarev automatic pistol.

RIGHT: The Nagant Model 1895 revolver. When operated the cylinder moves forward to form a gas-tight seal with the barrel, thus improving velocity and accuracy.

been bought for evaluation. Walter Christie's design used large running wheels so that the vehicle could be operated with or without tracks, and since one of the prime characteristics of his designs was speed, these tanks were seen by the Soviets as a class apart, 'fast moving' (*bystrochodya*) tanks (hence BT) to act in independent tank formations. The BT-2 weighed 11 tons, had a three-man crew, a 37mm gun and two machine guns, and could reach almost 70 mph on its wheels and 40 mph on its tracks.

The Kirov Plant at Leningrad produced the medium tank, known as the T-28, in 1932. This seems to have been a synthesis of the best British and German ideas of the time, and was a three-turret model weighing 18 tons and with a 6-man crew; the main turret carried a 76mm gun, while the others carried machine guns. In the heavy class the first design to appear was the T-32 of 45 tons, mounting no less than five independent turrets which carried, between them, a 76mm gun, two 37mm guns and two machine guns. All this required a ten-man crew to operate, and the T-32 could reach 18 mph on a good surface. It was succeeded by the T-35 in 1933, a similar design with improved armor which weighed 50 tons. These monsters were the ultimate in the 'land battleship' concept which had intrigued designers throughout the 1920s, vehicles which, by sheer size and firepower, could dominate the battlefield. Their weakness lay in the large number of men required to operate them, which presented considerable control problems; the large amount of storage space needed for the battery of armament; the relatively weak armor, necessitated by a need to keep the weight down to a figure with which the transmission and suspension could cope; and the fact that they made enormous targets. Relatively few of the heavy tanks were built, but they survived right through until the Second World War; some of their deficiencies were seen in the war with Finland, and the last of them went into action against the Germans in 1941.

In addition to tanks and trucks, the vehicle factories turned out large quantities of armored cars during the period of the Plan. A small four-wheeled vehicle, the BA-27 (BA=*Bronie Avtomobil*=Armored Car) had a chassis derived from the GAZ-A automobile,

onto which a rivetted body carrying a turret and 37mm gun was fitted. The GAZ-A was, in fact, the Russian-made Ford Model A, from which the alternative name of 'Bronieford' was derived. A more practical design was the BA-10, based on the GAZ-AAA six-wheel truck chassis and also mounting a turret with a 37mm gun; being a six-wheeler, tracks could be looped around the rear wheels to improve traction when operating cross-country.

The tractor plants were also turning out tracked and semi-tracked trucks to act as towing vehicles for the artillery, for the mechanization of this arm was the next priority after the development of armor. The artillery was always held in high regard by Russia, but by 1930 its armament was obsolete; apart from a 76mm infantry gun produced in 1927, the entire gunpark was of pre-World War One design and ripe for replacement. But the Five Year Plan placed the accent on mechanization first, with a limited modernization program of armaments in second place. This modernization consisted of re-working some of the older gun designs to improve their performance so that they could continue in service until fresh weapons could be designed from scratch. Thus the Tsarist 3-inch Gun of 1902 was given a longer barrel and the carriage improved to allow more elevation, changes which increased the maximum range from 7200 yards to 14,200. The 122mm howitzer of 1910 was similarly revamped to improve the range from 8300 to 9800 yards. Two new weapons which began to appear about this time were the 76.2mm field gun M1933 and the 203mm Howitzer M1931. The field gun was a new barrel unit mounted into the carriage of the obsolescent 122mm howitzer of 1910; the intention appears to have been to produce a long range divisional support gun, but in fact its maximum range of 14,200 yards was the same as that of the 1902–03 rework, while it weighed 300 kilograms more and was a cumbersome load into the bargain, so relatively few were built. The 203mm, on the other hand, was a heavy and powerful weapon mounted on an unusual tracked suspension—a product of the tractor factories—and firing a 220lb shell to 20,000 yards, and this remained in service throughout the 1930s and 1940s.

One field of armament which never

46

seems to have been tied in with any Five Year Plan was that of small arms. The manufacturing facilities for these had remained from the pre-Revolutionary days and were maintained and expanded during the 1920s, and the development of new weapons began as soon as the Civil War was over. One reason for this was the desire to outfit the Army with a standardized range of weapons, since the end of the war years found the Red Army in possession of an extremely varied collection. In 1921 a weapons design office was set up under the leadership of V. G. Federov, one of the most outstanding weapon designers Russia ever produced, and among his staff were Degtyarev, Shpagin and Simonov, all of who were to become prominent designers.

The first fruits of this office appeared in 1927 when, after a comparative trial, the Degtyarev light machine gun Model DP was approved for service. A gas-operated, drum-fed 7.62mm weapon, it was reliable and simple and it served as the squad automatic until 1946. A tank version, the Model DT was also produced. F. V. Tokarev had also produced a machine gun, which was tested against the Degtyarev, but when this was turned down in favor of the DP,

Tokarev set to work to produce an automatic pistol to replace the 1895 Nagant revolver as the official sidearm. Basing his design loosely on the American Colt .45 M1911 automatic, Tokarev made some innovative changes which simplified production and maintenance and improved field reliability. The lockwork and hammer, for example, were mounted in a removable unit which greatly simplified repair and cleaning, while the magazine feed lips, notoriously the weakest part of any automatic pistol, were actually machined into the pistol frame, a move which reduced the probability of a malfunction due to a damaged magazine.

Tokarev had also designed a submachine gun in 1926, but it was not particularly successful, one of the drawbacks being that it used the Nagant revolver cartridge, a long, rimmed round of low ballistics. The submachine gun was now tackled by Degtyarev, and he produced a design based on the best features of the Finnish 'Suomi' and the German 'Bergmann'. It was adopted by the Red Army as the PPD—Pistol Pulyemet (machine pistol) Degtyarev— in 1934 and was put into production at the arsenals of Tula and Sestoretsk. It does not appear to have

been made in large numbers, and it is probable that the Red Army were no more certain of the submachine gun's place in warfare than anyone else at that time. It is likely that they envisaged it as a weapon for internal security forces rather than for the Army, a role in which they were frequently found in other countries.

An interesting point about Soviet small arms is that all the infantry weapons—the rifle, carbine, submachine gun and pistol—were of the same caliber, 7.62mm, and, more remarkably, were all rifled to exactly the same specification; four grooves, right-hand twist, one turn in $9\frac{1}{2}$ inches. This meant that the same barrel-making machinery could be used to provide barrel blanks for every type of weapon; indeed, during the war years submachine gun barrels were made by making rifle barrels and sawing them in half.

The Second Five Year Plan of 1933–38 was the next stage in Red Army development. The first Plan had prepared the heavy industry foundation and had made a start in mechanizing the Army; the next step was to complete the mechanization and at the same time begin the re-equipping of the Army with new weapons. During the course of the second Plan the Gorki Automobile Factory (GAZ) was expanded to achieve a planned production of 300,000 automobiles a year; the ZIS factory at Stalingrad was expanded to produce 80,000 automobiles a year; a plant at Yaroslavl was stepped up to 25,000 heavy trucks a year; a Stalingrad factory producing 100,000 3-ton trucks annually was turned over entirely to tracked vehicle production; and some 30 factories were involved in

LEFT: The crew of a 45mm anti-tank gun survive a near miss.

ABOVE: The PPD-40 sub-machine gun with drum feed.

RIGHT: The SG-43 Goryunov heavy machine gun on a wheeled mounting. Originally a tank machine gun, it wa widely adopted by ground forces.

manufacturing tanks and armored cars, self-propelled guns, armored troop carriers and other 'hard' vehicles. Work began on the development of a high-power diesel engine suitable for tanks; electric welding of tank hulls was perfected, and tests were made on methods of casting armor to produce complex shapes, such as turrets in one piece.

One aspect of the spread of mechanization was the need to produce vast numbers of technicians—in 1933, accomplished drivers were not easily found among the annual crop of conscripts, and a massive instructional program had to be mounted. It was greatly aided by the activities of OSOAVIAKHIM (The Association of Societies for the Promotion of Defense and Aero-Chemical Development), a para-military training and youth organization which gave basic pre-military training to youths before their induction. In 1936 the Osoaviakhim claimed to have trained almost a million drivers for the Army since the inception of their special driver-training program in 1930. Voroshilov, at about the same time, stated that 50 per cent of the Army consisted of specialists of various grades.

In 1934 the Soviet leaders began to view the activities of Germany and Japan with some disquiet, and decided to strengthen the Army. It was expanded to 940,000 men, 77 per cent of whom were regular army and the remainder Militia, but the expansion did not stop when it had reached the target figure and by 1936 there were 1,300,000 men under arms. The 'Revolutionary Military Council' was abolished and replaced by the 'Higher Military Council', the sort of terminological double-shuffle which means little but charms the devious Marxist mind. More significantly, the Japanese threat led to a reorganization of the system of Military Districts so as to produce autonomous army groups on the Manchurian and Mongolian borders. Another straw in the wind in 1934 was the closing-down of the joint German-Soviet tank school at Kazan; the Soviets were beginning to think they had sucked that particular orange dry, and when Hitler came to power he was apparently enraged to find that his army had been doing deals with the hated Communists and ordered German participation to end forthwith.

By 1935 the Red Army felt sufficiently sure of itself to invite foreign

military observers to watch the annual maneuvers, held in the Kiev district in the autumn. This was the first time that the Red Army had been exposed to view and to professional criticism, and all that most foreign nations knew of it was hearsay. What the military attachés saw was an eye-opener; tanks of all sizes, performing faultlessly for days on end; impressive parks of artillery; military aviation, including such novelties as tanks slung beneath aircraft and parachute troops; full mechanization; columns of supply trucks; the crowning feature, commented on by every reporter, was a mass drive-past of 1000 tanks on the last day of the exercise, not one tank breaking down. This was a feat which could not have been performed by any other army in the world at that time or, for that matter, for several years afterwards. The report of the British Army representative was so forthright about the superiority of the BT tanks that the British government immediately purchased a Christie tank from America and began trials and design studies which eventually led to such British designs as the Crusader, Cromwell and Comet which served Britain during World War II.

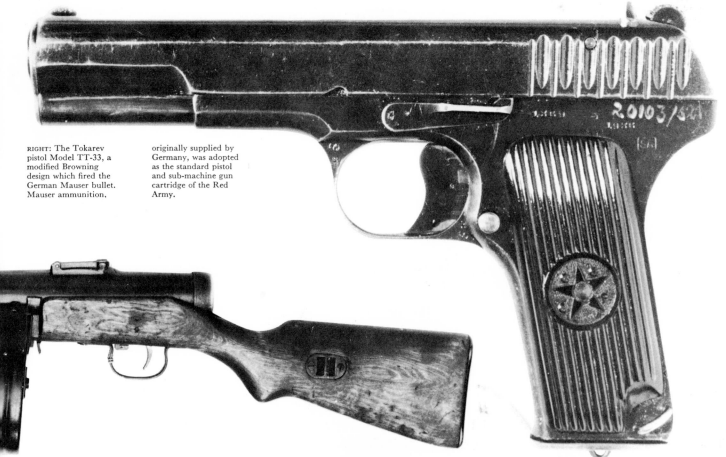

RIGHT: The Tokarev pistol Model TT-33, a modified Browning design which fired the German Mauser bullet. Mauser ammunition, originally supplied by Germany, was adopted as the standard pistol and sub-machine gun cartridge of the Red Army.

1 The Degtyarev Model 34/38 sub-machine gun. This was the first Soviet sub-machine gun to enter service, but it was considerably modified in the light of experience in Finland in 1940.

2 The PPD-40 sub-machine gun, which was the re-design of the 34/38 model. It was easier to manufacture and the drum magazine carried more ammunition than their early box pattern.

3, 4, 5 The Berdan rifles, which were originally issued to the Tsar's Army in the 1870s. Numbers of these survived in private hands and were put to effective use by partisan forces.

6 The Mosin-Nagant rifle Model 1891 with the bayonet fitted. This was the standard infantry rifle of the Red Army.

7 A Mosin-Nagant rifle manufactured by the Remington Arms Company of the USA in 1915.

8 The Model of 1944 carbine, in which the bayonet was permanently attached by a hinge and could be folded back when not in use.

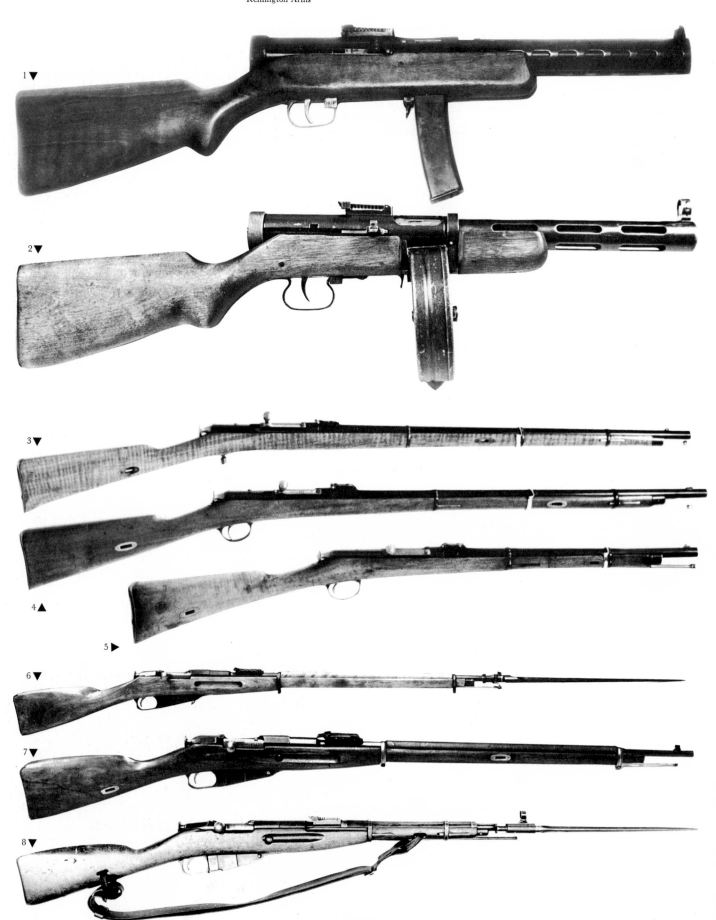

1 ▼

2 ▼

3 ▼

4 ▲

5 ▶

6 ▼

7 ▼

8 ▼

By the time of the Kiev Maneuvers the tank and gun designers had moved along a little further. The light tank range had been increased by the addition of the T-37 tankette, an amphibious model which was fitted with a propeller drive for use in water. Long track guards actually housed balsawood flotation to improve the buoyancy. Used as reconnaissance vehicles, the armament was originally no more than a light machine gun, but this was improved by substituting a 12.7mm heavy machine gun and in some cases by fitting a 20mm cannon. About 250 of these were built, at a time when amphibious tanks were considered to be a slightly ridiculous idea by the rest of the world, and in 1938 they were supplanted by an improved design the T-38.

The BT series was continued with the BT-5, armed with a 45mm high-velocity gun which had good armor-defeating power, and there were also close-support versions carrying a 76mm field gun in the turret. In 1936 the BT-7 went into production, a further improvement, which had a much better 450 hp engine, more fuel capacity to give greater operational range, and improvements in steering and transmission. The armament remained the same, and the BT-7 soon became the standard medium tank.

It was the artillery which benefited most from the Second Five Year Plan, so far as new designs were concerned. Between 1935 and 1941 fifteen new guns appeared in quantity in the Soviet armory, almost every one of which was a completely new model.

The first to appear, in 1935, was the 152mm howitzer BR-2. This used a split-trail carriage carried on a tracked suspension unit — a form of mounting which is uniquely Soviet and stemmed directly from the vast production capacity of the tractor plants; no other nation could have afforded to build tracked suspension for artillery at that time. For movement the trail ends were brought together and supported on a two-wheeled limber and the gun was then towed by one of the numerous designs of full-tracked prime mover which had been introduced for artillery traction. The BR-2 could fire a 108 pound shell to 29,500 yards, and weighed 17.9 tons in the firing position, a good deal of which was attributable to the heavy suspension unit.

In 1936 the 76.2mm Divisional Gun F-22 arrived, a most up-to-date and efficient design using a split trail and pneumatic-tired wheels. It was remarkable for its long barrel, 51 calibers in length, which was a good deal longer than was customary in a field gun, but this enabled it to throw a 14-pound shell to 15,000 yards for a maximum weight in action of the whole weapon of only 3500 pounds, remarkably light for such a powerful gun. It was also provided with an armor-piercing shell which could beat 70mm of plate at 1000 yards, striking at 30° angle, which was a lot better than most so-called anti-tank guns of the day could manage. Indeed the gun was so good that when the Germans captured large numbers of them in 1941 they found it profitable to modify them to suit their gunlaying methods, alter the chamber dimensions slightly in order to be able to use a standard German cartridge case, manufacture ammunition, and take the weapon into service as the '7.62cm Panzer Abwehr Kanone 36(r)' and use it as an anti-tank gun against its former owners.

The Soviets produced a 'proper' anti-tank gun in the following year, the 45mm M37. A 45mm gun had been developed as a tank gun in 1930, and some of these had been fitted to wheeled carriages in 1932 for evaluation. In 1936 a number of 37mm anti-tank guns had been purchased from Germany, the Rheinmettal-produced PAK 36, and

now numbers of these had the barrels removed and were fitted with an updated 45mm barrel. This fired a $3\frac{1}{2}$ pound shell at 2500 ft/sec to defeat 45mm of armor at 1000 yards range, which was on a par with contemporary anti-tank thinking.

The same year saw a strengthening of the medium gun park by the adoption of two 'partner pieces' using the same carriage, the 122mm Gun A-19 and the 152mm Gun-Howitzer ML-20. The carriage was a two dual-wheel split trail model in which the gun tube was pulled back in its cradle for travelling. The 122mm gun fired a 55-pound shell to 22,750 yards, while the 152mm Gun-Howitzer fired a 95-pound shell to 19,000 yards. Both were provided with armor-piercing shells as well as high explosive, incendiary and smoke ammunition.

Anti-aircraft defense was catered for in 1938 by the introduction of the 76.2mm M1938 gun, mounted on the usual pattern of four wheeled platform with outriggers. The carriage had selsyn receiver dials for AA fire control data from a predictor and it was also provided with anti-tank sights as a standard fitting. In its vertical role it fired a 15-pound shell to an effective ceiling of about 25,000 feet, while as a field piece it had a maximum range of 15,600 yards and was capable of piercing 75mm of armor at 500 yards range. It is indicative of the speed of production that while this gun was officially intro-

ABOVE: The Maxim Model 1910 machine gun, showing the mount folded up for carriage in a truck.

LEFT: The Federov Model of 1916 automatic rifle. This was the first of its kind to enter Russian service and was used in small numbers in 1917–18. It then formed the starting point for subsequent development.

BOTTOM: Twelve-cm mortars being packed for issue to the front in factory behind the Urals.

duced in 1938, a specimen examined some years ago was serially numbered 1372 and bore the date 1938; over 1300 had been produced in the first year of issue, a rate of production which could not have been matched by any other country at that time. The British 3.7 inch AA gun was introduced at about the same time, and it is extremely doubtful if 1300 had been made before the outbreak of war in 1939.

The 76.2mm caliber was, as can be seen, a popular one with the Soviets even though most other nations had moved to larger calibers for their field and AA guns. This was due to two things; firstly that it allowed a reasonably powerful and long-ranging gun for a moderate weight; and secondly that it had been a standard caliber in Russia since the beginning of the century, and there was a lot of machinery available for making ammunition. But a 14-pound shell was a poor projectile against modern aircraft; its lethal area was only about 25 feet in radius and

thus the probability of an effective burst, given the many variables in anti-aircraft gunnery, was low. So in 1939 a much better AA gun, the 85mm M39, was produced. This could fire a 20-pound shell at a rate of 20 a minute, to an effective ceiling of 27,500 feet, had a ground range of 17,000 yards and could pierce 110mm of armor at 500 yards.

Meanwhile the Spanish Civil War had broken out and the clash of ideologies was assisted by military aid from the totalitarian states, Germany, Italy and Russia. Apart from aircraft, the number of which are fairly precisely known, the exact degree of military aid provided by Russia to the Spanish (in exchange for 250 million dollars worth of gold) is difficult to assess accurately. Judging from the content of museums in the Iberian Peninsula, which exhibit weapons and equipment of the Civil War, it would seem that the Soviets took the opportunity to get rid of a lot of equipment of dubious value.

Early designs of machine guns which were produced experimentally in the 1920s found their last resting place in Spain, as did aging armored cars and tanks, 1910 model Maxim guns, and obsolete Tsarist field guns.

What was more important was what came back in the way of tactical lessons and equipment assessments, for small quantities of new designs were sent there to be given a field testing, but the Spanish Civil War was probably the most fecund source of false lessons and erroneous conclusions in military history, and the Soviets were little better at reading the right lessons than was anyone else. The worst assessment they made was that tanks were incapable of acting as an independent arm and should henceforth be subservient to the infantry. But one lesson came out of the war to stand the Red Army in good stead in the years to come: the revelation that the submachine gun was, after all, a viable weapon and well suited to a hurriedly-raised army which had little

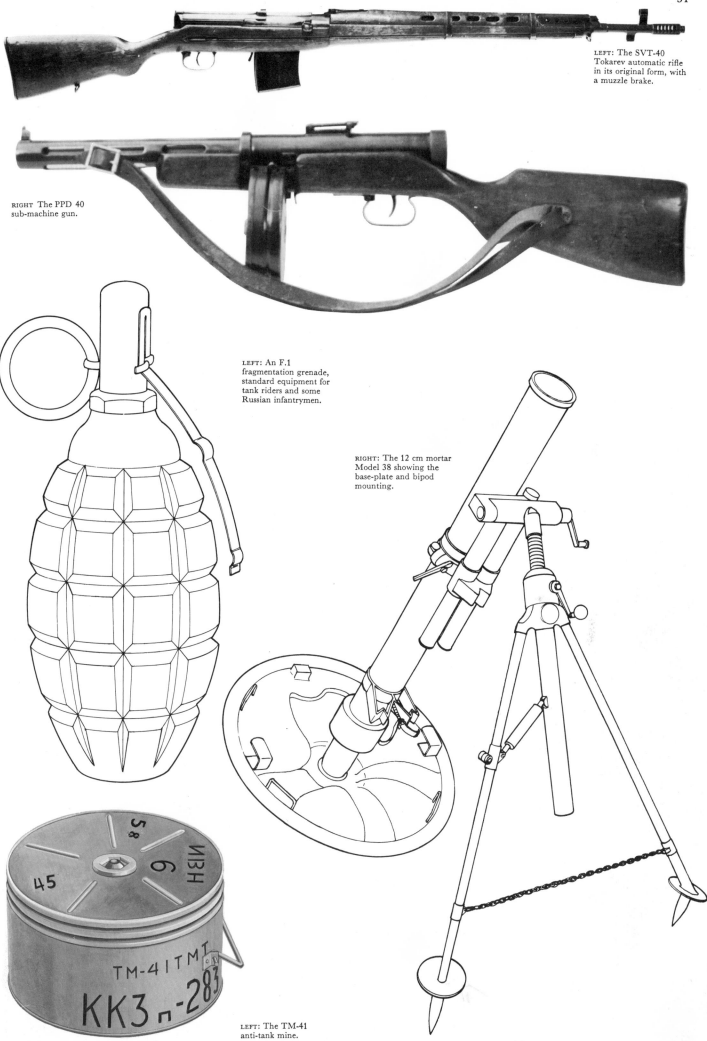

LEFT: The SVT-40 Tokarev automatic rifle in its original form, with a muzzle brake.

RIGHT The PPD 40 sub-machine gun.

LEFT: An F.1 fragmentation grenade, standard equipment for tank riders and some Russian infantrymen.

RIGHT: The 12 cm mortar Model 38 showing the base-plate and bipod mounting.

LEFT: The TM-41 anti-tank mine.

time available to devote to training. The submachine gun was cheap, lethal, easily learned, simple to maintain, quick to manufacture. Submachine guns in the hands of a mass army gave formidable firepower, and they were well suited to a conscript army of limited technical ability and intelligence. Moreover, they fitted the Russian style of fighting; with a submachine gun it is scarcely possible (despite posed propaganda photographs) to hide in a ditch and snipe at the enemy. You have to get out of the ditch and go after him. And as a result of all these factors, the Soviets gave the Degtyarev PPD submachine gun a higher priority and put it into mass production.

The standard infantry weapon at that time was still the rifle, and this was the Mosin-Nagant 7.62mm bolt action, a design which went back to 1891 for its origin. It had been overhauled in 1930, shortened, modified so as to simplify manufacture, and fitted with sights graduated in meters instead of the archaic 'arshin' of the Tsar's day. Then in 1938 a carbine version was issued, 9 inches shorter than the rifle and intended for more convenient carriage by mechanized personnel. But in 1936 the US Army had adopted the Garand

automatic rifle after years of trial, and other armies had been conducting trials of automatic ever since the end of the First World War; the day of the bolt-action magazine rifle was coming to its close, and an army as forward-looking and technically oriented as the Red Army was obviously not the one to be left behind in this sphere.

Trials of automatic rifles had taken place as early as 1930 in Russia, and a Simonov design had been selected for further development. Simonov had been apprenticed to Federov in the days when Federov was concerned with automatic rifle design, before the Revolution, and he never lost his interest in this type of weapon. His rifle, the AVS-36, was introduced into the Red Army in 1936, a 7.62mm gas-operated weapon. But like many another potential winner, the AVS-36 performed better in the laboratory than it did in the field. For reasons not entirely clear it gave excessive muzzle blast and recoil; to try and improve matters a muzzle brake was fitted, which did make things better for the man who was firing it, but made life very trying for anybody at his side since the muzzle blast now went sideways. The mechanism was prone to fouling and stoppages

BELOW: The 122 mm gun-howitzer Model 1938, the backbone of the Soviet divisional artillery.

LEFT: The SVT-38 automatic rifle. This was Tokarev's first design, but proved to be unreliable and was modified to become the SVT-40.

BELOW: A Soviet 37 mm anti-tank gun giving covering fire to an advancing infantry platoon.

BELOW: The 82 mm mortar Model 1937, which was the standard infantry company support weapon.

LEFT: The PPSh-41 sub-machine gun. This replaced the earlier PPD models, since it was much easier to mass-produce. It is principally formed from steel stampings, welded and riveted together.

LEFT: The 152 mm gun-howitzer Model 1937. The barrel has been drawn back and secured to the carriage for transport.

RIGHT: The 57 mm anti-tank gun Model 1942. At the time this weapon was introduced Britain and America were phasing out guns of this caliber.

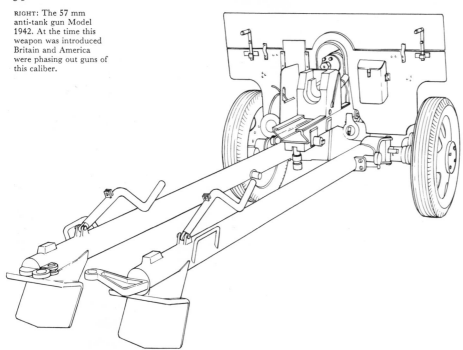

In the Winter War against Finland the Degtyarev PPD submachine gun had its first combat use, and it functioned well. The only complaint from the troops was that the box magazine only held 25 rounds, whereas the Finns were armed with the Suomi submachine guns which used a drum magazine which carried 71 rounds and thus gave the Finns the edge in a fire fight. So a drum magazine was rapidly produced, basically copied from the Suomi but of a slightly odd design since it had to fit into the housing designed for the box magazine. The other objection to the PPD was more serious; it was expensive and time-consuming to manufacture, requiring milling and turning processes to fabricate the gun body and jacket. So in order to overcome both objections, Degtyarev redesigned the weapon, simplifying it, altering the specification to call for lower grades of steel, simplifying the machine operations, and designing a new and better 71-round drum magazine which fitted to the gun in an easier manner. This became the PPD-40 and was being mass-produced by 1941.

from grit and dust entering the action, and the selective automatic fire option, which allowed the weapon to be used as a light machine gun, also gave trouble. As a result it was not issued in large numbers and, indeed, is extremely rare today. It was replaced in 1938 by the SVT-38, a design by Tokarev, which was also gas operated but which used a different and simpler mechanism. While rather more reliable than the AVS-36, it was less robust and a somewhat stronger model was later issued as the SVT-40. But even so, it was a

delicate design, somewhat temperamental, and it was never widely issued; most of them finished up in the hands of snipers, probably on the assumption that the sniper is a better-trained soldier and has more time and incentive to give a delicate rifle the care it needs to keep it functioning. Thus the automatic rifle never became a general issue until after the war, though its absence was less critical than it might have been had the submachine gun not become such a prominent feature of the Soviet Army scene.

RIGHT: The DP light machine gun. A drum-fed weapon, it was the base of fire for the infantry section. Designed in 1928, it served with distinction throughout the war.

RIGHT: The ShKaS 7.62 mm aircraft machine gun, a complicated but reliable weapon, and, firing at 1200 rounds per minute, one of the fastest machine guns in the world.

RIGHT: The PPS-43 sub-machine gun, developed in Leningrad during the siege. It was designed to make use of the limited materials and machinery in the besieged city.

RIGHT: The Mosin-Nagant Model 1938 carbine. Originally intended for cavalry use, it was widely adopted by infantry because it was a light and handy weapon.

RIGHT: The DT machine gun, which was the standard armament in all Soviet tanks.

The enormous losses of matériel, and also the loss of many engineering plants during the first days of the German invasion led the Soviets to look for weapons which could be easily and cheaply produced. Their experiences in Finland had convinced them of the value of the submachine gun, and now a designer called Shpagin appeared with a submachine gun, constructed largely from steel stampings, welded together, capable of being made by almost any metal-working workshop, cheap, roughly finished, but reliable and effective. Due to its simple design the rate of fire was 900 rounds a minute, a lot higher than the rate generally considered suitable, and this rate of fire caused the muzzle to climb during firing and scatter shots all over the place. To counteract this the stamped metal perforated barrel jacket was formed into a simple muzzle deflector which forced some of the blast upwards and thus pressed the muzzle down to compensate for the climb. This gun went into service as the PPSh-41, and is believed to have gone into mass production early in 1942; according to reliable estimates something like five million were made before the war ended, and the PPSh (or 'pepeshka' as it became known) became the hallmark of the Soviet soldier. Whole units were armed with nothing else, the most notable being the 'Tank Descent Troops' or 'Tank Riders', as they were known in the west. These men formed the immediate support infantry for armoured divisions, and rode on top of the fighting tanks, clinging to handles welded to the turret and hull. With a PPSh in their free hand and a stock of loaded magazines slung around their waists, these men rode into action and dismounted to shoot their way through any opposition. If their tank was knocked out, the survivors jumped aboard another. They appear to have been the toughest troops of World War II; their life expectancy was about three

weeks once battle was joined, and Western troops who came into contact with them in the closing stages of the war described them as being primitive to an animal-like degree, their channel of supply, apart from ammunition, being largely a matter of what they could loot and forage as they went. And for men like these, whose sole tactic was frontal attack, the PPSh was the ideal weapon.

While the PPSh-41 was the official and standard submachine gun, there was a second design, even cheaper (and, in my own view, better) than the PPSh, a design which appeared in unusual circumstances. In 1942 Leningrad was besieged by the German Army and the weapon situation was becoming a matter for concern. A technician-engineer, Alexei Sudayev, was in charge of arms production in the factories there, and he designed a submachine gun, working to an unusual form of specification. In most weapon designs the criteria are such matters as velocity, range, weight and so on; in Sudayev's predicament the prominent questions were 'What machinery is available and what materials can be found?' and the weapon designed to suit. The result was an all-metal (except for two slabs of wood on the pistol grip) design which was stamped, pressed, welded and riveted in the cheapest imaginable manner. Only the barrel was a precision job, and that was made by sawing up old rifle barrels. The PPS-42, as it became known, used a 35-round box magazine, since facilities for making the standard drum pattern did not exist; it had no means of firing single shots; it had the most rudimentary sights; and a folding steel butt based on the German MP40 design. But it was a sound and effective weapon which played a significant part in holding the Germans at Leningrad. The design had some slight improvements made in the following year to become the PPS-43, but the changes were matters of detail

in the design of the stock and safety catch and it takes a keen eye to detect the difference. About a million of both models are said to have been made but it was never standardized, nor did it replace the PPSh, though it was doubtless cheaper and quicker to make. After the war it vanished from Soviet service, being given to satellite nations (it was the primary submachine gun of the North Korean People's Army, for example) and it was widely copied in other countries. The lack of enthusiasm in the Red Army for this weapon is difficult to explain, though it has been suggested that there was a political motive behind it; the defenders of Leningrad were viewed with some suspicion in postwar Russia and their works were not perpetuated.

One of the most remarkable deficiencies in the prewar Red Army was the lack of any sort of infantry anti-tank weapon smaller than the 37mm gun. In every other army anti-tank rifles were standard, and although today they are looked upon with some scorn it must be remembered that in 1936–37, when most of them were introduced, their performance — about an inch of armor pierced at 500 yards — was adequate for the tanks of the day. Britain's 'Medium Mark Two', for instance, had 8mm of plate, the German PzKwIII 14.5mm, and the Soviet BT-5 13mm. Nevertheless, the Red Army ignored the high-powered rifle; it was a 'defensive' weapon, and the Soviet philosophy of war did not contemplate allowing an enemy to enter Russian territory and having to fight on the defensive. When the workers' revolution finally came, the Red Army would surge forth, all-conquering, and all its actions would be offensive.

In the event, of course, the Germans made nonsense of this theory, just as they made nonsense of a lot of others in their time, and having watched events in Poland and France and after their own experiences in Finland (where the Finns used an extremely good 20mm Lahti anti-tank rifle), the Soviets reluctantly admitted that there might be something in it after all, and during the latter half of 1940 two designers, Degtyarev and Simonov, began work. They both produced a design and, unusually for the Soviets and perhaps indicative of their apprehension in 1941, both designs were put into production. A special round of ammunition was devel-

BELOW: The Finnish Suomi 1932 sub-machine gun, an extremely reliable weapon which made a great impression on the Russians in the Winter War. The magazine arrangement was copied by the Russians in all their subsequent designs.

RIGHT: The Degtyarev DP light machine gun. This view shows the mounting of the recoil spring beneath the barrel, which led to overheating and spring failure. It was subsequently re-designed and the spring moved to a cooler position.

RIGHT: PTRD-41 anti-tank rifle. This single-shot rifle fired a 14.5 mm bullet, but by 1944 it had been overtaken by German tank design.

ABOVE: The 76.2 mm field gun, the standard Soviet field piece. As well as performing normal fire-supporting missions, it had a useful anti-tank capability.

oped first, a 14.5mm steel-cored bullet weighing just over two ounces, with a propelling charge which drove it at 3300 ft/sec muzzle velocity. The Degtyarev design, known as the PTRD-41, was about as simple as it was possible to be and still work; the barrel recoiled in the stock, and as it did so the bolt — just the same as that of an ordinary rifle — rode over a cam. As the barrel returned to its forward position, the bolt caught on the cam and was jerked open to extract the fired cartridge case; the firer then inserted a new round and closed the bolt manually. Although simple, it was heavy (38 pounds) and long (79 inches), as it needed to be to withstand the punch of the heavy cartridge, but it could defeat about 15mm of plate at 500 yards, which was very satisfactory for a shoulder-fired weapon.

The Simonov design, the PTRS-41, was vastly different; this was a gas-operated semi-automatic with a five-shot magazine — though this virtue lost its edge because the magazine had to be clip-loaded and the clip could only go in one way, an idiosyncracy which was of

no help at all in the heat of battle with a Panzer bearing down a hundred yards away. On paper the Simonov should have been the better weapon, but it was not robust enough to stand the hammering of that powerful ammunition and it frequently broke down in the field. Moreover it was even longer and heavier than the PTRD and just about the limit as a one-man weapon. In spite of these disadvantages, it, together with the PTRD, survived until the end of the war, long after every other major nation had discarded the anti-tank rifle.

The arrival of the Panzers in 1941 suddenly made the Red Army very anti-tank minded, and the short-comings of their 37mm and 45mm guns rapidly became obvious. Their first reaction was to upgrade the 45mm by giving it a longer barrel to improve the muzzle velocity and penetration. They then developed a tungsten-cored 'Arrowhead' shot which had a velocity of about 3200 ft/sec and could beat 70mm of armor at 500 yards. While this was a useful improvement it was

BELOW: A Soviet
anti-aircraft battery
defends Moscow.

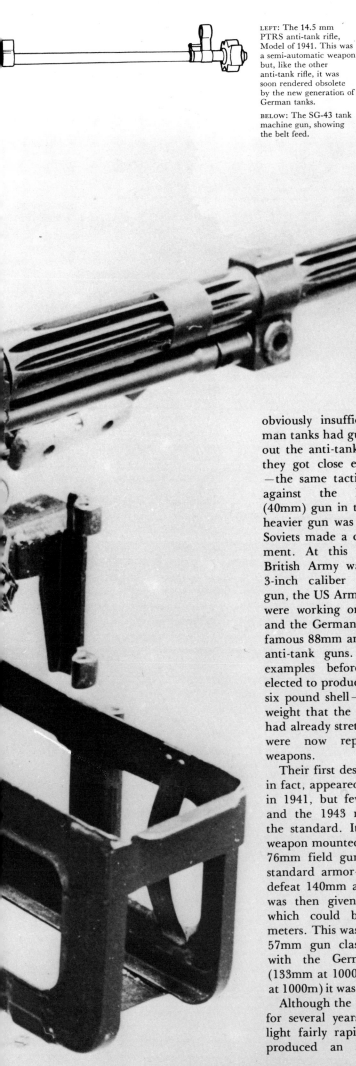

LEFT: The 14.5 mm
PTRS anti-tank rifle,
Model of 1941. This was
a semi-automatic weapon
but, like the other
anti-tank rifle, it was
soon rendered obsolete
by the new generation of
German tanks.
BELOW: The SG-43 tank
machine gun, showing
the belt feed.

obviously insufficient, since the German tanks had guns which could knock out the anti-tank weapons long before they got close enough to be harmed —the same tactic they had employed against the British two-pounder (40mm) gun in the Western Desert. A heavier gun was needed, and here the Soviets made a curiously wrong assessment. At this time—late 1942—the British Army was about to issue the 3-inch caliber 17-pounder anti-tank gun, the US Army had their 3-inch and were working on a design of 90mm, and the Germans, of course, had their famous 88mm and two different 75mm anti-tank guns. And yet with these examples before them, the Soviets elected to produce a 57mm gun firing a six pound shell—the same caliber and weight that the British and Americans had already stretched to its utmost and were now replacing with heavier weapons.

Their first design of 57mm gun had, in fact, appeared in small numbers late in 1941, but few of them were made and the 1943 model (ZIS-2) became the standard. It was a long-barrelled weapon mounted on the carriage of the 76mm field gun M1942 and with its standard armor-piercing shell it could defeat 140mm at 500 meters range. It was then given an 'Arrowhead' shot which could beat 100mm at 1000 meters. This was up to standard for the 57mm gun class, but in comparison with the German 75mm PAK 40 (133mm at 1000m) or PAK 41 (177mm at 1000m) it was pathetic.

Although the 57mm remained in use for several years, the Soviets saw the light fairly rapidly and in 1944 they produced an anti-tank gun which

certainly compensated for their misjudgement with the 57mm model. The 100mm BS-3 was an extremely powerful gun of excellent design. It is believed that the gun itself was derived from a naval high-angle gun, and it was mounted on to a two dual-wheel split trail carriage. Although weighing $3\frac{1}{2}$ tons, and a cumbersome handful to manhandle about the battlefield, it fired a 34-pound AP shell at 3000 .ft/sec to pierce 190mm at 500 yards, and with a high velocity arrowhead shot its performance was undoubtedly better, though no reliable figures are known. With a 35-pound high explosive shell it could double as a field gun, with a maximum range of 23,000 yards.

It must be borne in mind that the Red Army was less dependent upon 'pure' anti-tank guns than other armies. The Red Army view was that any gun which was capable of shooting at a tank was an anti-tank gun, and armor-piercing ammunition formed part of the outfit of all artillery pieces. In defensive actions the artillery was distributed around the perimeter of the position and allotted 'zones of fire', and the field artillery of the forward area were given a zone which extended from the gun's muzzle to the nearest skyline. As a result any and every gun could find itself shooting at tanks; and if, say, a 57mm anti-tank gun in the forward area was knocked out, its replacement was the next gun standing in the reserve park. It might be a 57mm; it might as easily be a 76mm field gun or a 122mm howitzer; whatever it was, it went into the vacant place. This interchangeability of role went a long way towards evening out the relative weakness in anti-tank guns in 1942–43. By the same

BELOW: The PTRS anti-tank rifle.

CENTER: The DPM light machine gun was a modification of the DP machine gun, in which the recoil spring was moved to the rear of the weapon in order to improve reliability.

BOTTOM: A photograph of the DPM machine gun.

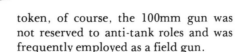

token, of course, the 100mm gun was not reserved to anti-tank roles and was frequently employed as a field gun.

Perhaps the greatest surprise to both the Germans and the Allies was the extensive use of rockets as an artillery weapon by the Red Army. Research into rockets had begun in the Leningrad Gas Dynamics Laboratory in 1930 under the guidance of an engineer named Petropavlovsky, and after his death in 1935 was continued by a design team headed by A. Kostikov. This led to an 82mm solid-fuel rocket carrying a 6½-pound high explosive or a 6-pound fragmentation warhead. Launching was done from an openframe type of launcher mounted on the back of a 2½-ton truck, either a ZIS-6 or a Lend-Lease Studebaker or GMC. This launcher held 36 rockets in three rows and could be elevated and traversed like a gun, though the rockets always were launched over the truck cab, which had to be protected by steel blast plates. Firing was done electrically from the vehicle batteries, and the rockets could reach a maximum range of about 6000 yards.

The first use of this rocket — known then as 'Kostikov's Gun' — was near Orszy on 21 July 1941. It soon received the name 'Stalin's Organ' from the Germans due to the peculiar note of the rocket's flight through the air, while the Soviet troops christened it 'Katyusha'. In spite of its frequent appearances in propaganda pictures, little definite information was ever released about it or any other wartime rocket, and Allied military visitors were never allowed to get near them. They were, in fact, never manned by Regular Army troops but by NKVD troops or military police, an additional measure of security.

Shortly after the 82mm had entered service it was followed by a heavier model, the 132mm, which used a 40-pound warhead and had a range of 9250 yards. This was also truck-mounted, using the M-13 launcher, a 16-rocket device which launched from a cluster of I-beam launch rails. Some of these launchers were also mounted on the chassis of obsolete T-60 and T-70

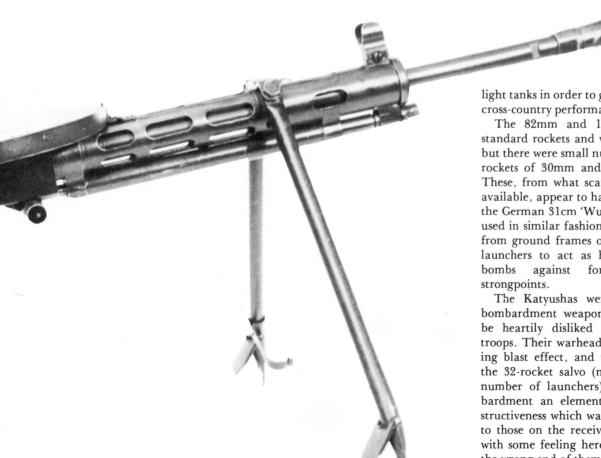

light tanks in order to give them a better cross-country performance.

The 82mm and 132mm were the standard rockets and were widely used, but there were small numbers of heavier rockets of 30mm and 310mm caliber. These, from what scant information is available, appear to have been copies of the German 31cm 'Wurfgerat' and were used in similar fashion, being launched from ground frames or truck mounted launchers to act as heavy demolition bombs against fortifications and strongpoints.

The Katyushas were a formidable bombardment weapon which came to be heartily disliked by the German troops. Their warheads had a devastating blast effect, and the dispersion of the 32-rocket salvo (multiplied by the number of launchers) gave the bombardment an element of random destructiveness which was most unnerving to those on the receiving end. I speak with some feeling here, since I was on the wrong end of them in Korea in later years.

BORDER CLASHES

THE MANCHURIAN AFFAIR

The Red Army's involvement in Manchuria began in 1929. Until then the Siberian Military District, an enormous stretch of country, was garrisoned by four infantry divisions and three cavalry brigades, and in line with Party policy the district was a command of the Red Army, pendant at the end of a long supply line. Although logic and the teachings of the Russo-Japanese War indicated the need for a completely autonomous force in the area, autonomous armies were considered likely foci for counter-revolution, so the teachings of history were ignored. But in the summer of 1929 a dispute arose over the Chinese Eastern Railway, the main artery of communication running across northern Manchuria to connect Chita and Vladivostok. This, since its inception, had been jointly managed by Russian and Chinese staff, but now the Chinese Army appeared and drove the Russians out.

As a result, a Decree of 7 August 1929 formed the Special Army of the Far East, placing General (later Marshal) Vasilly Blücher in command. Blücher lost no time in organizing his forces and in November swept across the Manchurian frontier, drove the Chinese Army back, and re-established joint control of the railway.

By 1932 Japanese intervention in

Manchuria had reached into the northern area and the Soviets began to sit up and take notice. The Special Army was gradually reinforced, growing to 11 infantry and 2½ cavalry divisions. Under the somewhat autocratic command of Blücher, this army was soon welded into an efficient fighting force. It included in its make-up the so-called 'Kolkhoz Corps', a force of trained reservists who were settled in collective farms close to the Manchurian border. While working the farms so as to provide the Army with food, these men were also liable to instant mobilization if the situation demanded it. By 1937 the Army's strength had grown to 15 infantry divisions, three cavalry divisions and four tank brigades, plus the Kolkhoz Corps, a strength of about half a million men.

During this time Blücher had lost no opportunity to pin-prick the Japanese and extend Soviet influence in China whenever the opportunity offered. In 1933, for example, the Chinese governor of Sinkiang had a Moslem rebellion on his hands, and he was aided by Blücher allowing Chinese troops, driven north by the Japanese, to be moved through Siberia to Sinkiang. When this proved insufficient, two infantry brigades, together with artillery, tanks and

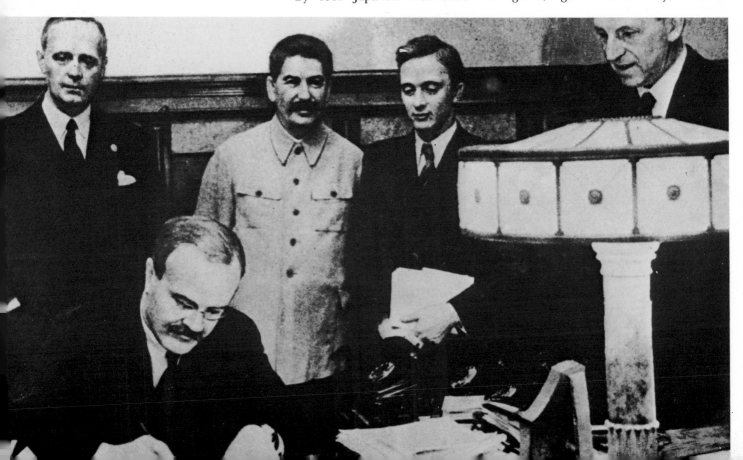

BELOW: Finnish soldiers man barricades made of strips of wood. Logs or wooden blocks were also used to blend into the heavily forested landscape of Finland to provide rudimentary but nonetheless effective barriers to the Russian invasion.

RIGHT: Lieutenant Platan of the Finnish Army directs a counter-assault against Russian forces.

BELOW RIGHT: Anti-tank obstacles are dismantled in a fortified area around Teriioki on the Russo-Finnish frontier.

aircraft, went into Sinkiang disguised in Chinese uniforms to render the necessary assistance. By this intervention Soviet influence in Sinkiang was strengthened, and the Japanese, who were also scheming to gain power in that area (and had financed the Moslem rebellion) were discomfited.

In 1938 came the first major armed clash between Russia and Japan, an affair which has never been satisfactorily explained. At that time the Japanese High Command were divided into two schools of thought; those who considered that the future lay in a strike against Soviet Russia—the 'Strike North' school—and those who thought Japan's destiny would be better served by aiming for South China, Indo-China and the Dutch East Indies—the 'Strike South' faction.

According to the generally-accepted version of events, the 'Strike North' school, encouraged by the apparent weakness and disorganization of the Red Army after the Great Purge, suggested a trial of strength with the Soviets. Hagaki, the Japanese Minister of War, together with the Japanese General Staff, laid plans for a move which, if successful, would allow an encirclement of Vladivostok and seizure of a sizeable piece of Soviet territory. The 'incident' occurred on 29 July 1938 at Changkufeng, a small hill of no particular significance on the eastern

border of Manchuria, close to Vladivostok.

However, a slightly different version of events came to light when the incident was brought up during the Tokyo War Crimes Trial in 1946. The Soviet Border Guard Commander at the time of the incident deposed that there was no dispute over the boundaries at that point, that the Soviets owned the eastern slope of the hill and the Japanese the western. The Japanese at the trial claimed that the Soviets had begun the dispute by occupying the crest of the hill, which had always been used by the local villagers for religious festivals without Soviet interference. The Chinese Consul-General in Vladivostok later said it was 'a direct Soviet challenge to Japan', while another source claims that Blücher deliberately provoked the incident to bring on a war with Japan, something he felt to be inevitable and which would be as well to precipitate at a time when the Far East Army was in good heart and the Japanese exceptionally stretched in China and Manchuria.

Wherever the responsibility lay the upshot was a series of confused patrol skirmishes at first. Then both the Japanese and the Soviets began to bring in reinforcements, including tanks and aircraft, but by this time the Japanese Air Force were forbidden to move in support. Instructions were given to settle the whole thing diplomatically. A truce agreement was reached, the Japanese Army moved back one kilometer to leave a neutral zone, and on 11 August the affair ended. The Soviets proposed a joint boundary commission

RIGHT: Japanese cavalry units from the Manchurian military academy on a charge near the Russian border. Skirmishes between Japanese and Soviet troops occurred frequently in the 1930s, occasionally blowing up into full-scale battles.

to settle the matter amicably, and produced a copy of a map drawn up as part of a Sino-Russian agreement in 1886, but since no agreement was ever reached about the validity or authenticity of this map, no border survey ever took place.

One consequence of the Changkufeng Incident, and probably the only one of lasting influence, was the sudden removal and liquidation of Marshal Blücher. He had survived the Purge, and his removal tends to support the view that he had been responsible for the affair. Even after he was 'rehabilitated' in the post-Stalin era, the final years of his career are ignored in the official histories.

After Changkufeng the Japanese Army was restive; they were still divided, and the 'Strike North' faction were still able to deploy some persuasive arguments, playing on anti-Soviet sentiments which had been aroused by a fishery dispute and troubles over the Japanese oil concessions in Sakhalin. But by this time the General Staff in Tokyo were coming round to the 'Strike South' policy and they were not anxious to stir up trouble in the north; a quiescent Manchurian border would suit them very nicely and would permit the withdrawal of some forces for service elsewhere.

Unfortunately the Japanese government and General Staff were not masters in Manchuria; the Japanese Kwantung Army holding the country was very much a law unto itself. It had, over the past ten years, forced the Government's hand on numerous occasions, notably the Mukden Incident which set the conquest of Manchuria in motion and the affair at the Marco Polo Bridge which began the China War. The Kwantung Army feared an alliance of Russia and China, an alliance which, by their intelligence service throughout China and Mongolia, they had ample reason to believe was proceeding apace. Moreover they were on the spot; they were there; they knew the answers better than the chairborne warriors in Tokyo. That was their version; it is equally true to say that they were so deep in the trees of Manchurian involvement that they were unable to see the wood of world politics beyond.

Whatever the rights or wrongs of the Mukden-Tokyo disagreements, the Kwantung Army once again decided to give events a push; they had done this successfully on two major occasions and they fancied their chances at bringing it off a third time. The Japanese had long been contemplating the annexation of Inner and Outer Mongolia; these were to some degree under Chinese influence but the Japanese claimed—with some validity—that the Chinese had no sovereign rights there, and they had formulated plans for increasing Japanese influence in these areas so as to lead, eventually, to full Japanese occupation and control. But the Outer Mongolian Government had signed a Pact of Mutual Assistance with the Soviet Union in 1936. Red Army troops were stationed in Mongolia under a Soviet commander who, in 1939, was Zhukov, the future Marshal. The question in the mind of General Ueda, Commander of the Kwantung Army, was 'How far will the Soviets go in support of the Mongols?' They resolved to find out.

On the northeast border of Outer Mongolia was a stretch of country tailor-made for the purpose. The border turned northeast across the lake of Bor Nor, then turned back southeast, making a salient into Manchuria; the logical border line would have followed the course of the Khalkin River, but it actually ran some 20-30 miles east of the river—and there could be no argument about the boundary, since it was well-marked with stone pillars bearing inscriptions. But the Kwantung Army decided to move forward to the river line and thus shave off much of the salient; if this went unopposed, they would move further until the salient was completely ironed out and the frontier re-drawn. A secondary advantage would be that a projected railway line from Hailan to Taoan would then be well away from the border and in a less vulnerable position.

On 11 May 1939 a brigade of renegade Mongolian cavalry, aided by troops of the Japanese 23rd Infantry Division, crossed the boundary line and advanced to the Khalkin River. The Mongolian Border Guards, in a log fort on the west of the river called up a local cavalry unit which crossed the river and drove the invaders back to the border. Three days later the Japanese reappeared with a regiment of regular cavalry in support and with aircraft which bombed the frontier posts on the Mongolian side of the river. The border

guards reported back and a Soviet Major, commanding a battalion of Red Army, was sent forward to see what was going on. He arrived just in time to witness an air raid and, convinced that the attack was serious, he called for a division of Mongolian cavalry and some Red Army infantry. As these troops began to arrive so the Japanese force on the river fell back into the broken and hilly country between the boundary line and the river, surrounding the village of Nomonhan.

On 22 May a force of Soviet and Mongolian troops crossed the river to carry out a reconnaissance and ran into an ambush prepared for them in the hills, being severely mauled before they could fight clear and fall back to the river. They re-crossed and prepared a defensive position on the eastern bank, but a Japanese force swooped out of the hills and pushed them back to the western side.

By this time the affair had reached substantial proportions; it has since been estimated that something in the order of 15 to 20,000 troops were now involved, with roughly equal numbers on each side. But the Soviets viewed the affair with some alarm; they appreciated that if the Japanese were allowed to get away with a minor incursion it would soon become a major annexation. So more Red Army units were rapidly ordered to the scene, the first being the 149th Motorized Infantry Regiment which drove straight into action, providing the necessary weight to push the Japanese back to the border line again.

Zhukov now appeared, to take charge of operations, but before he could begin, the Japanese brought up strong reinforcements from a nearby railhead at Halunarshan, marched them cross-country, and on 3 July had once again pushed forward to the river. By now the Japanese mustered about 40,000 troops, with 135 tanks and 225 aircraft. Zhukov, on the other side of the river, had 12,500 troops with 185 tanks and 225 armored cars.

The next Japanese move was an attempt to encircle the Soviet position by swinging north, throwing a pontoon bridge across the river, and then driving south on the western bank, sweeping the Soviets before them; meanwhile a second swing to the south would form a backstop so that the Red Army troops would be caught in a pincer movement.

This was a perfectly sound idea and it would probably have worked very well against a Chinese warlord or against the Mongolian Army. But they reckoned without the swift reaction of Zhukov and the powerful tank arm he wielded. As the northern flanking movement began to cross the river, Zhukov ordered up his mobile reserve; one tank brigade, one armored car brigade and a motorized infantry regiment. This force moved rapidly into a three-pronged attack on the bridgehead. At the same time aircraft of the Soviet Air Force bombed and strafed the Japanese on the far side of the river, while artillery laid down a concentration of fire which prevented Japanese reinforcements coming across the pontoon bridge. Zhukov's all-mechanized attack hit the Japanese before they had time to organize the defense of the bridgehead, and within a matter of hours the Japanese west of the river were destroyed, while those on the far side were still hurriedly trying to organize a counterattack.

The Japanese counter-stroke was launched the next day. The Soviets allowed it to cross the river before taking any action; once a sizable force was across, the Red Air Force destroyed the bridge and the army moved in to wipe out the now-isolated attackers. It was later estimated that 90 per cent of the attack force were destroyed. Over half the Japanese tank strength was wiped out and about 9000 Japanese troops were killed.

Even this bloody repulse did not daunt the Kwantung Army. They returned in strength, the 6th Army under General Ogisa, reinforced with additional Manchurian troops and with 80,000 men, 180 tanks, 300 armored cars, three artillery regiments and 450 aircraft, mounting a major attack on 23 July which was quickly brought to a standstill by heavy Soviet artillery fire and tank attacks.

Zhukov now decided that the only solution was to inflict a major defeat on the Japanese, and while his artillery and a tank screen held Ogisa's army in the Nomonhan Hills, he began preparations for an ambitious maneuver. It will have been seen that until this point the Soviet forces had behaved in a strictly correct fashion; their activity had been confined to repulsing Japanese forces after they had entered Mongolia. But Zhukov saw that this sort of action could go on indefinitely, with the Japanese trying again and again.

Every available Soviet vehicle was pressed into service to ferry supplies from Chita, the railhead on the Trans-Siberian Railway over 400 miles away across the Mongolian wilderness. Some 18,000 tons of ammunition and over 40,000 tons of other supplies, more guns and tanks were ferried in, and on 20 August 35 infantry divisions, 20 cavalry squadrons, 500 guns, 500 tanks and 350 armored cars were ready. Zhukov's plan was to turn the Japanese plan back on themselves, to encircle the force and annihilate it. The attack would be made by three groups, with armored forces on the flanks to make a wide swing around

BELOW: Finnish infantry
on skis take up positions
near Tolvajaervi. The
use of Finnish sporting
equipment during the
Winter War was another
surprise for the Soviet
Army.

each end of the Japanese position to meet in the rear of the enemy who would meanwhile be held by a frontal engagement. At 0545 hours on 20 August the attack opened with an air attack by 150 bombers and 100 fighters on the Japanese positions; as the last explosion died away 250 Soviet guns opened fire with a two-hour bombardment of forward positions, artillery positions and reserve areas, and shortly before 0900 the Red Army moved in to the attack.

Apart from momentary hold-ups in places where the Japanese had built field fortifications, the Soviet attack went forward smoothly. On the southern flank the armored column, accompanied by self-propelled guns and a number of flame-thrower tanks, roared clear of the battle in a wide sweep to cross the border into Manchuria and then move north to Nomonhan, the

pivot of the Japanese position. By 23 August the northern armored force had completed a similar swing and had joined up at Nomonhan; the Japanese 6th Army were surrounded, and Zhukov's men set about exterminating them with a cold and purposeful ferocity.

While the encircling armor held the ring and fought off an attempt to relieve the encircled army, the Soviet Air Force pounded the Japanese inside the trap, dropping almost 200 tons of bombs. Then the flame-throwers, tanks and armored cars moved inwards, blasting every pocket of resistance. By 31 August the battle was over; of the 60,000 Japanese and Manchurian troops caught in the trap, less than 10,000 escaped. Soviet casualties were said to be 10,000, though this is probably an under-estimate. The Japanese Army had suffered its worst defeat in history, and the full story was never publicly

revealed until after the war. But the Battle of Nomonhan failed to make the world's headlines; for on the day after Zhukov's troops accomplished their victory the German Army crossed the Polish border, and the world's eyes were focused on Europe.

In Manchuria the Japanese opened negotiations for a truce. The Soviet Government were happy to oblige, since they were casting anxious eyes on the Polish campaign, fearful that they might lose their chance of westward expansion. An agreement was reached whereby the armies remained where they were—in effect, reverting to the position at the start of the abortive campaign. General Ueda was removed from his post and replaced; a number of junior Japanese commanders committed ritual suicide after their failure in battle; and the 'Strike North' school was finally discredited.

THE WINTER WAR

BELOW: Another example of Finnish preparation for the Russian assault. Clad in white, weatherproof clothing in temperatures as low as –50°F, Finnish troops could withstand the unusual climatic conditions far better than their Russian enemies.

BOTTOM: Russian POWs in Finnish hands at a religious service. This Finnish propaganda photograph was meant to indicate that as prisoners Russian troops enjoyed a freedom of religion denied them in the Soviet Union. Its authenticity is open to question.

One of the constant problems of the Soviet government during the 1930s was the question of the Baltic states. The Finnish border was only a few miles from Leningrad and the northern coastline of the Gulf of Finland was owned by the Finns. Most of the southern shore of the Gulf was Estonian soil, and this meant that Russia's 'Window to the West' was, in theory, capable of being closed by any hostile action which could persuade the Finns and Estonians to act in concert. In 1938 the Soviets began discussions with the Finns, suggesting that the Finns might cede to Russia some of the islands in the Gulf in order that defenses could be installed there to safeguard the Russian right of passage to and from Leningrad. But the Finns, understandably, were not receptive to the idea.

The German-Soviet Pact of 23 August 1939 left the Soviets with considerable freedom of action, and when the German invasion of Poland began the Soviets exercised this freedom to acquire as much territory as they could. In September they took eastern Poland, and in October they seized effective control over Latvia, and Estonia and part of Lithuania. This regained them some of the old Tsarist territories and it also gave them the southern side of the Gulf of Finland. Now the diplomatic pressure on the Finns became greater; the suggestions turned into demands,

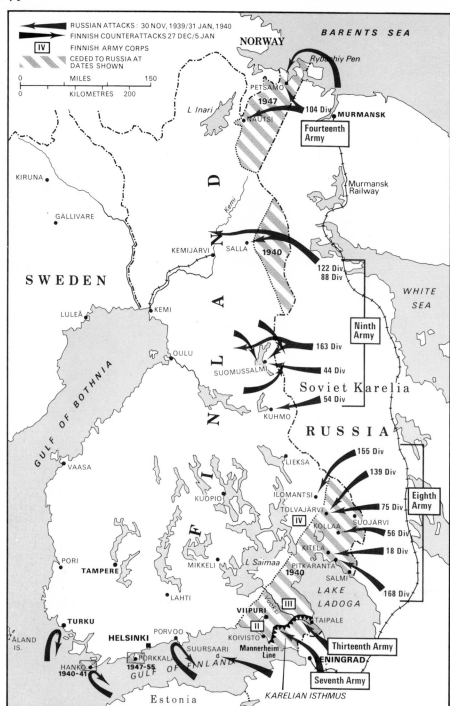

RUSSIAN ATTACKS: 30 NOV, 1939/31 JAN, 1940
FINNISH COUNTERATTACKS 27 DEC/5 JAN
IV   FINNISH ARMY CORPS
CEDED TO RUSSIA AT DATES SHOWN

and the demands increased at every repetition. Now the question of ceding a few islands was no longer enough; the Soviets now demanded a lease of the Hango Peninsula so that they could develop it into a naval and military defensive base; the lease of the Rybachi Peninsula and the port of Petsamo, Finland's only ice-free port; the ceding of the Koivisto region north of Leningrad so as to push the Finnish border further away; and political assurances that Finland would never join any other coalition of powers. In return for these grants, Russia would present Finland with 2000 square miles of worthless forested wilderness north of Lake Onega.

The Finns were not particularly happy about these proposals, but Marshal Mannerheim, Commander-in-Chief of the Army, advised the govern-

ment that it would be wise, in the circumstances, to swallow its pride and agree. The example of the fate of the Baltic states was before them, and in Mannerheim's view it would be better to accept the Soviet proposals and remain an independent state than to have the proposals eventually thrust upon them by force of arms or, worse, by Communist infiltration.

Mannerheim's advice was rejected; the Finns attempted to negotiate but received no encouragement from Moscow, and on 26 November 1939 the Soviets accused the Finns of provoking a border incident by shelling the Russian border village of Mainila. The Finns, certain of their innocence, offered to participate in a Joint Investigating Committee to look into the incident, but the Soviet reply was to launch an invasion on 30 November.

It hardly came as a surprise to the Finns, for the Soviets had been building up their strength on the border for several months, building new roads, storing supplies and concentrating troops. The attack was delivered in four different areas simultaneously, indicating careful planning. The official Soviet announcement said: 'Troops of the Leningrad Military District have crossed the Finnish frontier. They have occupied the town of Terioki, where a People's Government has been formed, headed by Comrade Kuusinen, member of the Comintern.' This was a half-truth; the troops were indeed of the Leningrad Military District, but it was a big district and there had been a partial mobilization of reservists beforehand, and there was no mention of the other areas of attack.

In fact there were four armies in

action. The 7th Army, based on Lenin-grad, struck at the Finns' strongest area, the well-fortified Mannerheim Line across the Karelian Isthmus. The 8th Army moved off from the area north of Lake Ladoga towards Sorta-vala to strike at the flank of the Mannerheim position. The 9th Army, stationed along the eastern borders of Finland, moved to cut across the country and reach the head of the Gulf of Bothnia, cutting Finland in half and preventing the possibility of Swedish assistance. And the 14th Army from the Murmansk region attacked the Petsamo district in order to isolate the port and prevent any possible seaborne re-inforcement from the outside world.

On the face of it this seemed a reasonable tactical plan which should have met with rapid success; the Soviets certainly thought so (their troops were

carefully instructed to respect Swedish neutrality when they arrived at the far side of Finland) and the figures were on their side. The Finn Army's strength was something in the order of 250,000 men, while the Soviets were throwing in 26 infantry divisions, 1½ armored corps and a mass of supporting artillery, an estimated 350,000 men. What the Soviets did not appreciate was the quality of the Finnish Army, well trained, well motivated, and fighting on their own ground in defense of their homeland. The Finns put up such a formidable defense that the Soviet attacks achieved little of their planned objectives.

The Soviet 7th Army made small impression on the Mannerheim Line; this was a defense in depth, well pro-vided with concrete and steel strong-points, anti-tank obstacles and mine-

fields, and in spite of continuous and prodigal frontal attacks the Finns held the line firmly. The 8th Army had some initial success near Taipale and Salmi and advanced about 40 miles before being brought to a standstill. The nor-thern arm of this army, moving through Suojarmi, suffered a consider-able setback when three divisions blun-dered into a Finn ambush and were cut to pieces. The 9th Army were routed at Liekaa, were held at Kuhmo, and two of their divisions, the 163rd and 44th, were soundly defeated outside Suomus-salmi. The 14th Army had the only real success; Finnish strength in the far north was minimal, since most of the troops had been moved south to more vital sectors, and Petsamo and the surrounding district were captured.

The reason for these successes against the odds lay in the Finn method of

LEFT: Finnish machine gunners wearing white camouflage train their eyes on the Soviet invader during the first weeks of the Winter War.

BELOW: A Russian tank advances in the Finnish snows.

warfare. The Finns, instead of attempting to hold a continuous line, a tactic which the Soviets expected and were confident of their ability to defeat, operated in small highly mobile groups of men on skis, groups which were familiar with the terrain and the climatic conditions and which were full of initiative. Armed with submachine guns, and with a high proportion of snipers in their number, they would appear, raid, and disappear before the Soviets knew what was happening. The Red Army, on the other hand, was hidebound; it was paying the price of the Great Purge in that commanders were largely over-promoted men who adhered closely to 'the book', were fearful to show any signs of nonconformity or originality and were in dread of their political commissars. Organization and supply were poor; discipline was shaky—one Soviet division is said to have mutinied after suffering a repulse—and the appalling winter conditions told more on the Soviets than on the Finns since the Soviet equipment, clothing and weapons were less well suited to extreme cold conditions.

In the sort of isolated battles which developed, the commander on the spot had to make quick decisions and the individual sub-units and soldiers needed to be capable of using their common sense and acting independently. But the Soviets displayed none of these characteristics and, as a result, the Finns, who exhibited these qualities at their best, ran rings around the cumbersome Red Army formations. Time after time mobile Finn columns would swoop from the forest, cut off a Soviet formation, and then systematically wipe it out, and this often went on with another Soviet formation nearby, a formation which should, if properly led, have been able to go to the assistance of the trapped unit. But if the Soviet commander had no orders, he wouldn't move, and the unfortunates in the 'Motti', as the Finns called these traps, were left to their own devices. In many cases the Finns simply isolated the Soviets and left them to starve and freeze to death; and considering that the winter of 1939–40 was one of the hardest winters for many years, this process didn't take long.

By Christmas it was obvious that the Finns, if not winning, were not really losing either. Moreover Britain and France were beginning to take an interest, and there was a distinct probability that they might decide to go to Finland's assistance—and if they had, the subsequent political alignments and the course of the war make an interesting subject for speculation. Also there was considerable international feeling against Russia, while the Red Army was being made to look ridiculous. In later years it was suggested that the Soviets actually used second-line units and obsolete equipment in Finland in order to deceive the world in general and Germany in particular, but there is no truth in this assertion; they were doing the best they could and it wasn't good enough.

All these factors convinced the Soviet government that the Finnish war had to be brought to a close, and quickly. The lesson so far seemed to be that with the Soviets in open country the Finns could do pretty well what they pleased; therefore the next phase of the war had better be conducted so that it was favorable to the Soviet arms and tactics and curtailed the Finnish freedom of movement. The only sector which satisfied this assessment was the Mannerheim Line, and therefore the Red Army now began preparations for a massive assault in the Karelian Isthmus, leaving the other sectors in a holding condition.

Throughout January preparations took place; one of the most remarkable results of this new phase was that the prisons and labor camps throughout the Soviet Union were scoured to find any officers who had been imprisoned as a result of the Purge and who had, by some freak of fate, escaped liquidation. These officers were rapidly rehabilitated and sent to take up commands in the new formations being assembled. Among them was Colonel Rokossovsky, who used this reprieve to such good effect that he finished the war as a Marshal of the Soviet Union, having commanded the Army of the Don at Stalingrad and 'liberated' Poland. Mobilization was extended to other military districts and troops were brought from as far afield as Siberia. Armor, artillery, and massive stocks of ammunition were moved up and substantial elements of the Air Force made available. Finally the command structure was re-organized; Marshal Voroshilov, People's Commissar for Defense, assumed overall command; the attacking force was divided into two, the 7th Army now commanded by Meretskov and the 13th Army commanded by Grendal. The 8th, 9th and 14th Armies were re-organized into the 'Northern Front' under General Shtern (who had been officially credited with the success of the action at Changkufeng on the Manchurian border in 1938. after the downfall of Blücher) and the Murmansk area was placed under the command of the Naval C-in-C Kuznetsov, his task being to prevent any seaborne landings by British or French troops.

All this maneuvering and organizing took time, during which the Soviet Air Force and artillery kept up bombardments and raids on the defensive line and on rear areas. Viipuri was heavily bombed on Christmas Day 1939 and several other towns suffered during the following month. This period of attrition was a serious drain on the Finnish manpower since they had no reserves left and no hope of reinforcement, and there was no way of relieving front-line units; they simply had to sit there and take the incessant shelling.

Eventually, on 10 February, the Russian steamroller moved. 13 divisions were thrown against a 20km front, with heavy artillery and tank support. Although initially checked, the Soviets finally achieved their breakthrough when all the defenders had been killed or wounded and there were no more replacements for them. This happened on 15 February and the remaining Finns then fell back from the Mannerheim Line to a reserve position in front of Viipuri. There the Soviets were again checked, and while the frontal attack concentrated on shelling Viipuri into ruins, a flank attack by six divisions was mounted across the ice of Viipuri Bay. By scraping up some troops from other sectors, even this threat was held off by the Finns.

How long the Finns might have held the Soviets remains an open question, for by this time both sides were making peace overtures in Stockholm. The Finns knew that their last reserves were committed and that there was no hope of outside assistance, so they wanted to make peace while they were still holding. The Soviets were anxious to end the embarrassing affair which was proving to be more costly than expected, was beginning to stir up anti-Soviet feeling abroad and was complicating the political scene. So on 13 March a peace agreement was signed in Moscow and the war came to an end.

figures of 48,745 killed and 158,863 wounded are considered to be vastly understated, and other sources speak of 270,000 dead and an unknown but much higher number wounded. The 'People's Government' under Otto Kuusinen made no impression and was hastily jettisoned after the war ended. The Finnish peasants and workers failed to rise and crush their oppressors; or rather, they did, but their idea of who was their oppressor was somewhat different to the Soviet view. The 'Finnish People's Army' which featured prominently in early Soviet propaganda announcements failed to materialize.

The defects of Soviet arms and tactics were the most serious result of the war, and correction of the various shortcomings was given high priority. Voroshilov was finally 'kicked upstairs' to become Deputy President of the Council of People's Commissars, and Timoshenko took his place as the People's Commissar and C-in-C of the Red Army. Technical and tactical training was stepped up, poor commanders removed, military ranks reinstituted. The equipment lessons, particularly in the tank and automotive fields, were carefully analyzed and passed to the design centers. The Soviet Air Force came under some hard scrutiny; it was largely its failure to deliver success by strategic bombing in Finland which led to its reorganization as a Tactical Air Force for more direct support of the army in the field.

The Soviet campaign in Finland was acclaimed by the Soviets as 'a brilliant victory with limited losses' but to the rest of the world it was a sorry spectacle. That the Soviets managed to profit from their mistakes is to their credit, and there is no doubt that without the Winter War to expose some of the worst defects the Germans in 1941 would have had an even easier victory. But it cannot be considered as having advanced the glory of the Red Army or its commanders. One Soviet writer observed that the army artillery had, in the course of the short war, fired eight million shells, three shells for every Finnish man, woman and child, without breaking their will to resist. And a Red Army veteran of the campaign is said to have wryly summed it up by saying that the Soviets managed to wrest from the Finns just enough earth in which to bury the Soviet dead.

Even so, it did not end without a piece of typical Soviet duplicity. The cease-fire was to take effect at noon on 14 March. During the course of that morning the Finns, appreciating that the war was over except for formalities, began leaving their positions, loading transport and generally preparing to move off. At 1145 every Soviet gun opened rapid fire and continued until noon. This sudden bombardment caught untold numbers of Finnish soldiers and civilians in the open, and killed and wounded hundreds. It was completely unnecessary and inexcusable, and the memory of that fifteen minutes was to color the Finnish relationship with Russia from that time to the present.

The Finns were made to suffer under the terms of the peace treaty. The Soviets took the Hango Peninsula, the Karelian Isthmus, Petsamo and large areas in the northeast. The Finnish Army had lost an estimated 60,000 dead and 200,000 wounded — in other words there was scarcely a man of the army left whole — while half a million civilians lost their homes and property.

The Soviets, though, had suffered more. The exact figures have never been made public; the announced

SURPRISE AND RETREAT: BARBAROSSA

BELOW: Russian roads
were notoriously bad,
and in many areas
non-existent. When the
autumn rains fell in 1941
the Wehrmacht was
bogged down in mud,
and their advance was
slowed.

It was impossible to distinguish that evening of 21 June 1941 from any previous Saturday night in that year. It was an ordinary night with Red Army officers, junior and senior alike, taking full advantage of their free time, watching numerous garrison shows and theatrical plays, in and around their postings. Although the evening seemed quite typical, heads of intelligence sectors up and down the border of Russia were receiving information that German troops were concentrating along the frontier areas. Intelligence officers like Colonel Blokin, Head of Intelligence for the Western Special Military District, reported to their chiefs-of-staff that the Germans were moving, having been brought to full combat readiness, and much of the frontier was in a state of alarm. Reports such as these were referred to as 'some kind of rumor', propagated by alarmists and extremists. However, this opinion was held not only by the Army and District Commanders, but through-

out the chain of command to Stalin himself.

At 2100 hours on that Saturday, as Colonel Blokin was meeting Colonel-General Pavlov, Commander of the Western Special Military District, a German deserter named Alfred Liskow crossed over the Soviet Frontier. Liskow claimed that he was a Communist sympathizer and passed information on to an area officer at the front. During interrogation he made the assertion that he had overheard German officers discussing an upcoming attack at 0400 hours Sunday morning, 22 June. He also claimed that German guns had

RIGHT: Two officers of the 68th Infantry Division study a road map in the early stages of Operation Barbarossa. Their destination is clear.

FAR RIGHT: German infantry advance near Kharkov. The Russian Army was caught in a pincers movement which caused the loss or capture of hundreds of thousands of Ukrainian troops by Army Group South.

moved into their firing positions. This intelligence was at once passed throughout the chain of command along the front of the 5th Russian Army in the Kiev Military District area. In spite of information of this magnitude, nothing more than a doubling of the guard along that frontier evolved.

In most cases the information passed to no figure of authority, as the majority of Soviet officers had already taken advantage of their free Sunday. In this case to be with their wives, families, or just to relax in Lvov. But this was to be a rather different sort of Sunday.

RIGHT: Two officers of the 68th Infantry Division study a road map in the early stages of Operation Barbarossa. Their destination is clear.

FAR RIGHT: German infantry advance near Kharkov. The Russian Army was caught in a pincers movement which caused the loss or capture of hundreds of thousands of Ukrainian troops by Army Group South.

FAR LEFT: Early German successes on the Eastern Front brought smiles to the faces of their advancing troops.

CENTER LEFT: An evacuated building ablaze in Belorussia during the 1941 summer offensive.

LEFT: The town of Vitebsk was virtually razed to the ground as its inhabitants fled. The refugees clogged the roads blocking the Soviet retreat. Stalin subsequently issued orders that Soviet citizens remain in their localities to give the Russian Army freedom of movement.

BELOW: The remains of a Russian plane destroyed on the ground. Much of the Soviet air forces were wiped out before they left their airfields in the first two days of the war, which turned out to be a mixed blessing. Stalin was forced to bring new aircraft into production at a rapid pace, and the replacements were vastly superior to those destroyed.

All along the frontier incidents were taking place. A Lithuanian deserter, interrogated by the Staff of the 5th Rifle Division, also predicted a German 0400 attack. Even as late as 0220 hours, 22 June, the Soviet 4th Army Command finished interrogating yet another German deserter who set the latest confirmation of an invasion as due in less than two hours. The staff of 4th Army Command, contrary to much of what transpired along the frontier that night, attempted to report the incident to its superiors. The information was never to be received. At 0100 hours German commandos of the Elite Regiment 800—the Brandenburgers—had infiltrated and parachuted into areas behind Soviet lines and had begun to conduct Fifth Column and demolition activities against Soviet communication and power sources. They also secured bridges vital for the German movement, and were responsible for cutting many telephone lines. These included the 4th Army's links to higher command, halting their intelligence input.

BELOW: German soldiers
are greeted
enthusiastically by a
woman in a Ukrainian
village as they advance
toward Kharkov. In the
first stages of Barbarossa
the Ukrainians greeted
the Nazis as liberators.

BELOW: Infantrymen move
across a river in the
Ukraine during their
summer advance in 1941.

By 0230 hours on 22 June, only thirty minutes before German artillery commenced the pounding of Soviet forces along the frontier and the German Army kicked off what is often held to be the greatest military conflict of all time, Russia still closed its eyes to the impending Nazi aggression which loomed as a shadow of destruction extending from Western Europe, covering the continent to the Russian frontier.

Why was Russia caught in a state of such unpreparedness? The Russian Army was still recovering from the Stalin Purges of earlier years and was seriously understaffed in senior field commanders, not only in their numbers but in competency. Many of these senior commanders were part of the Stalin-supporting cavalry clique, and in other cases were merely 'yes men' to Stalin's policies. Another factor was the over-exaggerated propaganda instilled about the invincibility of the Red Army. This feeling of invincibility within the Soviet Army had its roots in the Draft Field Regulations of 1939, the fundamentals of which stated that any enemy who attacked the Soviet Union would be literally crushed by the Red Army. In such a case they would not only cast out the invaders from Russian soil, but would carry a fierce aggressive offense of retaliation into the attackers' homeland. In its closing lines it also

stated that the Red Army would achieve its decisive victory at a small cost in Soviet blood. This document was not only overestimating in its proposed capabilities, but denied the effectiveness of the current military ideas of German Blitzkrieg tactics which were proving so successful. The Soviets believed in the 'offense' and that all previous nations defeated by the new German tactics fell from a lack of will to fight and win, and from Fifth Column activities, rather than from the effectiveness of modern German warfare.

The lack of proper war experience in the Red Army, as compared to the Germans, was another aspect. Russia had not been involved in a 'modern war' up to that time. Most of the experience gained during the years of civil war and the revolution was lost either to age or during the Stalin Purges. The war with Finland was won more to the extent of sheer weight of numbers and attrition rather than on fighting ability. The only actual battle-hardened veterans the Soviets had to call upon were the Siberian troops who had fought against the Japanese in three separate conflicts in Manchuria. These troops were later to play an important role in the Battle of Moscow, but their combat experience was nowhere to be found along the frontier in the opening days of war with Germany.

Other facets ranged from Russian rail capacity, which was three to four times lower than Germany's during this period; to the low educational and training standards of the Red Army; to the frontier fortification along the new border, which were still not complete. The old 1938 border fortifications had already been dismantled to help build the strongholds along the new border. This, if for no other reason, demonstrates the Soviets' inability to hold a line of resistance along the frontier all the way back to the original borders.

Despite these numerous 'causes and effects' there are still four points which stand out more than the others in that initial Soviet downfall. Stalin had given strict orders not to fire on nor attempt to shoot down German reconnaissance aircraft flying over Russian territory. In the opening hours of the German invasion, this point alone contributed to the destruction of the Soviet Air Force, and to the mass disruption of the Soviet lines of communication. Frontier troops were also ordered to avoid armed conflict with German troops on border violations. Again, this proved disastrous in the early morning hours as many Russian frontier troops balked away from confrontation with the invading German soldiers as they streamed across the border. Thirdly, the Soviets made do with the existing facilities along their frontier, while the

Germans modernized their railways, railheads, roads and airfields.

The final and most critical basis for the early Soviet defeats and near loss of the war rested with the Russian General Staff which did too little, too late, not only to counter the German menace across the frontier, but the invading forces as well. Many Russian troops received no basic orders until late on the day of the invasion, and only after many units were destroyed, disorganized, surrounded or retreating.

So it was when at 0300 hours, 22 June 1941 — on the eve of Napoleon's Grand Invasion of Russia in 1812 — Hitler launched Germany into Operation Barbarossa. For the Russian people this time and date was to catapult them into a nightmare which would not end until 1945, and then only after 25 million Russians had lost their lives. While on that morning artillery shells ripped and scarred Russian soil, her people were being mentally scarred by a horror the memory of which influences Soviet military policy today, to never again allow the destruction of those years to recur.

As German troops lunged across the Soviet border, Russian troops rallied as quickly and ably as they could amid the confusion, destruction, and complete disorganization of the Soviet military machine. The rumbling of the heavy artillery rained fire into frontier defense

positions. The Luftwaffe conducted both strategic and tactical raids against a multitude of Soviet targets with frightening success. Incidents were not uncommon among the disorganized Russian troops where Luftwaffe bombers were allowed to make their runs with complete freedom of movement over their targets. Operating under the orders of Stalin and the Soviet Army Staff not to provoke the Germans into war. Russian anti-aircraft units assigned to defend such targets were restrained by their officers—who seem-

ingly refused to accept that this event had already come to pass. Frontier troops, who were to be the first line of defense, ran from their barracks headlong into slaughter by the combination of Stukas, tanks, and infantry already overrunning their positions. In the Soviet 15th Infantry Corps it was reported that the wives of the frontier troops not only carried water and ammunition to their husbands' fighting positions, but manned the weapons dropped by their bullet-riddled spouses and fought as valiantly as any soldier possibly could.

Throughout the day Soviet troops tried to resist and defend against the oncoming Germans, but sheer weight of numbers and heavy casualties took their toll, and the Soviets began to withdraw. Communications between Soviet units was minimal to non-existent, and it was rare that divisions, corps or armies even attempted to maintain communications with one another, or support each other in defense or withdrawal. As the German attack continued, Russian regiments and divisions were surrounded and isolated. Such pockets were in most cases destroyed in piecemeal, but one outstanding thing occurred. For reasons which have been listed as stubbornness, fear, and desperation, several of these pockets of Russian troops turned and fought their way out of encirclement to rejoin other units. Many cases have been cited where officers took control of no more than 40 or 50 men and began pushing east in a breakthrough attempt when they

88

would come across other small groups pursuing the same objective. By the time the actual 'escape' was completed the groups often numbered 4000 to 8000 strong. This is not to say that the Soviets did not lose large masses as dead or prisoners, but such determination, regardless of the odds against them, showed that the Russians were going to give the Germans a fight which, if properly handled and kindled, would only end with the destruction of one side or the other.

By noon the facts of the situation were becoming more apparent. Germany was launching its attack in a basic triple thrust movement which the Soviets thought would probably have the far reaching objectives of Leningrad, Moscow, and the Ukraine. The German Army Group North, under von Leeb, struck from East Prussia with 26 Divisions, including one Panzer Army, against the Soviet Baltic Special Mili-

LEFT: German Red Cross units follow Panzer divisions across the Russian frontier in June 1941.

BELOW LEFT: Wehrmacht private carries mines to their positions on the southern sector of the front in August 1941.

BELOW: A long motorized column moves east during the long, hot summer of 1941. At first the entire German advance seemed like a parade.

tary District which was commanded by Kuznetsov. Although the Soviet 8th and 11th Armies tried desperately to hold a feasible line of defense, German Panzer Group IV, under Hoppner, struck out across the River Niemen into Belorussia for the city of Dauguvpils and the River Dvina.

Army Group Center, commanded by von Bock, struck the Soviet Western Special Military District with a massive 51 Divisions including two Panzer Armies. Von Bock had organized his forces with Panzer Group III, under Hoth, and Panzer Group II, under Guderian, on the extreme flanks of his sector filling the center with the IV and IX German Infantry Armies. By doing this von Bock's main plan was to push both Panzer Armies in long sweeping thrusts behind the Russian line of defense, encircling and pocketing Russian troops before they had a chance to escape. These encirclements complete, it would be for the slower moving infantry to move forward and destroy them. This strategy met with great success during the opening hours. Guderian took the bridges crossing the River Bug by storm to the north and south of Brest-Litovsk with the XXIV Panzer Corps, and by evening this Corps and the XLVII Panzer Corps were located in Kobrin and Prushany respectively. This was a gain of almost 50 miles in the first day of battle. Although Guderian was having such remarkable success, Hoth's III Panzer Group was rocking the Russians back on their heels with even more force.

of their counterparts further north. Earlier on that Sunday, at 0715, the People's Defense Commissar, Marshal Timoshenko, broadcast a ludicrous message to the Russian troops.

1. Our troops are to attack the enemy forces with all the strength and means at their disposal, and to annihilate them, wherever they have violated the Soviet border.

2. Our reconnaissance and combat aircraft shall ascertain where the enemy aircraft and land forces are concentrated. By striking mighty blows our aircraft are to smash the main enemy troop concentrations and their aircraft on its airfields. These blows are to be struck anywhere within 60 to 100 miles of German territory. Memel and Königsberg are to be heavily bombed. Until further notice no further air attacks are to be made on Finnish or Rumanian territory.

Not only had he taken his objectives and bridgeheads across the River Niemen near the cities of Merkine and Olyta intact, but he had pushed nearly 60 miles into Russian territory by the end of that first evening. This success of the Panzer Groups was even greater than experienced in France and Poland in prior years, and von Bock was faced with the problem not of attaining his objectives, but keeping his Panzer leaders from racing away from the infantry armies.

Success seemed to be coming more easily than the Germans had expected. Army Group South, commanded by von Rundstedt, met the heaviest of Russian resistance, and although the Germans were making headway they were not enjoying the sweeping success

BELOW: A convoy of
Panzers makes its way
across Russian terrain
during an early autumn
advance.

BOTTOM: Russia had little
motorized transport at
the opening of the war
with Germany. What
they had was soon
destroyed or made
non-operational.

КЛЯНЕМСЯ МСТИТЬ
ГИТЛЕРОВСКИМ ЗАХВАТЧИКАМ !

LEFT: Russian poster urges young and old to throw back the Nazi invader.

BELOW LEFT: Wehrmacht troops use a flame thrower to clear a Soviet bunker.

BELOW: Motorcycle-infantry of the Wehrmacht check their road maps at a crossing during the thousand-mile advance in Operation Barbarossa.

BOTTOM: A bridge and motorized transport wrecked by heavy aerial and artillery bombardment somewhere west of Moscow.

These statements, or blanket orders issued by Timoshenko, proved the ignorance under which the Soviet High Command was operating in these early hours. The Russian Army was in almost complete disarray and the throwing back of violators as ordered was quite impossible. Moreover, by that point the Soviet Air Force was virtually eliminated in the forward areas and could not possibly carry out such directives.

As the Soviet Army fell back, certain concentrations, such as those surrounded in the Citadel at Brest-Litovsk, held out. Although German forces were by-passing such areas, troops still had to be left behind to destroy such loopholes of resistance. By nightfall of the first day Stalin and his General Staff finally began to come to grips with the situation and to take the reins of command which had slipped from their grasp. The mobilization of reserve and rear echelon units began. Very senior staff officers such as Zhukov were being sent forward to support the frontier commanders, and new fronts were activated. It was evident that chaos and confusion reigned along the frontier. At 2200 hours on 22 June, the urgency of the situation, although clearly apparent to many in the

General Staff, did not affect the communiqué which was issued to the Russian people on the day's events:

Regular troops of the German Army, during the course of 22 June, conducted operations against the frontier defense units of the Soviet Union attaining significant success in a number of sectors. During the second half of the day, with the arrival of forward elements of Field Forces of the Red Army, the attacking German troops along most of the length of our frontier were beaten off and heavy losses inflicted on the enemy.

This statement was released 45 minutes after Stalin issued his disastrous Directive Number Three. The directive called for all Soviet forces to stop their retreats and to take an offensive role along the front lines. Soviet troops made desperate counter-attacks against the massive German assault. The coming of 23 June made it apparent that only a handful of counter-offensives had halted any of the German advances that first night. The number of Soviet troops wasted in these attacks spread the Russian Army so thinly that gaps 80 miles wide appeared in the Soviet front

line. The Soviet Army of the frontier was broken, dispersed, and incapable of effectively halting the German progression.

With the initial battles for the frontier over, Army Group South finally overcame the Soviet Army's resistance by capturing Lvov on 30 June. By 2 July Army Group South had swung once again into the attack, and after smashing the Soviet 6th Army at Lvov, Panzer Group I of Army Group South, commanded by von Kleist, breached the Berdichev-Zhitomir Line. The III Panzer Corps of General von Mackensen was prepared to move into Kiev, taking the bridges along the Dniepr River. Although the III Panzer Corps could have taken Kiev, Hitler halted von Mackensen, forcing him to wait on the outskirts until a link-up with the German VI Army was made. Panzer Group I then turned and headed southeast, and by 2 August near Pervomaysk on the River Bug, the German VI and XVII Armies were united. This linking of the German armies cut the line of retreat for the Soviet 6th, 12th, and 18th Armies which were part of both the Kiev and the Odessa Special Military Districts, and spelled the doom for those caught in the snare. Trapped in the Uman Pocket, the Soviets lost 100,000 prisoners, over 300 tanks and 850 guns. This was all that remained of the seven corps of the three armies. The destruction of a total of 22 divisions exposed the Russian southern flank. As a result, by 5 August German troops had reached the Black Sea and were outside Ochakov. German–Rumanian contingents laid siege to Odessa, which held out for 73 days.

Army Group Center, with Luftwaffe support, smashed through with two Panzer Groups and completely sealed off a pocket of Russian troops of the Soviet 3rd and 10th Armies in the Minsk area. By 29 June this body was divided into three groups, situated around the cities of Bialystok, Vovlkovysk, and Novogrudok.

On 3 July, after Stalin had taken personal command of the war effort, he broadcast a speech to the Russian people. It had a welding effect on them,

LEFT: German private gives a light to a captured Soviet soldier.

BELOW: German artillery moves across a hastily constructed bridge in the march toward Leningrad.

and seemed to stiffen their will to resist. Stalin called for the resistance of all Russia's people against the invaders, and spurred on the soldiers' heroic battle against the odds which confronted them toward a 'patriotic war against the Fascist enslavers'. Two other points were stressed. First, that the Soviet people should allow the Germans no refuge or supply, and to that end Stalin ordered his people to institute a scorched-earth policy. Those who were already behind German lines, were to fight as partisans and keep faith among themselves, fighting for the day when Russian armies returned. Although the speech was very moving, Stalin began it by saying, 'Friends, comrades . . .' This removed the mistrust many felt after Stalin's purges and made the people see him more as an able leader of the Russian people.

Twelve Soviet divisions were cut off in the Bialystok and Vovlkovysk areas. Fifteen divisions were encircled at Novogrudo, and although some members managed to break free, by 9 July the Minsk pocket had yielded no less than 2900 prisoners, 2500 tanks and 1400 pieces of artillery. This event enabled Army Group Center to swing again into its pincer movement, closing another trap in the Smolensk-Vitebsk-Orsha area. By mid-July the dry route to Moscow lay as a straight road ahead.

Army Group North had advanced steadily in a series of penetrations and envelopments, destroying roughly twelve Soviet divisions west of the River Devine. With the Russian air force crushed and the Luftwaffe holding air superiority, German units split the unification between the Soviet 8th and 11th Armies. On 26 June Daugavpils fell to the LVI Panzer Corps. On 30 June a bridgehead across the Devine was secured between the cities of Yekabpils and Vivani. The successful crossing of this river enabled the IV Panzer Group to take the city of Ostrov and by 4 July they lay some 200 miles south of Leningrad. By 10 July German Army Group North's Panzer units had moved into Pskov and the German XVIII Army·captured Riga, moving on to occupy all of Latvia. As a result Russian troops fell back in two directions. The Soviet 8th Army retreated into Estonia, heading for Tallinn as their last point of defense. The 27th and 11th Armies moved south of Lake Ilmen where they prepared to hold a line in the surrounding swamps.

It was on that day, 10 July, that Finnish troops of Mannerheim's Karelian Army headed southeast out of Finland to expell the Soviet troops from the Karelian Isthmus. By 4 August the Finns had recaptured much of the territory given up in the Winter War with Russia, they proceeded no further by 1 September. By that time the Germans held a northern advantage of 2.5:1 superiority in men, a 4:1 superiority in guns, and had complete superiority in tanks and aircraft.

To halt the anticipated advance on Leningrad, a Soviet line of defense along the River Luga was made. Reserve troops from Leningrad manned the positions alongside improvised Opolcheniye units. These units were comprised of nearly every type of male citizen, from workers battalions to student and schoolboy battalions. Over 100,000 civilians were mobilized early in July to build three lines of trenches surrounding Leningrad and its approaches, the outermost ring of which was to be the River Luga. When these defenses were finally completed there were no more than four regular Infantry divisions and three Special Soviet Civilian Divisions to defend the positions. Although German forces were slowed by these units, they succeeded in forging a number of bridgeheads on the northern side of the city. Meanwhile, other Army Group North forces had

cut off the retreating Soviet Army in Estonia and while some forces laid siege to Tallinn, others turned north toward Lake Peipus to unite in the effort of bridging the Luga. On 19 August an all-out attack on Tallinn commenced, but the city managed to hold until 26 August. Of the 20,000 Russian troops trapped there, the Russian Navy managed to accomplish their own style 'Dunkirk' and convoy the greater part of the navy and several thousand troops to Kronstadt and Leningrad.

Panzer Group IV had broken through the Luga bridgehead on 8 August and managed to reach Novgorod and the River Volkhov by 16 August. This event tolled the death of the Luga line and left the Russians totally disorganized. Not until the beginning of September and the arrival of General Zhukov did the defense of Leningrad really take shape. But by 28 August Leningrad was totally besieged.

Army Group Center was far from idle during this July-August period. On 19 July they closed the trap around Smolensk. Over 100,000 prisoners, 2000 tanks, and nearly 2000 guns were captured, while some fourteen to twenty Soviet Divisions were crushed. Although the German forces achieved great success in destroying this pocket, the Soviet 4th, 6th, 13th, and 20th Armies managed to hold a line approximately 20 miles to the east of that city. This action was the first productive check of the German Blitzkrieg, and though a major German victory was acclaimed, the Soviet soldiers proved that it was possible to stop the German advance.

In August Hitler began reorganizing not only his military forces, but his entire train of thought on the destruction of the Soviet forces as well as his projected strategic goals. He ordered Hoth's III Panzer Group to Army Group North, and Guderian's II Panzer Group to the support of Army Group South. Army Group Center, which had always managed to maintain the largest concentration of German troops, reverted to little more than an infantry army, with orders to march on Moscow. This movement met with violent opposition from his generals, but Hitler held to the belief that Russia was only mounting infantry armies against this sector of the front, giving him the opportunity to carry out such reorganization in protection of his flanks. On 21

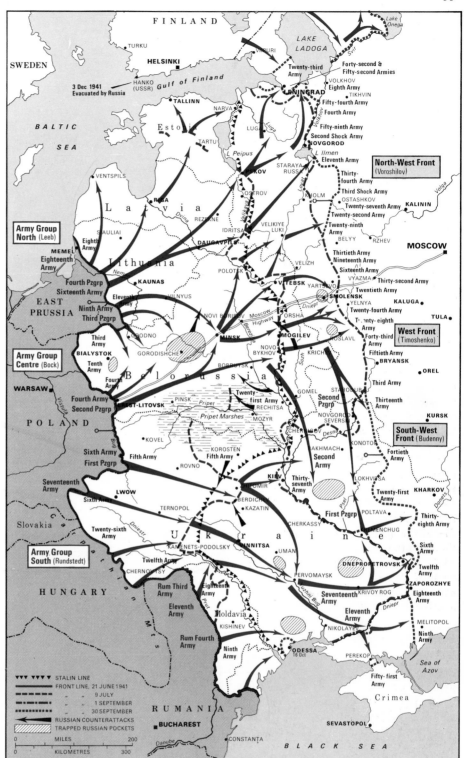

BELOW: A dead horse is left behind as weary German infantry drag equipment across a stream in November 1941. By this time the advance had been dramatically slowed by early winter snows.

BOTTOM: Homeless Russian peasants, carrying a few meagre belongings, leave their burning village.

RIGHT: A long trail of motorized transport, bringing food and supplies to the Wehrmacht deep in the Ukraine.

FAR RIGHT TOP: Cavalry dispatched from East Prussia during the invasion of the Baltic states.

FAR RIGHT BELOW: Rifles mark the graves of the fallen.

BOTTOM RIGHT: A fresh German advance on Moscow in the autumn of 1941.

August Hitler made the decision that Moscow was no longer the primary objective. In fact, it would become the target only after Leningrad was finally encircled. He decided that Army Group South must take priority in its capturing of the Ukraine. This region was the essential basis of the Soviet economy and war effort because of its wealth in food production, minerals, ores and factories. Guderian swung his Panzer Group southeast around the Pripet Marshes, and although openly exposed to the Russians he managed to link with the 1st Panzer Group on 16 September.

The objective was made obvious to the Russians; Kiev was to be the next brick in the Soviet wall destined to fall. In this light Stalin issued the order that 'no Russian soldiers should take one step back', as opposed to the previous idea of 'save what you can for as long as you can'.

Although the German steamroller proceeded with the trapping of the Soviet 5th Army in and around the swamps, Russian troops were succeeding in slowing the advances. Soviet units continually harassed the flanks of the Germaan Armies. Kiev's isolation

LEFT: Russian militia men surrender in the Ukraine. Partisan activity increased considerably as Nazi rule was imposed.

BELOW: Rumanian troops load rifles during their Ukrainian advance. Hitler's allies took the opportunity to settle old scores and regain lost territories during the initial stages of Barbarossa.

brought about a controversy between Stalin and General Nikita Khrushchev. Stalin, who did not want to abandon Kiev, insisted that troops be taken from other sectors in support against the advancing Germans. Khrushchev, along with Major-General Tupelov, Chief of Staff of the Southwest Front, felt that the Russian position had become so catastrophic that a withdrawal of the four armies of the Southwest Front should be made before the Germans closed the 20-mile gap between Lokhvitsa and Lubny. The Soviet General Staff agreed with Stalin, refusing to accept the withdrawal proposal, until on 16 September the German forces made their connections. At 1140 hours, 17 September, authorization was given to abandon Kiev. Two days, during which the Soviet Armies could have slipped away, were wasted. As a result the abandoning breakout turned into an incoherent rout, during which it was 'every unit for itself'. Only a small number of the General Staff caught in the encirclement managed to escape, and tens of thousands of Russian soldiers were killed or captured.

What were Stalin's intentions in holding this area? True, the defense had upset the German timetable for the conquest of the Ukraine, but this was not the key reason for clinging to the Kiev area. In fact, the commitment here wasted the precious time Germany

LEFT: A motorized division is slowed by Russian mud during the autumn rains of 1941.

BELOW: Horse-drawn carts and infantry cross a bridge in Lithuania during the early progress of Army Group North.

needed to take Moscow before winter, and although German armies had torn a 200-mile gap in the Ukraine, the next two months were going to be spent in combating Soviet counter-offensives.

During the latter part of September, in preparation for a fresh offensive, units which had been taken from Army Group Center were recalled. As far as possible this reconsolidation of German troops had to be accomplished with utmost secrecy. Even with reconsolidation efforts in progress Army Group South swept through Kharkov, Rostov, and the Crimea, while Army Group North continued to besiege Leningrad.

The German command decided against an all-out attack on Leningrad, feeling that the city could easily be taken by demoralizing citizens and troops through a constant bombardment by artillery and the Luftwaffe. It was considered that a German victory, bloodless to its own forces, would give a moral and strategic advantage to their assault on Moscow. By 10 September German troops lay within ten miles of Leningrad, and communications between that city and the rest of Russia were severed. The receipt of supplies

BELOW: Siberian infantrymen, warmly clad for the winter campaign unlike their German enemies, carry anti-tank weapons up to the front protecting Moscow.

BOTTOM: Fighting became more intense and the Wehrmacht was forced to regroup.

RIGHT: Russian reinforcements move up to the Moscow front. The Soviet Army made its stand in December and threw back the Nazis.

was limited to air and river traffic, which was inevitably under constant interdiction by Finnish and German troops. The outlook was terribly grim for Leningrad and martial law had existed since the opening phases of the war. Although over 100,000 refugees and the whole of the Baltic Fleet had become dependent on the dwindling supplies, the solid backbone of total resistance, which the Germans had encountered in their bombings of London, appeared in Leningrad. Within the besieged city the relentless bombing and shelling became the cornerstone of the peoples' resistance.

Throughout December the people of Leningrad banded together to conserve food and energy supplies. Thousands of inhabitants swept floors to gather particles of grain which might have fallen. Ships and railway cars were minutely searched for some edible scrap which might have been overlooked or left behind. People banded together and foraged outside Leningrad for potatoes and other root vegetables. It meant certain death if they were spotted by the German soldiers located there. Regardless of these conditions the people of Leningrad continued the clearing of rubbish and sewage, and the burying of their dead in an attempt to keep the levels of social order intact — a difficult task when explosives were being used to open the frozen earth where family and friends were buried in mass graves, scores perished daily of starvation, and the Nazi invader lay in wait on the surrounding landscape.

After months of isolation, and the starvation of thousands in Leningrad, resistance to the siege continued and in spite of the freezing conditions of that winter, a 200-mile life line was thrown

to the people of the city through a road that ran to Zaborie. On 6 December, the date on which other Soviets launched a counter-offensive around Moscow, the people of Leningrad had a means, however small, of resupply. On 9 December Soviet Leningrad troops, led by General Meretskov, recaptured the railhead at Tikhvin. With this counter-offensive, German forces were pushed back 50 miles to the far side of the River Volkhov. It was a matter of time before Russia could permanently supply Leningrad. Although Soviet forces continued the rebuilding of railroads and destroyed bridges, preparing the way for increased supplies which were soon flowing into Leningrad, approximately 4000 people continued to starve in spite of the efforts. The death toll within the city by the end of December 1941 totalled 50,000.

With Army Group South's near complete conquest of the Ukraine, and Army Group North in a siege-stalemate, Hitler turned his eyes, and the German Army, in the direction of what he now believed would be the final objective — Moscow. German strategists felt that by capturing Moscow the industrial areas that remained in the Urals, since the Germans controlled the important Ukraine, could be easily bombed by the Luftwaffe from Moscow bases. The Soviets' ability to wage war would be at a standstill once those remaining industrial complexes were eliminated.

From the beginning of the war the people of Moscow had prepared the city's defenses and turned it into a fortress, surrounded by trenches, pill-boxes, and anti-tank ditches. No less than 400 miles of anti-tank ditches and 300 miles of breastwork were construc-

ted. Over 800 miles of barbed wire, 30,000 firing points, and 1000 miles of wooden obstacles were erected in the forest areas surrounding the city. The Moscow defenders also prepared against the Luftwaffe, which they knew would try to reduce the city to rubble. By creating massive rings of anti-aircraft guns positioned around the city, Moscow won the battle of the air by allowing only 120 of the 4000 German aircraft launched against it to get through from July to September 1941. These Luftwaffe crews were the same men who had boasted of their blitz of Poland, France, and the Battle of Britain. The people of Moscow formed partisan groups who themselves carried out many essential operations.

The Soviets realized that the Battle of Smolensk had detained the German military timetable by almost two months. The German offensive against Moscow was not only being stalled by the poor weather conditions facing the Germans, but by the new strain of resistance instilled in the Russian Army. It wasn't until Hitler's success in the Ukraine that he decided to carry through with Operation Typhoon, designed to eliminate the Soviet capital. On 26 September Germany concentrated no less than 77 divisions, including 14 Panzer and eight mechanized divisions. Nearly 2000 tanks, 20,000 guns, and 1000 combat aircraft were redeployed to Army Group Center from the Leningrad and Ukraine Fronts. Opposing this force were the Soviet Armies of the Western Front, commanded by General I. S. Koniev, Marshal Budenny, and General Yeremenko. On paper the Soviets had an equal amount of divisions as compared to the opposing Germans, but in actu-

ality those divisions were only one-third the strength of their German counterparts. The Germans had a superiority of 2:1 in tanks and artillery and 3:1 in aircraft.

On 2 October, with the pincer coalition of the II Panzer Corps from the south and the III and IV Panzer Corps of the north, the Germans began their attack on Moscow. Although the Soviets attempted a quick counter-attack, the Panzer forces had accomplished deep penetrations and the main forces of the Soviet Western and Reserve Fronts were surrounded near Vyazma and Bryansk. These pockets held no less than four Soviet Armies, and in General Zhukov's memoirs he said that 'on October 7th the road to Moscow was opened'.

At that time two events of great importance occurred. The encirclement of Vyazma and Bryansk tied up 28 German divisions and gave the remainder of the Soviet Army time to reorganize a defense on the Mozhaysk Line. In further aid of the Soviet forces, 8 October brought heavy rains which bogged down German armored units.

The Soviet High Command (STAVKA) began pulling urgently needed troops for the defense of Moscow from Siberia, the Far East, and the Volga Military Districts. The troops from Siberia and the Far East were the basis on which the Soviets were later to turn the tide of battle against Germany. They were battle-hardened veterans accustomed to the harsh weather conditions of Siberia, who had fought the Japanese under Zhukov in prior years, and were being released from watching Japanese armies in China and Manchuria to fight the Russian Western war. Stalin had been convinced by his principal spy in Japan, Richard Sorge, that the Japanese were not looking for further conquests against Russia, but had turned their thoughts more toward the Pacific and the United States, ruling out the risk of Russia being faced with a two-front war. For the first time in the war, Stalin willingly gambled his strategic policy on the advice of one of his agents. No less than fourteen rifle divisions and forty artillery regiments were placed under General Zhukov, who had been transferred from Leningrad to form a single Western Front command whose object was the protection of Moscow. As the Soviets continued to form new armies, fighting along the Mozhaysk Line was especially fierce around 10 October. Soviet forces seemed to be able to stand their ground and stubborn resistance was causing heavy losses to the Germans. Nevertheless German forces still held superiority and managed to penetrate the Mozhaysk Line in a number of places, while Kalinin, Mozhaysk, Volokolamsk and Kaluga fell under German attack. From 14–20 October Russian resistance in the Vyazma and Bryansk pockets was finally crushed. The Soviets lost 650,000 killed or prisoners on that fateful week, but a large number of troops still managed to return to their own lines. The situation looked terribly grim in some areas, but with each passing day Soviet reinforcements were reaching the Mozhaysk Line in greater numbers. By the end of October-beginning of November Hitler's armies were ground to a halt and forced into a defensive posture some 45 to 75 miles away from Moscow. It was the German situation which now appeared grave. As each day passed the Soviet forces grew stronger. In Army Group North the German forces had become so weak that they were unable to continue their offensive against Leningrad, Army Group South was nearly 200 miles east of von Bock's Center Army.

On 13 November Hitler gave orders for the Northern and Southern Armies to go into a defensive posture in order that they might collect and renew their strengths, and both he and the German

BELOW: Russian soldiers captured near Kharkov. There were hundreds of thousands more who suffered the same fate.

BOTTOM: German heavy artillery bombards Russian positions.

General Staff agreed that Moscow had to be taken for both military and psychological reasons. The second offensive against Moscow was planned.

Despite the easing of the German offensive and the receipt of 300 tanks, 2000 guns, and 100,000 troops, the Soviet Western Front remained in a difficult position as Army Group Center again established a stable footing. Tikhvin, in the north and Rostov in the south were retaken by Soviet forces. More than at any other time in the war the Soviets were in need of victories.

On 15 and 16 November Army Group Center marched for Moscow once again. The German October superiority of almost 2.5:1 was rapidly dwindling. It was at this time that the Soviet Air Force actually had a 1.5:1 superiority over the Luftwaffe. On the Volokolamsk Highway a Soviet rifle division of the 16th Army stopped a large German tank thrust. During the battle a valiant force of 28 Soviet soldiers were killed almost to a man in destroying 18 tanks, preventing an enemy breakthrough. In spite of stubborn resistance and an increased capability for counter-offense within the Soviet Army, the Germans managed to penetrate to within ten to 25 miles of Moscow in some sectors. The Soviet

defensive line was bent in an arc around the city, and though weakened in many sections managed to hold the line. Although in the last days of November scattered German reconnaissance elements reached to the outskirts of Moscow, it was apparent to General Zhukov, if not perhaps to the German generals, that Operation Typhoon was about to die.

By 1 December all German units were taking a defensive stance, while being constantly harassed by Soviet counter-measures. South of Moscow the Soviet 2nd Cavalry Corps threw back Guderian's II Panzers as they made an

attempt to attack northwards. All along the front Soviet forces prepared for a large counter-offensive. Within twenty days of the commencement of the German second offensive against Moscow, 150,000 Germans had been killed, wounded or frozen to death. The Soviets' great ally was once again the winter snows, which had fallen since November. As in Napoleon's attack on Russia in the summer of 1812, the weather destroyed the morale and fighting ability of the German Army, whose 'six-week Barbarossa' conquest of Russia was already six months old with no end in sight.

THE TURNING TIDE

BOTTOM: Ill-clad German infantrymen find their first Russian winter almost as hard as Napoleon's forces discovered in 1812. They were stopped as much by General Winter as by General Zhukov.

RIGHT: Russian troops re-occupy an abandoned German trench outside Leningrad in the early spring of 1942.

FAR RIGHT: Soviet tanks move up the nearly abandoned Moskovsky Prospekt on the way up to the front on the outskirts of Leningrad.

By the end of November 1941 Marshal Georgi Zhukov knew that the German objective of taking Moscow would be stopped by the defending Russian armies. On 29 November Zhukov approached Stalin with a planned counter-offensive, using the First Shock and 10th Armies as its basis. Although Stalin listened he gave no reply until the next day when it was decided that a counter-attack should be launched along the entire front. The principal idea of the counter-offensive was not only to drive the Germans back from around Moscow, but to hit them with as much force as possible around Leningrad and the Ukraine. The STAVKA issued orders for all front commanders to prepare for a counter-offensive between 3–6 December.

On 3 and 4 December Soviet forces struck out on their right flank at Klin and Solnechnogorsk and headed towards Istra; while on the left southern flank Zhukov sent his armies to outflank and circle behind Guderian's II Panzers. Their objectives were Uzlovaya

and Bogoroditsk with the 10th Army, for which Zhukov had asked days earlier, at the spearhead of the assault. These counter-attacks by Soviet troops gained momentum as the days went on, and German troops, who were not only morally and physically beaten by the arduous Barbarossa campaign but by the freezing weather, reeled in the wake of the Soviet onslaught. The weather conditions made it impossible for the thinly-clad German troops to fight, and immobilized German tanks and aircraft, whose lubricants were not designed for such sub-zero temperatures. It was not an uncommon sight for Russian troops in the early days of the counter-offensive to come upon abandoned German equipment, left behind because of the weather's force.

By 5 December Zhukov had pushed his remaining armies through the center, trying to force a situation whereby the Germans were unable to deploy their forces to the flanks, which were beginning to collapse.

Stalin had endorsed the STAVKA

FINLAND

HELSINKI

LENINGRAD — Leningrad Front

Estonia

NOVGOROD

Army
Group
North

STARAYA
RUSSA

Latvia

Lith.

MINSK

SMOLENSK

Volkhov Front
TIKHVIN

L Ilmen

North-West Front
Kalinin Front
KALININ

MOSCOW

West Front

VYAZMA

KALUGA

BRYANSK

Bryansk
Front

TULA

South-
West
Front

Army
Group
Centre

Pripet

GOMEL

OREL

YELETS

KURSK

ZHITOMIR

KIEV

Dniepr

KHARKOV

IZYUM

Don

Donets

Army
Group
South

DNEPROPETROVSK

South
Front

RUMANIA

ODESSA

ZAPOROZHYE

ROSTOV

Dniestr

Danube

Sea
of Azov
KERCH

Crimea

Caucasus
Front

SEVASTOPOL

Crimean
Front

BLACK SEA

LIMIT OF AXIS ADVANCE, 5 DECEMBER 1941

REOCCUPIED BY RUSSIAN FORCES, 6 DECEMBER 1941
TO END APRIL 1942

FAR LEFT: Progress on the Eastern Front during the winter of 1941–42.

LEFT: Russian citizens line up with pails to collect their water from a broken main in a Leningrad street during the siege.

BELOW LEFT: Soviet citizens dig out rubble from a street destroyed by German artillery a few miles away outside the city of Leningrad.

113

BELOW: Soviet defenders of Leningrad in a trench on the perimeter during the spring of 1942.

plans for a major counter-offensive with the stipulation that the Soviet forces would first eliminate the German threat to Moscow. Further operations in the North and Ukraine would depend on the success of the forces around Moscow. At that time Zhukov realized that if he were to deal the Germans a serious defeat he would need more tanks and artillery to accomplish his objective. Though Zhukov personally asked Stalin for such re-enforcements, Stalin insisted that he had no reserves, especially in tanks, to give. Stalin then asked the STAVKA what strategic reserve might possibly be given to Zhukov. After long deliberation Stalin decided to pull aircraft from the outlying fronts, giving them to Zhukov to support his attacks. By 5–6 December the Soviets launched flanking attacks extending 38 miles in the north and 60 miles in the south. The counter-offensive was becoming a grim reality to the Germans.

The Soviet 20th Army reached Solnechnogorsk and dislodged the German forces by the evening of 12 December. The First Shock and 30th Armies reached Klin by 13 December and cleared it of German resisters by the 15th. In the south Guderian's Panzer Army was stunned by the attack of the Soviet 10th Army, supported by the 5th Army, and retreated to Venev. In this attack the Soviets captured no less than 70 tanks which had been abandoned not because they were destroyed, but because the cold had rendered them useless.

At the same time the early December counter-offensives were gaining momentum, Stalin received the news that his gamble with the relocation of Russian Far Eastern troops had paid off. On 7 December Japanese naval aircraft struck Pearl Harbor and Stalin's fears of a Japanese front opening in the East were laid to rest. Stalin and the Soviet High Command were in agreement that a two-front war was no longer a possibility, and strategic reserves could at last be pulled from the Far East and Siberian Fronts.

Between 13 and 24 December the Red Army pushed the Germans back to a position which was equivalent to that of their starting line for Operation Typhoon in November 1941. To try to bottleneck retreating German forces, Stalin urged on his Army commanders. Even with the odds in their favor Soviet

commanders hesitated on almost every occasion when deep penetrations into and behind German troop concentrations were involved. Though they knew that the Germans were retreating and there was little likelihood of Soviet troops receiving heavy German counter-attacks, junior Soviet officers were nevertheless afraid that the Germans would somehow cut off and destroy them in isolated pockets as had happened so often in the first six months of the initial campaign.

By 1 January 1942 the right wing of the Western Front had pushed the Germans back to the Rivers Lama and Ruza. STAVKA had ordered the 30th Army transferred to the Kalinin Front to re-enforce that Soviet attack. In the center the 5th, 33rd, 43rd, and 49th Soviet Armies were moving toward Mozhaysk, Borosk, Maloyaroslavts, and Kondrovo destroying German resistance wherever it was met. On the left wing General Belov's group of the 50th and 10th Soviet Armies pushed German troops back in the direction of Kirov, Yukhnov, and Mosalsk. On the Kalinin Front, north of Zhukov's Western Front forces, the Soviets were fighting fiercely against German resistance on the River Lama while keeping up their support of Zhukov's right flank. The Bryansk Front, which had been newly formed on 18 December, they were fighting the Germans along the River Oka, but were not managing to keep up with the left wing of the Western Front. But the situation was looking brighter for the Red Army. Although troops still fought with obsolete equipment, Russian morale had taken a great surge forward as the counter offensive around Moscow seemed to be succeeding. By 5 January the December counter-offensive to relieve the threat around that city was accomplished. Stalin at that time turned his objectives forcing back German troops from around Leningrad and the Ukraine.

Those bitter cold winter days of December 1941 brought Germany to the reality that the Army, which had conquered Western Europe, Scandinavia and had achieved such success in Africa, was faced with its first defeats since the beginning of the war in 1939. Countless causes added up to the defeat, but one of the main factors seemed to be Hitler's meddling in the affairs of the German General Staff. Before the beginning of the Russian

winter counter-offensive Hitler's generals wanted to fall back and establish a defensive line which they knew they could hold, but Hitler refused. Mainly because of that conflict of ideas, Hitler conducted a purge. On 18 December von Leeb, von Rundstedt, Brauchitsch and others had retired from the Eastern Front for reasons which ranged from 'ill health' to open disagreement with Hitler's policies. On Christmas Day the brilliant Guderian was dismissed by his Führer for disobeying orders once too often. The independent initiative which Guderian showed on the field of battle had no place in Hitler's running of the Front. Von Bock was removed as commander of Army Group Center and put in charge of Army Group South; Field Marshal Kluge took command of Army Group Center, while Field Marshal Kuechler replaced Leeb as commander of Army Group North.

Although the German troops had suffered greatly in December, the physical defeat in no way compared with the moral defeat which seemed to grip the German Army as winter fell over Russian landscape. For the first time German troops heard criticism of their commanding officers. An example of this was when Goebbels, Hitler's Propaganda Minister, referred to Brauchitsch as a 'vain, cowardly wretch and a nincompoop'. It was amid this type of slander that 35 generals were removed and disgraced.

On the morning of 5 January 1942,

RIGHT: Snow covers the Nevsky Prospekt in Leningrad.

BELOW: A carload of bodies of Soviet citizens killed by the Germans when the food supplies ran low. The German soldiers' food came first. Those people unable to feed themselves were slaughtered.

by which time the Russian troops had seen that the German aggressor could be beaten, Stalin's plans for extending the offensive were being discussed in Moscow. STAVKA met with Zhukov, Marshall Shaposhnikov, the Chief of the General Staff, his deputy General Vasilevski, and N. A. Voznesensky, head of the State's Planning Organization. At that meeting Stalin expressed his personal plans for trying to recover areas he considered important. Around Leningrad the Armies of the North-western Front and the Baltic Fleet were to combine in an effort to break the blockade and relieve the city. In the south both the Southwestern and Southern Fronts were to retake the Dombas, while the Caucasus Front and the Black Sea Fleet were to push into and take back the Crimea, forcing the German XI Army out. Even with these new priorities, Stalin wanted the main offensive directed against Army Group Center. The thrust at the German center was an attempt at keeping the Germans in a state of constant retreat, thereby gaining back as much as possible of their lost territory before the Russian lack of supply and German resistance broke the advance. On 10 January heavy artillery bombardment was directed at the Volokolamsk area, while the First Shock Army, the 20th Army, and the 2nd Cavalry Corps began their offensive against Army Group Center. Within seven days the Russian right wing had progressed as far as Lotoshino and Shakhovskay. Due

LEFT: Soviet dogsleds bring up supplies to a village outside Leningrad as the siege intensified.

BELOW: A child is evacuated on his sled from Leningrad in the late autumn of 1942. By this time communication across Lake Ladoga, the only outlet for the city, had been regularized.

BOTTOM: German Panzers on the move once again in the late spring of 1942, when the offensive was renewed by Army Group South.

to this success, on 19 January the First Shock Army was withdrawn and put into the strategic reserve of General Headquarters.

The Western Front was being severely weakened by the transfers and withdrawals which were then being made, and with the 20th Army making no further progress the Soviets tried another counter-attack which included the dropping of two battalions of the 201st and 250th Airborne Units. Between 18–23 January these units were dropped approximately 20 miles south of Vyazma. The Soviet 33rd Army was basically the only force still available and capable of exploiting a break and linking with the airborne and partisan troops. From 23–27 Jan. troops under the command of Lt.-General Yefremov pushed forward to link up with the exploited areas. By the end of January the German defenders fell back from Vyazma, but on 3 and 4 February they counter-attacked and restored their lines, cutting off the Soviet forces which had recently made the breach. This seemed to stabilize that front and from that date until mid-March the troops stayed locked in their positions.

All along the front Soviet troops had pushed the Germans back, but with resources becoming scarce and the spring thaws hampering mobility, the counter-attack waned and a defensive line was formed. By saving Moscow and halting the Germans, the Soviets gained a great victory and the Germans some 500,000 men, 1300 tanks, and 17,000

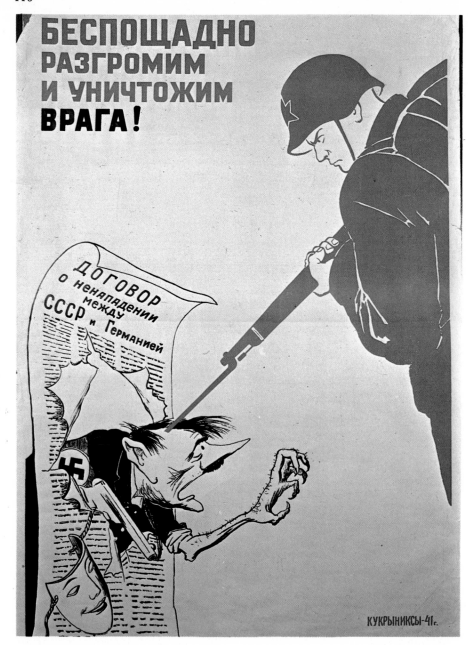

БЕСПОЩАДНО РАЗГРОМИМ И УНИЧТОЖИМ ВРАГА!

LEFT: A Soviet poster showing Hitler driven out of Russia. A reality in 1944, it was an optimistic sentiment in 1942.

equipment so necessary in keeping the production lines flowing.

Two days after the war with Germany had begun, the Evacuation Council was put into action. By 30 June 1941, the GKO—State Defense Committee—had organized all the heavy industry in Russia of strategic military importance under it, not only for the management of military production but for the relocation of displaced industries. In the first few months of the war large scale reorganization of laborers, trades, and production was undertaken by the GKO. The Soviet Union came to grips with two major problems: relocation and the shifting of a peacetime economy onto a wartime footing. In those early months production schemes which included retired pensioners returning to work without loss of pensions, and the introduction of overtime working hours, were put into effect. With overtime working alone some industries were given up to three days extra production. This meant a 20 percent to 25 percent increase without having to enlarge the number of people needed to man the factories. This point was very important as the Soviet Union would need vast quantities of human resources to fight and would not be able to give up that vital human aspect for the industries. Through the early months the Soviet military budget was increased from seven percent to 29 percent of the Gross National Product in 1941 and 57 percent was reached by the end of 1942.

In the evacuation plans the GKO envisioned moving most of the large-scale military industries into regions of the Volga, Urals, Western Siberia and Central Asia. In doing this the Soviets showed how far they were willing to go in trading land for time before indeed having to draw a line and hold. As ineffective as the military appeared, the evacuation was something just short of pure genius. Hundreds of thousands of railway cars pulled Soviet industries to a safe refuge. From July to November the Soviets completely disassembled and moved over 1500 industrial complexes, including 1300 major military enterprises, the majority of which were relocated in the preplanned Volga, Ural and Siberian areas.

During the mass exodus it must be remembered that the German forces made no less than 5000 air raids in an attempt to interdict lines of communication on which movement was being

assorted guns and vehicles. Though Hitler held where Napoleon retreated, the German Command knew they must call upon their allies and shift troops from previously conquered theaters to regain numerical superiority over the Russians. Moscow had proven to be a harder nut to crack than the Germans had believed possible. Leningrad, which was receiving supplies, however sporadic and inadequate, remained defiant to the Nazi and Finnish troops which tried to besiege it. With those two fronts at a standstill it seemed that Hitler had only one choice—to exploit the Ukraine and confiscate the Russian agricultural and manufacturing areas, and the oil-rich Caucasus, vital to the continuation of the Soviet war effort despite Allied promises of support.

In the early days of the blitz against Russia the Red Army showed complete unpreparedness for fighting a war against Germany. One would have thought that throughout the whole of the Russian planning that stream of incompetence would continue. How-

ever, as disorganized as the Russians seemed in the early days, the evacuation of Soviet industries from the areas which were being overrun were probably the most complete and efficiently planned strategies that the Russians put together. The Soviets originally believed in a false premise which in the long run became a partial reality. The Soviets believed that their armed forces could initially repel the Germans, and that their industry would shift over for a long war of attrition. The Russians felt that if the Germans did invade, certain areas of the country would fall before a great counter-offensive could be launched. In such areas Soviet industry would have to be evacuated. Although this plan originally called for only certain areas in the projected front to be immediately evacuated, the plan held true throughout the dark days of 1941 and into much of 1942. In some places Soviet industries were moved as far as 3000 to 4000 kilometers to the east, and in many cases with very little loss of the much needed supply of heavy

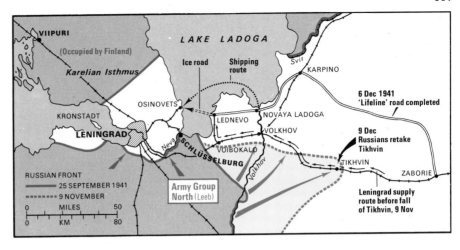

RIGHT: Map of the besieged city of Leningrad.

BELOW LEFT: Russian troops carrying rifles and machine guns move through a trench on Leningrad's perimeter.

BELOW RIGHT: Poster exhorting Soviet armed forces to drive the Nazis from Russian soil.

made. They dropped 50,000 heavy bombs on economic targets, some of which were intended for evacuation. Countless examples of Russian determination and fortitude were shown as Russian workers dismantled factories and evacuated them while under constant harassment from the air by the Luftwaffe, and in many cases while under fire on the front lines.

Once 1942 began, and German forces were halted by the Russian winter counter-offensive, Soviet industry settled down to the task of re-equipping a Red Army which could break the back of the German war machine. In the early days of the blitz large quantities of Russian equipment, tanks, aircraft, artillery, and even basic infantry weapons were lost to the Germans. This equipment, although in desperate demand in those frantic days, was fundamentally obsolete and was slowly being replaced by the war industry. This meant that the Red Army was trading the loss of

obsolete armaments for front-line German equipment on the battlefield. This one factor alone was to be felt by the Germans throughout the rest of the war. The Germans had not anticipated such heavy losses of their supplies, and it was the duty of Soviet industry to see that the German rearmament program—which never came close to equalling Soviet output—remained at a disadvantage. In military terms the total production of aircraft, tanks, artillery and ammunition increased by 18.5 percent in some areas, and 76 percent in others between June 1941 and June 1942. In the Soviet tank industry alone, production of the KV-1 and T-34

during the first half of 1942 increased threefold over 1941 production. This meant that by the winter of '42 three Tank Armies and 23 detached Mechanized Corps were ready. The Soviet aircraft industry had in production fourteen new models of fighter and ground attack aircraft. If the Russian Army could hold the Germans at bay for at least another year, Russia would undoubtedly win a war of attrition over the German industries. This meant that in the critical year of 1942, the year which would make or break the Soviet Union, the manufacture of essential war materials and the production of steel would have to outstrip that of the

German industry. It was almost entirely through forethought and the blood of the Russian people in the evacuation and relocation of the Soviet industrial complexes that the Soviets produced· 340 percent more planes and 600 per cent more tanks per million tons of steel than their German counterparts. Even with the heroics on the battlefield, the war could only be won by the Russian workers' outproducing the Germans, which they did.

By March 1942 the Red Army had fought itself to a standstill all along the Front. Although the Soviet forces had dominated in the Moscow counter-offensive and the winter months that followed, no substantial German defeat

materialized. It was true that in the first year of fighting the Germans had lost nearly a quarter of a million men and large numbers of tanks, guns and planes, but the Russian Army had only managed this in the destruction of German divisions—not on the massive scale of corps and armies as the Germans had accomplished against the Soviets. As the snows left and the weather turned to the advantage of the highly mobile German forces, Stalin and the STAVKA realized that the year of 1942 was to be even more critical than the last.

In January 1942 a declaration had been signed by 26 separate nations of the Allied Powers for continuing the

fighting until the war was over. On 26 May the Anglo-Soviet Treaty was signed in London, and on 11 June the US-Soviet Agreement was signed. Both were pledges of support to the Russian people. Within these agreements was the Anglo-American position of continuing the Lend-Lease program to the Russians on a massive scale. Stalin knew that his armies needed such supplies until the Soviet factories could swing into full production to support their own efforts. However, Stalin's main concern in these agreements was for a second, Western European front to be opened by the English and Americans to draw off German troops and bring the odds more into Russian favor. Such a second front never materialized as Stalin had envisioned, the only combined Allied operation against German forces taking place in November in North Africa, which was of little use to Stalin's desperate needs.

It appeared that Stalin was to face another year of trying to defeat Hitler's forces with an army that, while growing in confidence, was still basically unprepared for fighting and holding off the invaders.

The Russians knew that the Wehrmacht was going to continue their drive in the spring. Confusion as to where that offensive would take place seemed to be the stumbling block of Russian strategy in those early summer months. The German Army had increased by 700,000 troops more than had been initially committed to Operation Barbarossa the year before. Swelling the ranks of the forces were large numbers of Hungarian, Rumanian, and Italian troops pulled in from the Axis Alliances, as well as volunteers from pro-Fascist sympathizers in many of the conquered countries. By May 1942 Hitler's army stood at over six million men on that Eastern Front with nearly 60,000 guns and mortars, 3200 tanks and over 3000 combat aircraft.

Although these numbers seem very impressive, several points must be made concerning Hitler's new army. The non-German troops which were being committed were not of the same high caliber as the German soldiers they fought alongside. With inferior equipment and without intermixing these units with German units, their fighting ability was very much in question. Another point was that although German tanks were excellent in the 1939–41 period, by the summer of 1942 the new Russian T-34s and KV-1s were beginning to prove more than a match when handled proficiently. The new Russian models were still few in number, but it was evident that unless the Germans re-modernized they would soon be overtaken by the developing Russian factors.

Stalin strengthened his forces around Moscow, believing that the new German spring and summer offensive would push in that area. Though thoroughly convinced of this he continued in carrying on smaller Russian offenses along the front at key strategic points which he felt had to be retaken. In reality Hitler only had the supplies and manpower to strike in one major sector of the front. The front he chose was in the Ukraine and Caucasus. The year

before German troops had had great successes in those open plains, and Hitler planned a strike in two directions from the Caucasas. First his forces would swing south toward Rostov, from where they would move into the oil fields of the Caucasus. The second thrust was to have the major target of Stalingrad and with it the severing of the Volga River. To this end Hitler shifted massive armored forces south in preparation for the assault he believed would finish the war with Russia.

Only days prior to the commencement of Hitler's summer offensive Soviet forces massed in the Kharkov area, and on 12 May on the Southwestern Front an attack was launched which cut through the German VI Army, and advanced to within 16 miles of Volchansk. Although the Russians landed the first blow, through Stalin's misinterpretations of the fronts, no consolidated Soviet superiority was held in the area and by 17 May German forces began throwing back and cutting off the Soviet shock troops. Once again Stalin and Khrushchev come into conflict. Khrushchev personally called Stalin saying that in his opinion the army should stop its advance on Kharkov and be pulled back into a defensive position in order to cope with any

BELOW: A long column of German troops moves toward the Caucasus in mid-1942. The breaking of Army Group South into two sectors, one heading toward Stalingrad and the other toward the Caucasus, placed the Soviet Army in a position to launch a counter-offensive.

BOTTOM: German artillerymen instruct a young recruit in the Ukraine. During 1942 the front stabilized near Leningrad and Moscow, but the Nazis advanced hundreds of miles in the Ukraine.

RIGHT: Soldiers of the Wehrmacht move through a Ukrainian wheat field.

CENTER RIGHT: Bulgarian allies of Hitler in the Ukraine.

FAR RIGHT: German infantrymen approach a house as a Pzkw-IV protects them.

German counter-offensive which might ensue. Stalin disagreed and insisted that the advance continue. Although Khrushchev objected to the idea and made insistent attempts to convince Stalin to revoke his orders, Stalin refused to talk to him, saying that everything would remain as it was. After several weeks of fighting in the small salient, German forces surrounded the Russian armies and annihilated them.

By 25 June the Russians had lost nearly 250,000 men and German forces had begun their sweep into the Caucasus. In another sector of the same front, Sebastopol was under siege. Although it held for 24 days with constant pounding by the German XI Army, it was lost by 3 July. After a total siege of 250 days, 26,000 Russians were said to have been lost within the city, very few actually having been evacuated. Through the fall of that Soviet stronghold the doorway was truly open to the Caucasus. Russian resistance melted away all along that front. Soviet commanders on the southern flank were well aware that the tremendous loss of men would make it impossible to fight the Germans in a pitch battle and decided to trade space for time. Hitler was overjoyed and felt sure that it was the beginning of the end of the Russian campaign.

On 7 July Army Group South was reorganized. The I Panzer, XI and XVII Armies were joined together to make up the new Army Group A,

under the command of List. By 9 July the remainder of Army Group South fell under the redesignated Army Group B, with Hitler relieving Bock and replacing his command in favor of General von Weilchs. Hitler pushed his armies forward in the takeover bid of the Caucasus. German troops were making exceptional headway and meeting such little resistance that the German Command were convinced that the Russians were completely crushed in the south. The next advance was the push south of the I and IV Panzers along with the XVII Army to grab the Novorossisk naval base and the Maikops oil fields. This transfer left the German VI Army, stripped of fuel and armor, to make its way to Stalingrad alone. It became a race for the Germans; to catch the fleeing Russian troops, cross the Don River in the north, and seize the oil fields in the south.

During late July many things became obvious. The Russian retreat in the Caucasus could not be stopped, despite orders from Stalin to continue to fight and not give up ground. Army Group A's progress was slowed due to Hitler's transfer of the IV Panzer Army back to Army Group B. By 1 August German troops were spread out and over-extended along a 500-mile front. In spite of the over-extension Soviet troops were unable to stop the German advance, and by the end of August German troops had crossed the Don,

repulsed all Russian counter-attacks, and had reached the Volga a few miles north of Stalingrad. The Germans could see victory ahead, but several faults in the German operations appeared. First, in several places along the northern flank of the German VI Army's movement along the River Don, Russian troops had managed to maintain their bridgeheads. Secondly, the German forces had gathered their siege equipment from the Sebastopol offensive and sent it north to the Leningrad area to help continue the siege and break the expected Russian attempt to link the Leningrad and Volkhov Fronts in August and September 1942. This equipment should have been sent forward in the Stalingrad offensive. But perhaps most important was the fact that German Panzer units were running out of their vital life blood—fuel.

It was at this point in time that Stalin put one of his favorite troubleshooters in as new commander of the Southeastern Front: the 39-year-old Col.-General Yeremenko. Yeremenko shared the defense of Stalingrad with the insufferable General Gordov—Commander of the Stalingrad Front—to his north. As the German VI Army pushed on toward Stalingrad, it seemed to halt suddenly on the outskirts of the suburbs of the city. On 23–24 August the Luftwaffe pounded the city and its defenses in the heaviest air raids since June 1941. Throughout Stalingrad buildings

BELOW: German and Rumanian troops move through the ruins of Sebastopol in September 1942 when the Crimea and the whole north coast of the Black Sea fell into Nazi hands.

BOTTOM: A Cossack uses his horse as a cover during the intense fighting in the Ukraine.

BELOW: The German advance through the Ukraine toward the Volga astonished both the Russians and their own commanders. Rather than consolidating positions the Nazis lengthened their supply lines further and continued to move east.

BOTTOM: German troops embrace each other after a few were released from Communist confinement.

burned and many civilians were killed, but the Russian troops doggedly remained in their defenses. Stalin decided that rather than evacuate the civilian population of Stalingrad, it would be far better to leave them in the city. The troops would fight more fiercely for a 'live' city rather than give it up. As the German IV Panzer Army approached on the southern flank of the city, the Russians, fearing an encirclement, withdrew into the city itself. On 25 August it became clear to the German forces that the great Russian retreat of the previous months was over and the Russians were determined to make their stand then and there. The Soviet 62nd and 64th Armies withdrew into the city on that day, as the Regional Party Committee proclaimed a state of siege in their speech which has become famous throughout Russia ever since:

'Comrades and citizens of Stalingrad! We shall never surrender the city of our birth to the depredations of the German invader. Each single one of us must apply himself to the task of defending our beloved town, our homes, and our families. Let us barricade every street; transform every district, every block, every house into an impregnable fortress'.

Such was the mood and thought behind the forces which Germany chose to meet in their last major offensive.

Meanwhile, in the Caucasus the Germans were reaching the end of their supply lines. The oil fields which Hitler had thought would deprive the Russians of fuel, while making a new source available for German consumption, turned out to be a blazing inferno ignited by the retreating Russians when

the I Panzer Army reached it on 9 August. The Soviets continued refusing battle and German Army Group A was hindered only by the unreliability of its vehicles, not by Russian resistance. All attention seemed to have turned to Stalingrad, and on 12 September, the day before General Paulus was to launch his attack into the city, Hitler was confronted by both Paulus and Weilchs at his headquarters. Hitler had called the two generals back to emphasize his orders for clearing the entire west shore of the Volga. He wanted every available man pushed into the fight in order that Stalingrad and both banks of the river would be captured as soon as possible. The generals faced Hitler with their concern about the problems of having both flanks of the VI Army and IV Panzer Army covered by the Rumanians and

BELOW: Russian prisoners in the Caucasus celebrate their 'liberation' by German arms. Soviet minorities welcomed the Germans initially as they did in the Ukraine in 1941, but disillusionment rapidly set in.

RIGHT: Soldiers of the Wehrmacht display fatigue as the fight for Stalingrad was about to begin.

Italians, and asked whether these units should be strengthened by German soldiers to improve their morale should there be a counter-attack on either flank. Hitler told them not to worry, for as those troops arrived they would be more than adequate for protecting the flanks. Hitler himself was still under the impression that the Russian armies on the entire southern front had been completely destroyed by the early summer drive, and he honestly believed that Stalingrad would fall within a matter of weeks. However, as an addition to Paulus' forces in the VI Army, Hitler dissolved the German XI Army and sent three divisions as re-enforcements to the VI Army area. Just as Hitler believed that the fall of Stalingrad would be the key in the final defeat of the Russians in the south; Stalin decided it was time for a change. He removed Timoshenko from command of the Southwestern Front and sent in the same winning team of Voronov—the artillery specialist, Novikov—chief of the Red Air Force, and Zhukov—the genius behind the counter-offensive at Moscow, and the only Soviet general who could boast of being undefeated in any battle.

From 4–13 September fighting was mainly concentrated in the suburbs of Stalingrad. The Germans had managed to break through to the Volga on the south of the city, and the Russian 62nd Army found itself in an isolated position. General Chuikov took over command of the 62nd, determined not to give an inch and to retain his bridgeheads for as long as possible.

Both the Russians and the German troops fought a dogged house-to-house, 'street-fight' battle throughout the city. For the Germans it seemed that every building, every pile of rubble, every ditch was alive with Russian troops. Soviet soldiers fought desperately, and in many places fought on to the death, never retreating or surrendering until their ammunition ran out. One Russian officer after the battle commented that the Russian soldiers did not think of giving up a position in a fortified building until the floor below was engulfed in flames and their clothing was smoldering. The city streets became a place of carnage as the stink of death rose over the city.

History has recorded the relentless struggle in which the Russian and German troops were gripped around the destroyed factories and burning rubble of Stalingrad. Both sides were grimly determined to gain signs of victory. By nightfall of 14 September the Germans had thrown everything against Chuikov's forces and held nine-tenths of the city; but Chuikov, with all his reserves committed that day and his support from the far bank of the river, snatched victory from Paulus' situation. It was evident that the Russians would hold.

Without trying to take anything away from the battle which raged in Stalingrad itself, the true scope and purpose of the battle seemed to be unfolding behind and on the flanks of the city. Chuikov had gained a near miracle and locked the Germans into the man-eating hell of Stalingrad.

By 18 November Zhukov had completed his plans for the counter-offensive which he hoped would not only trap the German Army around Stalingrad, but would actually sweep out, cutting across to Rostov, trapping the Army Group A in the Caucasus. Zhukov's plan was basically twofold. First, his bridgeheads in the north across the River Don, which the VI German Army had failed to clear in its earlier thrust to Stalingrad, were to be the jump-off point for his five armies in the north. In the south below Stalingrad the 51st and 57th Armies of the Stalingrad Front were to launch their attacks around the three lakes of Sarpa, Tsatsa, and Barmantska.

Paulus' fears were being realized, and with the arrival of November and the cold weather he knew that his troops were not going to take their objective as planned and wanted to fall back and consolidate a defensive position on the Don. Hitler refused for reasons which totally lacked stability. Since 10 October the VI Army had been flanked by the III and IV Rumanian Armies, with the VIII Italian and II Hungarian Armies flanking the III Rumanian to its north. These armies were the satellite forces which Hitler had told Paulus not to be concerned about. Hitler believed, through the intelligence and in agreement with the Chiefs of Staff, that the Russians had no reserves with which to execute any major counter-offensive in the area. Against the judgement of many of his senior officers Hitler had committed himself so totally to the offensive that the Germans had less than four divisions in reserve to supplement a 300-mile front. In the grave situation the Rumanians, who had no tanks and only a few anti-tank weapons, stood on the threshold of destruction. Their fate would spell disaster for Paulus and the German VI Army.

At 0730 hours on 19 November Zhukov launched his counter-offensive and closed the snare around Stalingrad which Chuikov and his men had fought so desperately to lay. The Katyushas rocket artillery, which had begun to gain fame in the Battle of Stalingrad when one salvo from a battery had completely decimated a German battalion, opened up with a general bombardment along the Southwestern and Don Fronts. After the brief prelude, the Russians concentrated a heavy artillery bombardment against the Germans and Rumanians with approximately 90 guns per mile of the Front. The heavy concentration of artillery fire was deployed by the Russians not so much for its devastating effect but as a measure against the fog which lay along the landscape that morning. The Russians were taking no chances on missing their targets, and by 0850 hours Soviet troops and tanks pierced through the haze and flung themselves mercilessly against the shattered Rumanians. On the Southwestern Front the 5th Tank Army and

the 21st Army had exploited large gaps in the Rumanian defenses. By nightfall two Soviet Tank Corps broke into the Rumanians' rear, causing widespread panic, and began their sweep toward the River Don and Kalach. Encirclement of the Rumanians seemed certain.

On the Don Front the 24th, 65th and 66th Soviet Armies were running into stubborn resistance in the XI German Corps, which formed the southern left flank of the VI Army. These Russian armies were not making the headway of the other armies due to the XIV Panzer Division's counter-attack, which managed to fill the gaps that the Russians had opened in the early hours.

On 20 November Colonel-General Yeremenko swung the 57th and 51st Armies against the IV Rumanian Army.

At 1000 hours the attack began, and by early afternoon the Russians had virtually eliminated three Rumanian divisions. However, the German XXIX Motorized Division, in reserve, managed a counter-attack which slowed the situation. This unit, although it gained a small success, could not stem the tide of the battle. The Rumanians were already in full rout. By the next morning Yeremenko's 4th Cavalry Corps took the city of Abganerovo and within minutes of its capture Khrushchev appeared on the scene to congratulate and rouse the troops on to victory.

By this time, in the north the 4th Tank Corps and the 3rd Guard Corps of the Soviet 5th Tank Army were pushing deep and exploiting their day-old attack to the rear of the

126

Rumanians. The Soviet 21st Army had encircled the Rumanian V Corps and after the entrapment turned south to support the Soviet 5th Army's movements.

Before dawn on 22 November the Soviet 26th Tank Corps was within striking distance of Kalach and the Don River after covering over 60 miles within three days. By late morning a detachment of two Infantry Companies under Colonel Philipov snatched a bridge over the Don. The 23rd of November seemed truly a day of destiny for the Russians. At 1030 hours Yeremenko's 4th Mechanized Corps had linked from the south with the 4th Tank Corps of the Don Front near a small village by the name of Sovietskiy. It had been less than four days since the attack had begun, and it was clear that both the Rumanian III and IV Armies were crushed and routed. The Germans themselves were totally confused. For the first time Russian troops had executed a major offensive which did not merely trap divisions in isolated pockets as in the Moscow offensive, but had now completely encircled the entire German VI Army.

If the 23rd was a day of destiny for Russia, it was a day in which the shadow of doom stretched over the Axis forces and the VI Army. That night Paulus, surrounded by his corps commanders, appealed to Hitler to allow him to relinquish the city of Stalingrad and begin a breakout from the Soviet encirclement. Hitler, after reading the message, told Paulus that he was better

BELOW: Russian children
play in an abandoned
and unrepairable sedan
after their territory was
overrun by the Germans.

BOTTOM: The ruins of a
suburb of Stalingrad after
a Stuka attack. Both the
Russians and the
Germans decided to make
the fate of the city a
symbol.

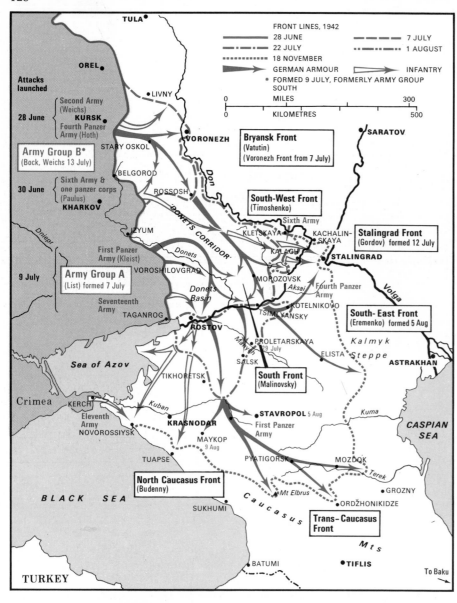

FRONT LINES, 1942
— 28 JUNE
—·— 22 JULY
···· 18 November
▶ GERMAN ARMOUR
• FORMED 9 JULY, FORMERLY ARMY GROUP SOUTH
––– 7 JULY
–··– 1 AUGUST
▷ INFANTRY

MILES 0 — 300
KILOMETRES 0 — 500

Attacks launched

28 June { Second Army (Weichs) — KURSK — Fourth Panzer Army (Hoth) }

Army Group B* (Bock, Weichs 13 July)

30 June { Sixth Army & one panzer corps (Paulus) }

9 July

First Panzer Army (Kleist)

Army Group A (List) formed 7 July

Seventeenth Army

Bryansk Front (Vatutin) (Voronezh Front from 7 July)

South-West Front (Timoshenko)

Sixth Army

Stalingrad Front (Gordov) formed 12 July

South-East Front (Eremenko) formed 5 Aug

South Front (Malinovsky)

Fourth Panzer Army

North Caucasus Front (Budenny)

Trans-Caucasus Front

First Panzer Army

TULA • OREL • LIVNY • VORONEZH • SARATOV • STARY OSKOL • BELGOROD • ROSSOSH • KHARKOV • IZYUM • VOROSHILOVGRAD • Donets Basin • TAGANROG • ROSTOV • Sea of Azov • TIKHORETSK • Crimea • KERCH • Eleventh Army • NOVOROSSIYSK • KRASNODAR • MAYKOP 9 Aug • TUAPSE • BLACK SEA • SUKHUMI • BATUMI • TURKEY • KLETSKAYA • KACHALIN-SKAYA • KALACH • STALINGRAD • MOROZOVSK • Aksai • KOTELNIKOVO • TSIMLYANSKY • PROLETARSKAYA • SALSK • STAVROPOL 5 Aug • PYATIGORSK • MOZDOK • Terek • GROZNY • Mt Elbrus • ORDŽHONIKIDZE • Caucasus Mts • TIFLIS • To Baku • Kalmyk Steppe • ELISTA • ASTRAKHAN • Kuma • CASPIAN SEA • Volga • Don • DONETS CORRIDOR • Donets • Dniepr • Kuban • Manych 29 July

LEFT: The position around Stalingrad in the autumn of 1942.

BOTTOM LEFT: Soviet poster stresses the solidarity of industrial workers forging munitions and the men at the front.

BOTTOM: Another poster emphasizes Russian industrial power.

RIGHT: Russian infantrymen fight to defend every house in Stalingrad.

FAR RIGHT: The Germans took most of Stalingrad.

BOTTOM RIGHT: Some of the 80-odd tanks left behind by retreating Nazi forces in Peskovatka west of Stalingrad.

The VI Army needed no less than 700 tons of supplies per day, according to Paulus' figures. Goering convinced Hitler that he could manage to fly in 500 tons and that the VI Army would have to tighten its belt and do without the other 200 tons. Throughout November and December 1942 the Luftwaffe tried in vain to maintain its commitments, but through severe weather and repeated mismanagement fell drastically short of the objectives. Overall the Germans lost 400 aircraft and 1000 air crews in the supply attempts as Russian anti-air fire and flight mishaps took their toll. The only credit that can seriously be given was in the air force's evacuation of some 25,000 sick and wounded from within the besieged city.

Hitler relegated the task of freeing the isolated troops to Field Marshal von Manstein. On 26 November Manstein began his counter-offensive with the newly arrived VI Panzer Division from France, and during that time scored a rather inglorious victory over the Soviet 4th Cavalry Corps. It happened that one of the Soviet brigades in that Corps was made up of camel-mounted troops from Central Asia, who fared none too well against tanks. In the early days of December repeated attempts were made to push through to Stalingrad, but the IV Panzer Army, under Hoth's command, could make no headway in the winter landscape, and by 15 December the Germans realized that fighting their way into Stalingrad

informed on the situation and that Paulus need not be anxious about the encirclement. Hitler had decided that the VI Army would not be moved on any account, and that he would try to break into the army with a relief force; or if that proved impossible, resupply Paulus by air. Goering was again coming into the picture. Earlier the year before he had managed to supply isolated German units during the previous Russian counters. He felt certain that his air force could resupply German forces in Stalingrad.

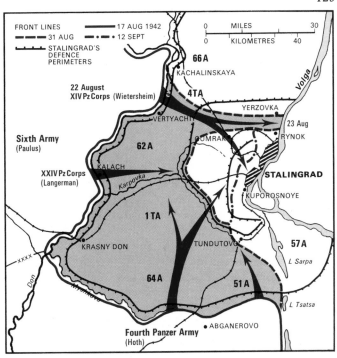

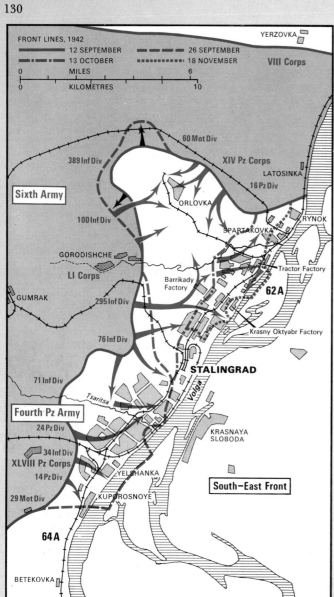

FRONT LINES, 1942

| | 12 SEPTEMBER | | 26 SEPTEMBER |
| | 13 OCTOBER | | 18 NOVEMBER |

MILES 0 — 6
KILOMETRES 0 — 10

YERZOVKA

VIII Corps

60 Mot Div

389 Inf Div

XIV Pz Corps

LATOSINKA

16 Pz Div

Sixth Army

100 Inf Div

ORLOVKA

RYNOK

SPARTAKOVKA

GORODISHCHE

Tractor Factory

LI Corps

Barrikady Factory

62 A

GUMRAK

295 Inf Div

76 Inf Div

Krasny Oktyabr Factory

STALINGRAD

71 Inf Div

Tsaritsa

Volga

Fourth Pz Army

24 Pz Div

KRASNAYA SLOBODA

34 Inf Div

XLVIII Pz Corps

South–East Front

14 Pz Div

YELSHANKA

29 Mot Div

KUPOROSNOYE

64 A

BETEKOVKA

BELOW: A German soldier
marches through the
ruins outside Stalingrad's
railway station.

BOTTOM: The fighting
became intense as the
Germans moved through
Stalingrad. Only shells
of buildings remained.

RIGHT: A Soviet factory in Stalingrad taken by the Germans. Soviet industry across the Volga and beyond the Urals more than made up for the loss of what was once 90% of Russian industrial capacity which by now was in German hands.

BELOW RIGHT: The ruins of another abandoned Soviet factory outside Stalingrad.

was impossible. Although they had reached to within 30 miles of the city, the exhausted battle-worn German troops fell back to the west bank of the Don River. To make matters worse, through the lapse in time, Paulus' troops had so little fuel left that any attempt on their part to stage a release from the city was out of the question.

With the German counter-offensive halted, the Soviet High Command put phase two of the winter 1942 offensive into effect with Operation Saturn. This was intended to be a pincers movement in the north between the Voronezh Front and the Southwestern Front to decimate what was left of the units of the Rumanian III Army—holding along the Chir River—and the Italian VIII Army—still holding its original position behind the Don. Once more Zhukov was in charge of the attack. On 16 December more than 5000 guns concentrated on that front, and the Russian 3rd Guard, under Lieutenant-

General Lelyushenko, broke the Rumanian resistance and forced them to abandon their positions. At the same time the 1st Guard Army crossed the then-frozen Don along with the Soviet 6th Army and within 48 hours had obliterated what was left of the Italians. Seeing the critical position, German forces were asked to be rushed into the area by the commanders of the crumbling Rumanians and Italians. The German XXVII Panzers were the only reserve unit in the region, and although given the task of strengthening the front, there was little they could do as they had only 50 tanks remaining in their unit.

The sweeping success of the Russian forces' attacks had pushed the Axis troops back all along the front, and by Christmas Eve 1942 they were preparing themselves for the crushing of Paulus' VI Army. Christmas Day brought phase two of the Soviet attack as forces headed toward Rostov, pushing the German IV Panzer Army further back so that its resupply by the Luftwaffe was a near impossibility. The 500 tons per day in supplies that Goering had promised to the VI Army had dwindled to less than 100 tons by January 1943. The Soviet Army knew that it was on the threshold of a great victory. Once more the combination of the inexhaustible supply of manpower of the Soviet Union, and the deadly cold of the Russian winter had united to destroy the German armies. The early days of January brought no relief to Paulus' beleaguered troops as the temperature dropped to −35°C. Not only were German troops exhausted, cold and hungry, but their ammunition and fuel were almost totally depleted. The STAVKA saw that the German forces were in no position to launch another counter-offensive and turned their attention away from the front, concentrating no less than seven Soviet armies against the German VI Army in Stalingrad. The German pocket which in time would have starved itself to death became an obsession which Soviet troops had to destroy. To many it was no longer just a matter of defeating an enemy; it became the turning point which Soviet soldiers knew would start the road to throwing the invaders out of Russia. The poorly armed, ill-equipped Soviet soldier was becoming a thing of the past. Through Lend-Lease supplies and the Soviet industries, which had been saved in the early months of the war, came the equipment with which they fought the Germans on an equal footing. In many cases the artillery, tanks, and planes were overtaking the Germans in quality, while their quantity grew with each passing day.

It was over these newly-equipped troops that Lieutenant-General Rokossovsky took command to destroy the VI Army. No less than 90 Soviet brigades and divisions stood on line to destroy the starving 22 German divisions left in Stalingrad. For Voronov destruction of the VI Army would mean his promotion to Marshal. For Major-General Rudenko the new weapons meant that his 16th Air Army could swing the balance of power in the Soviet favor and destroy the Luftwaffe aircraft attempting to supply Stalingrad. For once the battle was going completely the way the Russians desired. Every officer and each man knew that victory was within their grasp.

On 8 January 1942 two Soviet officers made their way across the rubble of the besieged areas and offered Paulus surrender conditions which Voronov and Rokossvsky had drawn up. The terms were extremely simple. German troops would cease fighting and give up all arms and equipment, handing it over in good condition, to Soviet forces. Along with this went guarantees for the safety of German troops and assurances that no retaliation of any sort would take place. These surrender terms even went so far as to allow German officers to keep their ceremonial daggers. This one point alone seemed rather noble and out of place after the bloody, desperate fighting which had previously taken place. Paulus made no reply. He knew that he had to fight for as long as possible, keeping as many Soviet armies concentrated on himself and giving other German units time to reorganize the defenses. On 10 January at 0800 hours the fate of the defenders of Stalingrad was sealed as more than 7000 guns thundered a barrage which only previewed the coming Soviet assault. By 14 January the Soviet 24th, 21st, 65th, 57th and 64th Armies had recaptured more than half the area formerly occupied by Germans to the west of the city, and by 22 January German resistance was confined to the city limits and only a few of the suburbs. On that day Paulus sent a message to Hitler telling of the situation and asking Hitler to allow him to surrender. The Führer gave an emphatic 'no'.

On 26 January German units were split into two pockets within the city, a link up having taken place between the 21st Soviet Army and Chuikov's brave defending 62nd Army. The link up took place on the Mamaev-Kurgan Hill. Soviet forces knew that it was only a matter of days.

On 30 January Paulus was promoted to Field Marshal by Hitler, more in order to keep Paulus from surrendering than for any other reason. Hitler was well aware that no German Field Marshal had ever been captured or surrendered and expected Paulus to commit suicide rather than let either event take place. By that time, however, Paulus and his staff had accepted the inevitable and surrendered to General Shumilov, commander of the 64th Soviet Army. In spite of Paulus' surrender, German resistance in the southern sector of the city continued until 31 January. The

northern sector held out until 2 February, when the German XI Corps finally laid down their arms.

A great Soviet victory had been attained. An entire German Army was totally destroyed and the Caucasus and Southern flanks were saved. The Germans had lost nearly 150,000 troops killed in the Stalingrad pocket, and the Russians hed captured nearly 100,000 German and Rumanian troops—including 24 Generals, 2500 officers and one Field Marshal. It was indeed the turning of the tide in the war with Germany. Soviet leaders knew that the road ahead would not be easy, and that the war would go on, but Stalingrad was the turning point.

THE RUSSIAN NAVY

The Russian Navy that served in World War II proved by and large a disappointment, despite the large number of ships built and the money lavished on it. But mere numbers of ships are not an index of efficiency, and it takes no great degree of perspicacity to identify the fundamental problems of the Russian Navy.

Of all the major prewar naval powers the Russians were uniquely unfortunate in having suffered three major catastrophes in less than 40 years. The first was their defeat at the hands of the Japanese in the Far East in 1905, when the entire Baltic Fleet was sunk or captured. The second was World War I, which broke out before a massive program or rearmament had made much progress. The two revolutions in 1917 did further damage to morale and ships, followed by sabotage at the hands of the Germans, Anglo-French forces during the Intervention, and both sides during the Civil War. The last blow was self-inflicted; in 1937 Stalin began a 'purge' of the military hierarchy, and during the next two years a large number of senior naval officers were executed or disappeared into what we now know as the Gulag Archipelago. No navy can dispense with the store of knowledge and experience accumulated by its officer corps, and there can be no doubt that the purges did as much damage as anything that had happened before to the Red Fleet.

There was another problem, one which was dictated by nature and geography. As she occupies the largest land mass in the world, the Soviet Union is flanked by four oceans, the

Baltic, the Black Sea, Arctic and Pacific. This has always forced Russia to divide her naval resources between four areas which are separated by long distances. The intervening territory is also controlled by unfriendly or even hostile powers, and so four fleets have to be maintained. Once a ship is deployed in the Arctic it is no easy matter to transfer her to the Baltic, and even harder to transfer ships to and from the Pacific or the Black Sea. After the disasters of the Russo-Japanese War the Pacific Fleet had been maintained at a weak level, and only light forces were kept in the Arctic, leaving the Baltic Fleet as the main force and the Black Sea Fleet somewhat weaker but also a strong force. As tension developed between Japan and Russia in the 1930s the Pacific squadron was strengthened, but this balance between the four fleets remained roughly constant.

When the Moscow government began to rebuild the Navy in 1922 it was clear that a major job lay ahead. Not only were the surviving ships in very poor shape but even the political reliability of

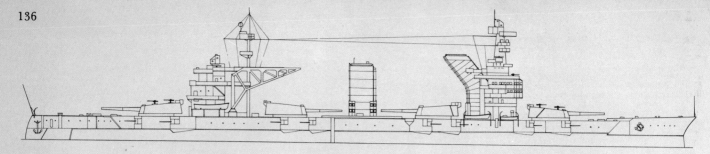

the Fleet was suspect. The Kronstadt rising of the year before had been bloodily suppressed, and Lenin in a vengeful mood proposed the scrapping of the entire fleet, on the grounds that it was troublesome, useless and expensive. It was apparently Trotsky who persuaded Lenin to change his mind. But the suspicion remained, and so right from the outset the new Red Fleet was subject to tight political control at all levels. Furthermore, its strategic aims were thought of as purely subordinate to Army requirements.

The first step was to draft 3000 Komsomols (Young Communists) into the naval schools for training as seamen. By 1927 over 10,000 Komsomols had entered the Navy to form cadres of trained ratings and junior officers. Many of the existing warships were in such bad condition that they had to be scrapped, and it was felt to be more worthwhile to finish some of the warships still incomplete since before the Revolution. After ruthless weeding out of useless hulls the Russians were left with the following:

Serviceable Ships

3 battleships (in commission or refitting)
5 cruisers (2 in commission, 3 still under construction)
17 destroyers (10 in commission, 7 under construction)
19 submarines (not all in commission or complete)

The battleships were sister ships, and all three received suitable Marxist names, *Gangut* becoming *Oktyabrskaya Revolutsia* (October Revolution); *Sevastopol* becoming *Parizhskaya Kommuna* (Paris Commune) and *Petropavlovsk* becoming *Marat*. A sister ship, the

Poltava had proved to be beyond repair and was used for spares, although the hull was still in existence in 1941. They had a unique profile, with four triple 12-inch gun turrets widely spaced along a flush deck. All were originally in the Baltic, but in 1929 the *Parizhskaya Kommuna* was transferred to the Black Sea, and after 1928 all were repaired and modernized. This resulted in what was known as their 'hammer bow and sickle funnel', a reference to the trunking of the forefunnel into a very ugly shape, and their icebreaking bows. They were given oil-fired boilers in place of the original mixed coal-and-oil arrangement, and at least one was re-engined, but they remained an antiquated design and no match for foreign battleships. The best feature was their guns, as the 12-inch could range up to 25,000 yards, and their worst was their accommodation; the kindest comment about them was that they were 'unsanitary' and exceedingly ill-ventilated.

The cruisers were an ill-assorted lot. Retained more out of sentiment than for any military value was the *Aurora*, the old 2nd Class cruiser first commissioned in 1902 which had fired the first (blank) shots of the October Revolution. She had another distinction as one of the few ships to escape from the Battle of Tsushima. Her main value was for training, and after 1930 she was permanently stationed at Leningrad, where she can be seen to this day. In the Black Sea there were three light cruisers. The oldest, the *Komintern* had to be re-engined after British forces had sabotaged her at Sevastopol in 1919, but even so she could only reach 20 knots

and had to be used for training. During the 1930s there was talk of converting her to a seaplane carrier, but she had been afloat for 30 years and even by Russian standards she must have been too old. Two more three-funnelled cruisers, the *Chervonaya Ukraine* (Red Ukraine) and *Krasni Krim* (Red Crimea) had been launched in 1915 for the Tsarist Navy. After a lengthy period of repair and rehabilitation they were completed to a slightly modified design in 1927–28. The *Krasni Krim* had been built in the Baltic, but she was transferred to the Black Sea in 1929 with the battleship *Marat*. Although originally designed for a speed of 32 knots they never made more than 29 when new, and by 1941 neither could exceed 25 knots.

The oddest cruiser of all was the *Krasni Kavkaz* (Red Caucasus), which had been launched in 1916 as the *Admiral Lazarev*, a sister of the *Chervonaya Ukraina*. In 1924 work began again, but to a modified design. The Russian designers achieved what would have been a most complex conversion job even for an efficient Western navy, turning the ship from a light cruiser with 5.1-inch guns in broadside casemates into a heavy cruiser with 7.1-inch guns in four single centerline turrets. When she was completed in 1932 she had been under construction for nearly 20 years, a record even for Russian shipyards. To add to her troubles she was badly damaged in collision with the *Komintern* shortly after completion and was subsequently lengthened by 14-15 feet. Like her onetime sisters she had a speed of 29 knots, and she was no

LEFT: The battleship *Gangut* became the *Oktyabrskaya Revolutsia* (October Revolution) in 1935. She bombarded Finnish coast defenses in the Winter War, but was penned in Leningrad from 1941 onwards and was used as a floating battery for the defense of the city.

RIGHT: Russian gunners aim a twin anti-aircraft machine gun against planes of the Luftwaffe.

BOTTOM: Russian flying boat passes over a destroyer of the *Silny* or VII-U Class and two 'Tral' Class mine sweepers.

match for foreign heavy cruisers in protection or gunpower.

The oldest destroyer had been a remarkable ship in 1914. As the Tsarist *Novik* she had been the fastest and most heavily armed destroyer in the world, with a speed of 36 knots, five 4-inch guns and nine torpedo-tubes. A further 53 improved versions had been ordered during World War I but only nine survived by 1922. One of the war casualties was refloated and a further six were completed. With the original *Novik*, now renamed *Yakov Sverdlov*, they were divided into Types I to VI, and the last were completed in 1925. Originally 12 were stationed in the Baltic and five in the Black Sea, but between 1933 and 1936 five were transferred from the Baltic Fleet to the Northern (Arctic) Fleet, and from there two went via the Northern route to the Pacific. By 1941 they were all very slow and suitable only for use as escorts.

As many as 33 submarines survived the Revolution and Civil War, but only 19 were recommissioned, 13 in the Baltic, five in the Black Sea and one in the Arctic. Submarines are unlike other warships; if they become unsafe to dive they are unusable, whereas surface warships can always perform useful tasks as long as they can steam and fire their guns. Most of the Tsarist submarines were the Bubnov type, which had not proved particularly successful in service. The best were the 'AG' or 'Amerikanski Golland' type bought from the USA in 1916. The survivors became the four 'A' Class in the Black Sea Fleet, and a fifth was salvaged and returned to service as *A.5* in 1928.

BELOW: British and subsequently American convoys brought vital weapons and other strategic supplies through the Arctic to the northern ports of Archangel and Murmansk. This map shows how close the winter and summer routes were to German air bases in northern Norway.

RIGHT: Crewmen of the Soviet heavy cruiser, probably the *Voroshilov*, practice loading drill for their 45 mm anti-aircraft guns.

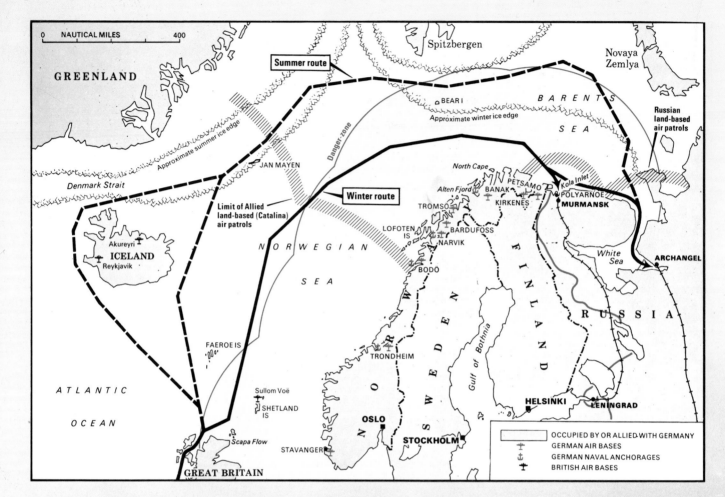

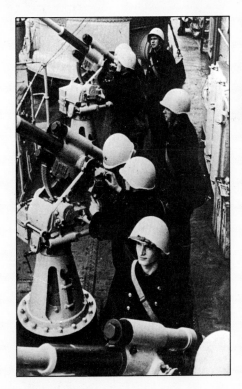

LEFT: The after 10.2 cm guns aboard an old destroyer. Many Soviet destroyers were relics of the Tsarist Navy.

BOTTOM: The Red Fleet's first public display was in 1937, when the *Marat* represented the Soviet Union at the Coronation Naval Review in Great Britain. Her icebreaker bow and unusual funnel shape attracted considerable comment.

Russia's lakes and rivers required an enormous number of small craft, in addition to those needed for coastal patrol work and minesweeping etc. During World War I 40 special landing ships had been designed for a projected landing on the Turkish coast, but only ten were completed. They anticipated many of the features of LSTs and LCTs of World War II, and were used during the Civil War. The remainder of the Russian auxiliary flotillas comprised a weird and wonderful assortment of ex-warships and mercantile conversions, for the Russians were always able to keep ships going.

However weak the Red Fleet was in the early 1920s its political masters never gave up the idea of expansion. In February 1924 the naval powers which had not been signatories of the Washington Disarmament Treaty met in Rome to discuss how to limit their own fleets. Russia broke up the conference by insisting on a capital ship tonnage of 490,000 tons, a figure which nearly equalled the total allowed to Great Britain and the USA at Washington. In return for an offer to reduce this total to 280,000 tons (the existing battleships totalled about 75,000 tons) the Russian delegation demanded the

BELOW: The destroyer *Soobrasitelny* (right) comes alongside the crippled flotilla leader *Tashkent* to rescue survivors. *Tashkent* had been attacked by German aircraft off the Crimea in June 1942.

RIGHT: The *Dekabrist* Class submarines were the first new warships ordered for the Soviet Navy in 1927. Designed in Italy, this class posed innumerable problems from the outset, and only six were built.

BELOW RIGHT: A sub chaser of the Northern Fleet (Red Banner Division) drops depth charges. The sailor is holding a portable range finder.

BOTTOM RIGHT: Two torpedomen carry out maintenance. Russian torpedos were rugged and reliable.

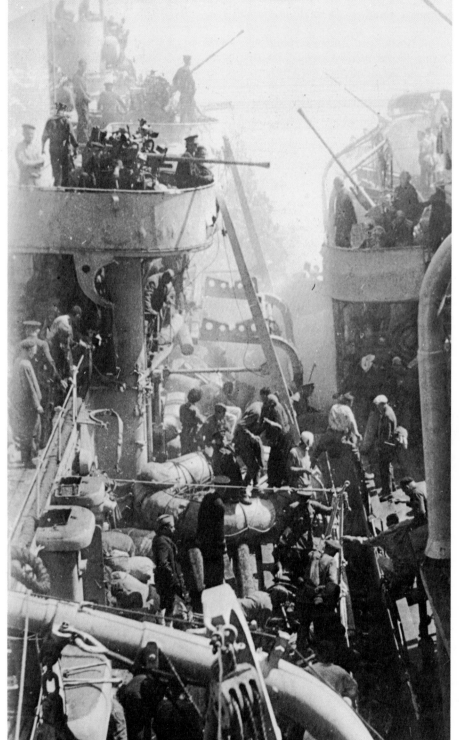

exclusion of foreign warships from the Baltic and the Black Sea, and the demilitarization of the Straits of Korea. Although they wrecked the Rome Conference the Russians pursued a policy of settling differences with their neighbors, wisely acknowledging that their fleet was inadequate for anything more than coast defense.

The role of the fleet was quite clearly laid down, to provide protection for the seaward flanks, particularly by defending major centers like Leningrad, by preventing enemy landings and by providing gunfire support to the Army. The principal enemies were seen as Japan in the Far East, Great Britain and Germany in the Baltic and Turkey in the Black Sea. The British depredations in the Baltic during their 1919–20 intervention had not been forgotten, and the revival of Germany had not gone unnoticed. Naturally the strength of the Japanese Navy in the Pacific was also alarming, and it was recognized that China ought to be supported to discourage the Japanese from trying to seize territory in Manchuria.

The first steps toward rebuilding the fleet came in 1927, and its hardly a coincidence that the decision was made at the time that the German Reichstag started its discussions on building the *Deutschland*, first of the 'pocket battleships'. The year before a German naval mission under Admiral Spindler had visited Russia, and talks had taken place about technical assistance. The Germans were bound by the terms of the Treaty of Versailles, and were looking for ways to pursue military research outside Germany, but without going so far as to build up a future rival. Plans of the World War I UBIII type of U-Boat were handed over among other things, and if this seems rather niggardly it should be remembered that the same type was developed by the Germans into the highly successful Type VII only ten years later. The Russians made good use of it too, and their 'S' class was a very successful variant. It is amusing to read that the Germans regarded the captain of the battleship *Marat* as a 'sound coxswain type'.

At the end of 1927 the first new warships were laid down at Leningrad, three submarines of the 'D' or *Dekabrist* class. The Italians had furnished some assistance, but the boats revealed so many faults on their trials in 1930 that

completion was delayed until 1931–32. When the faults had been rectified a further three were ordered for the Black Sea Fleet. To gain as much experience as they could the Russians raised the old British boat *L.55* which had been sunk in the Gulf of Finland during the Intervention. She was recommissioned in 1931, still under her British number, and her features were incorporated into a new 'L' or *Leninets* class. As coastal defense was so important large numbers of medium and small submarines were ordered. The 570-ton 'Shch' or *Shchuka* (Pike) class and 160-ton 'M' class were built in large numbers from 1930 onwards.

Not until 1932 did the Russians consider anything but submarines. In that year they started building the first

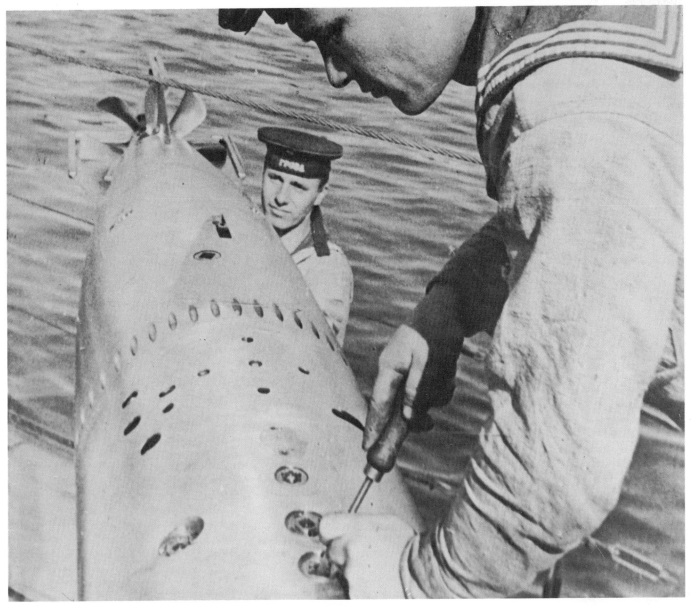

Major Warships Laid Down 1927–1941

Year	Battleships Battle-cruisers	8-inch Cruisers	6-inch Cruisers	Destroyers Leaders	Destroyers	Submarines
1927						3
1928						
1929						22[1]
1930						4
1931						3
1932			1			15
1933				1		3
1934						20
1935		2	1	1		6
1936		2		2	14	32
1937				2	13	35
1938	2[2]		2		16	48
1939	2[2]	2	3	2	15	18
1940		2	1		2	44
1941		4		2	10	44
Total	4	12	6	11	71	297

[1]This was the total authorized, but the program was spread over several years. [2]Suspended 1940.

of two flotilla leaders. In 1933 Marshal Voroshilov approached the French for technical assistance, and asked if it would be possible to have cruisers, submarines and destroyers built in France. The French had already provided plans for the two flotilla leaders, but on this occasion they were not willing to provide any help. The Japanese attack on Manchuria in November 1931 resulted in a redeployment of submarines to the Far East; three *Shchuka* class boats were sent in sections by rail to Vladivostock in 1932, and two years later three *Leninets* class were laid down. To counter what the Russians saw as a sinister *rapprochement* between Turkey and Great Britain, submarine building was stepped up in the Black Sea yards.

The turning point was 1935, for in that year it was finally recognized that Nazi Germany was the main enemy. In May 1935 Russia concluded alliances with France and Czechoslovakia. There was good reason for alarm, for in June the Anglo-German Naval Agreement conceded the right to the German Navy to build up to 35 per cent of the strength of the Royal Navy in surface ships and up to 100 per cent in submarines. The political apprehension was mirrored in the first major surface warship program since 1917. Two heavy cruisers were laid down, the *Kirov* at Leningrad and the *Molotov* at Nikolaev in the Black Sea. Seven fleet destroyers of Italian design, the 1660-ton *Gnevny* class, were laid down in the Baltic, with two more of the French designed leaders and a home-grown product, the ultra-high speed experimental destroyer *Serge Ordzhonikidze*.

The *Kirov* class cruisers, known as Project 26, were built with considerable Italian assistance. They strongly resembled contemporary Italian cruisers, with two widely spaced, raked funnels, but the armament comprised nine 7.1-inch (180-mm) guns in triple turrets. This was the same gun that had been tried experimentally in the *Krasni Kavkaz*, and according to Russian sources it made excellent shooting at ranges up to 39,000 yards. As could be expected from any ship with Italian ancestry speed was impressive, and one of the class reached 35.94 knots on trials, although the service speed was nearer 31 knots. Four more of the class were ordered between 1936 and 1939, but they incorporated several changes in accordance with the latest Italian ideas and were known as Project 26B. The most important difference was the fire control, which was mounted on a tower instead of a quadrapod foremast. The *Maksim Gorki* was completed in December 1940 for the Baltic Fleet and the *Voroshilov* joined the Black Sea Fleet in June 1941, only a week before the German attack. The other two, *Kalinin* and *Kaganovich* were ordered from the Koinsomolsk Yard on the Amur River in the Far East in 1939, but they were not ready until the middle of 1944.

In 1938 six more big cruisers of the *Frunze* class were authorized. Although they displaced some 11,000 tons as compared to the 8800-ton *Kirovs*, they adopted an armament of twelve 5.9-inch guns with 50° elevation to give some measure of protection against aircraft. Three were laid down at Leningrad in 1938–39 and another three were laid down at Nikolaev in the Black Sea in 1939–40, but all were stopped during the war. Six more heavy cruisers, possibly displacing as much as 20,000 tons and armed with twelve 7.1-inch guns were planned. Two were laid down at Leningrad in the winter of 1940–41, followed by two more in 1941 and one at Nikolaev. The whole project is shrouded in mystery, for some Russian sources indicate that the design was for a 22,000-ton armed with nine 10-inch guns and capable of 33 knots. According to these same sources the design was recast to a 38,000-ton battle cruiser to be known as the *Strana Sovietov* class. What is definite is that in 1941 the Germans found the hull of a cruiser, apparently to be named *Sevastopol*, on the slipway at Nikolaiev. It was over 800 feet long, which puts it in the capital ship category.

At the same time as the *Frunze* class cruisers were started, the plans of a new class of battleships were ready. Here again we are indebted to German intelligence records for the few positive facts known about these ships. As early as 1934 the Naval Staff had contacted various American firms such as Midvale Steel, Newport News Shipbuilding & Dry Dock Co., and Gibbs & Cox for help in producing not only designs but machinery, armor, gun turrets or even complete ships. Despite the US Government's adherence to the international treaties governing size of battleships one consortium of American firms produced a design for a 62,000-ton battleship armed with 16-inch guns. The US Government was prepared to permit the construction of a 45,000-tonner in a government naval yard, and gave tentative agreement in June 1938 — a deal which would have taken a lot of explaining to the other signatories of the treaties. But fortunately for the good name of the United States and capitalism the Soviet government suddenly withdrew on the excuse that the plans were not suitable. Negotiations were still under way in 1939, but when the US Navy embarked on its own expansion program in 1940 it no longer had spare capacity, and so the subject was dropped.

After an abortive enquiry in France about the possibility of buying 17.7-inch

guns from Schneider-Creusot the Russians turned to Italy. The Ansaldo yard at Livorno produced a design based on the new *Littorio* class which were planned for the Regia Navale, but as with the Americans the negotiations led to nothing, and it is possible that both exercises were undertaken merely to pick the brains of foreign designers. After the signing of the Molotov-Ribbentrop Pact in 1939 the Germans were asked to produce the plans of their new *Bismarck* class. The German Naval Staff, presumably acting on orders from above, did as little as possible to help, and very little information of any value was handed over. They did, however, accept an order for 16-inch and 15-inch gun turrets and other ordnance, and the Swiss firm of Brown Boveri and others received orders for machinery parts. None of this material had been delivered when war broke out.

The building of an ocean-going navy was the product of a big shift in strategic thinking. In 1935 there had been changes in the administration of the Navy, starting with the abolition of the rather bogus egalitarian nomenclature and the reintroduction of a rational rank-structure. But Stalin also took the first steps to tighten his control over the Navy by promoting his proteges, particularly L. M. Galler, who became Flagman (Admiral) commanding the Baltic Fleet, and N. G. Kuznetsov, who rose to flagman from the command of a cruiser. V. R. Orlov, who had been the head of the Navy, was confirmed as Supreme Naval Commander, while M. V. Viktorov, the leading submarine specialist, became commander of the Far Eastern Fleet. Orlov and the Chief Commissar Muklevich had been the advocates of a limited coast-defense role for the Navy, an unambitious strategy which they accepted without question, submarines being cheap to build and able to lay both offensive and defensive minefields. But their superior, Marshal Voroshilov, who became Commissar of Defense in 1934, was close to Stalin and echoed the dictator's thoughts of expansion. It was Voroshilov who had initiated the attempts to get German and French

BELOW: The new destroyer *Svobodny* was one of the first casualties of German air attacks on Sebastopol in the summer of 1942.

BOTTOM: Siberian soldiers of a rifle brigade embark on board the *Tashkent* for the perilous journey to Sebastopol in the Crimea.

support for the construction of heavy units, and he was probably behind the new revision of strategy.

The divergence of ideas first became evident to the outside world during the Anglo-Soviet discussions on naval limitations in 1936. The British wanted to bring Russia and Germany into line with the London Treaty of Naval Limitation of March 1936, by which the United States, Great Britain and France had agreed to maintain the spirit of limitation on naval armaments enshrined in the Washington Treaty and the 1930 London Treaty. It was particularly intended as a sop to France, who was very concerned about German rearmament. During the negotiations the Russians revealed that they intended to lay down two battle-ships armed with 16-inch guns and ten 8000-ton heavy cruisers. After a weary

round of haggling the Russians agreed to cut the cruisers down to seven, but would not abandon the 7.1-inch gun, despite the fact that the European Powers had already agreed to build only 6-inch gun cruisers.

The debate was continuing all the while inside Russia. In January 1936 Marshal Tukhachevsky announced the intention of going over to the building of large warships, whereas in November Orlov was addressing the Eighteenth Congress of Soviets and proudly claiming that the submarine strength had been increased 700 per cent and the coastal defense forces 300 per cent since 1933. But the 1936 program included two heavy cruisers and a large number of destroyers. The lack of destroyers was most serious and certainly not compatible with the new strategic thinking. But the destroyers, like the battleships,

were so specialized that their construction could not be undertaken until the country's industrial capacity had improved. In 1936 more of the Italian-designed *Gnevny* or Type VII destroyers were ordered. Unfortunately they turned out to be structurally weak and not sufficiently seaworthy for the weather conditions encountered in the Arctic and the Pacific, and so a new design was begun in 1938. Known as the Type VII-U (*Uvelicheniye* — extension), they proved much more successful. The original plans were for nine flotillas of six destroyers each, three for the Baltic, two for the Black Sea, three for the Pacific and one for the Arctic. By the outbreak of war in June 1941 eighteen of the Type VII destroyers had joined the Baltic Fleet and ten had joined the Black Sea Fleet, but only nine of the Type VII-U were ready.

During the early part of 1937 the 'defensive' school enjoyed its last moments of influence. Only two destroyers were laid down, and one large destroyer leader, the *Tashkent* was ordered from Italy, as against 35 submarines. The first sign of Stalin's displeasure was the arrest of Marshal Tukhachevsky. He had already been replaced by Admiral Orlov as the chief delegate representing Russia at the British Coronation, but Orlov's supporter Ludri was replaced by Galler as Deputy-Commander, Soviet Naval Forces. Then in July Muklevich was arrested by the GPU. In January 1938 Molotov made a startling announcement to the Supreme Soviet, claiming that the Soviet Navy must be built up to overshadow the Royal Navy. In the same month Orlov was replaced as People's Commissar for the Navy by an

BELOW: Rear Admiral
Vladimirsky addresses
the crew of a destroyer of
the Black Sea Fleet.

BOTTOM: Crewmen drag
an injured comrade from
a wrecked gun turret of
a destroyer leader in the
Black Sea.

obscure officer called Smirnov, who was made directly answerable to Andrei Zhdanov and the Naval Soviet.

All this was merely a curtain raiser to the full horror of the purges. That summer Orlov was summarily tried and executed, along with Muklevich, Ludri and Admirals Zivkov, Koschanov, Dushkanov and Kadotskii-Rudnev, respectively the commanders of the Baltic Fleet, Black Sea Fleet, Northern Fleet and Amur Flotilla. Among the many denunciations flung at their heads was the accusation that they had talked 'twaddle about the possibility or impossibility of supremacy on the sea'. It is also significant that one of the indictments which procured the execution of Marshal Tukhachevsky was his alleged opposition to giving the Navy new surface ships. Much worse for the Navy was the purging of the senior officers of the Naval Academy, Alexsandrov, Stashkevitch and Petrovich and a host of senior officers commanding squadrons and flotillas, for it crippled the officer-corps. Throughout the Great Patriotic War, which was only three years away, the junior officers showed reasonable professional training and great bravery but a total reluctance to perform any duty which had not been sanctioned by the Supreme Command. With the memory of the purges so fresh in their minds these inhibitions are not hard to understand.

Those few high ranking officers who survived the purges of 1937–38 were inevitably the believers in a large surface fleet. Admiral Galler, one of the original flagmen, became the Chief of the Soviet Naval Staff in 1938, while his fellow big-navy advocate, Admiral Kuznetsov, took over command of the Far Eastern Fleet. However, the building program for that year continued the emphasis on submarines, and only one cruiser was laid down. In March 1939 Kuznetsov moved upwards again, and replaced Smirnov as Naval Commissar. At the Soviet Congress he announced that the Soviet Union could and would build first-class ships of any size. Kuznetsov and Tevosyan, the head of the Naval Construction Commissariat, made frequent references to the building of 'a most mighty attacking fleet', and it was at this point that the keels of two battleships were laid, one at Leningrad and one at Nikolaiev. They were to be named *Sovietsky Soyuz*

BOTTOM: A flying boat circles over a *Stalinets* Class submarine. This class drew heavily on German technical assistance and was the most successful prewar type.

RIGHT: The Type VII destroyer *Bezposhchadny*, one of 27 built with Italian technical assistance in the 1930s. In service they proved top-heavy and too lightly built to withstand rough weather.

and *Sovietskaya Ukraina*, and as two of the biggest capital ships ever built they make an interesting comparison with the Japanese giant *Yamato*.

Construction slowed down in the Spring of 1940 because of an acute shortage of steel, and in October work stopped altogether. The laying down of two more battleships at Leningrad was deferred, and the outbreak of war prevented anything further being done. When the Germans overran Nikolaiev in August 1941 they found the hull of *Sovietskaya Ukraina* 66 per cent complete and only nine months away from launching, but they did nothing to her until 1944 when the giant hull was severely damaged by demolition parties.

The Molotov-Ribbentrop Pact signed in August 1939 was used, as we have seen, as an excuse to pump the German Navy for technical information. But in the area where the Russians most needed outside guidance they had chosen an ally who knew as little as they did. Aircraft carriers would be needed if the new surface fleets were to undertake any extended operations in the Arctic and Far East outside the range of shore-based aircraft. The Germans refused to pass over plans of their carrier *Graf Zeppelin*, which was just as well, since

Sovietsky Soyuz Class and Yamato Class Battleships

A comparison between the *Sovietsky Soyuz* Class and the *Yamato* Class battleships. This chart indicates the remarkable similarity in dimensions, since the *Yamato* Class is known for being the biggest ever built.

	Sovietsky Soyuz class	*Yamato* class
Displacement (normal/full load)	59,000/65,000 tons	64,000/69,980 tons
Length (OA)	889 ft	863 ft
Beam	127¾ ft	127¾ ft
Draught	33½ ft	34¼ ft
Armament	Nine 16-inch	Nine 18.1-inch
	Twelve 6-inch	Twelve 6.1-inch
	Eight 3.9-inch AA	Twelve 5-inch AA
	32–37-mm AA	24–25-mm AA
Aircraft	Four	Six
Machinery	4-shaft steam turbines	4-shaft steam turbines
Speed	28 knots	27 knots
Armor	16¾-inch belt	16-inch belt
	6-inch deck	9-inch deck
	19½-inch turrets	25.6-inch turrets

that ship incorporated many retrograde features and would almost certainly have been a failure if completed. We know that the German design staff was plagued with problems affecting the equipment of the *Graf Zeppelin*, which leads one to suspect that they may have been unwilling to admit to the Russians the extent of their own ignorance. The Third Five Year Plan for 1938–42 included provision for two aircraft carriers, but on Stalin's orders the ships were not laid down, and this decision may in turn have influenced the slowing down and eventual suspension of the

two battleships and the battlecruisers in 1940. As no information whatsoever has been discovered about the design of these carriers, it must be concluded that the Russians had not completed any design studies and were hoping to get everything from their allies.

Seaplane carriers were no substitute for proper aircraft carriers, but they could form a useful adjunct to the fleet by providing reconnaissance. The abortive attempt to convert the old cruiser *Komintern* has already been mentioned, the work being abandoned when it was realized that she was too slow. Just

BELOW: A *Stalinets* Class submarine running on the surface. Russia had the largest submarine fleet at the outbreak of World War II, but its many units were non-operational in mid-1941 when Germany attacked.

BOTTOM: The submarine *Naradovolets* in an Arctic anchorage. The best feature of Russian submarine design was their suitability for operating in icy conditions.

RIGHT: The cruiser *Kirov* displaced 8800 tons and was armed with nine 180 mm (7.1-inch) guns. The *Kirov* fought in the Winter War and was damaged by German bombs twice. She was one of the few heavy units to see active service in the Baltic.

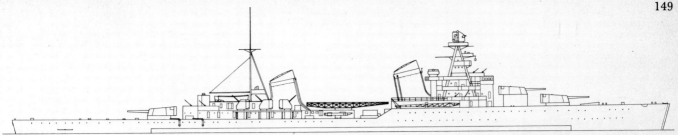

before World War II a pair of seaplane carriers were authorized for the Far East, but as far as we know they were cancelled.

One other attempt was made to get technical help from the Germans. Requests were made for the supply of machinery, armor and armament for four heavy cruisers, or sufficient technical help to build two *Admiral Hipper* class 10,000-ton cruisers in Russian yards; as a last choice, the purchase of two *Admiral Hipper* class was suggested. By the spring of 1940 the Germans were fully occupied in building U-Boats and were only too happy to sell the incomplete hull of the *Lützow*, and the ship was towed to Leningrad. The Soviet Navy had not asked for this, reckoning that they did not have the technical capability to cope with German machinery, but Stalin forced the deal through as a political gesture. Despite the help of 70 German technicians the work proceeded with difficulty. In June 1941 she was still incomplete with only three 8-inch guns aboard, and she was used as a floating battery in the defense of Leningrad.

In the vital field of scientific research the Soviet Navy does not appear to have done very well. The two technical advances of the 1930s, radar and sonar, do not appear to have been known to Soviet scientists until they were made available by the British and Americans during World War II. Torpedoes were rugged and generally reliable, but they lacked refinements such as magnetic pistols or electric propulsion. Fire control instruments were not comparable to their equivalents in other navies, but on the other hand the design of

guns was sound. The principal weapons were the 12-inch in the battleships, the 7.1-inch and 6-inch mounted in cruisers, the 5.1-inch (130mm) used in destroyers and the 45mm and 37mm anti-aircraft guns.

One factor which hampered the training of the Baltic Fleet was the freezing of the Baltic for three or four months of every year. As all the bases were inside the Gulf of Finland this meant that the entire fleet was ice-bound, and the Molotov-Ribbentrop Non-Aggression Pact of 23 August 1939 included a secret clause whereby Germany undertook not to obstruct Russian ambitions against the Baltic States. As a result when World War II broke out the Russians forced Estonia and Latvia to sign mutual assistance pacts which granted the Baltic Fleet new bases at Baltischport, Windau and Libau, on the islands of Dago and Ösel and in the Irben Strait, the very bases which had been Russian in World War I. An attempt to coerce the Finns into signing a similar pact led to the outbreak of the Russo-Finnish War in November 1939.

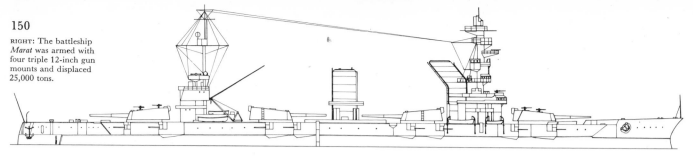

RIGHT: The battleship *Marat* was armed with four triple 12-inch gun mounts and displaced 25,000 tons.

BELOW LEFT: The 12-inch guns of the battleship *Sebastopol*, formerly the *Parizhskaya Kommuna* (Paris Commune), with the cruiser *Krasny Krim* (Red Crimea) in the background during operations in the Black Sea.

RIGHT: Strength of the Russian Navy in mid-1941.

BELOW RIGHT: The 'Shcha' or 'Shchuka' (Pike) Class submarines were built in large numbers for coast defense.

BOTTOM RIGHT: The large fleet submarine *K*.21, which was reputed to have torpedoed the *Tirpitz* in 1943. This claim was never substantiated in German records.

Russian Navy Fleets

	Baltic	Black Sea	Arctic	Far East	Total
Battleships	2	1			3
Heavy cruisers	1				1
Light cruisers	3	6			9
Leaders	2	3		2	7
Destroyers	19	13	8	12	52
Submarines	76	51	6	7	140

Russian naval forces did no better than the land forces in the 'Winter War'. The combined Arctic and Baltic Fleets and the Lake Ladoga Flotilla outnumbered the Finnish Navy by about ten to one, and yet they had no success in maintaining a blockade or even destroying any coastal fortifications. The total Finnish losses were an auxiliary patrol vessel and five merchant ships sunk and one captured. The Finns were heavily outnumbered, and no friendly countries were willing (or able) to run the risk of a simultaneous war against Germany and Russia at the eastern end of the Baltic. In March 1940 Finland signed a peace which ceded the Karelian Isthmus and the Hangö Peninsula, the areas wanted for bases by the Russians.

When war broke out between Germany and the Soviet Union on 22 June 1941 there were three battleships, one heavy cruiser, nine light cruisers, seven flotilla leaders, 52 destroyers and about 140 submarines complete. These were distributed as shown on the chart.

The figures give no idea of the state of readiness of the respective fleets. Certainly a very low percentage of warships were on station when war broke out. With so many ships still under construction or only recently completed efficiency was bound to be doubtful, and the expansion of training facilities had not kept pace with the shipbuilding programs. But looking further it is clear that the whole big-navy program was a megalomaniacal enterprise. The idea of 'overtaking' Great Britain, let alone the United States or Japan at that stage betrayed an astonishing lack of realism. The big ships seem to have been desired by Stalin and his henchmen purely for prestige and status, and there is no evidence of any strategic doctrine for employing them usefully. There was some empty rhetoric about carrying the war at sea into the enemy's waters, but no discussion of how and where this was to be done.

The Far East was the only area in which a Russian surface fleet could have avoided being cooped up as it had been in World War I, and as it was doomed to be once again in 1941–45. The Soviet Union told its wartime allies that the two battleships would have been deployed in the Far East, and that would have suited the British and the Americans. On the other hand the

152

BELOW: Loading a torpedo aboard a ship of the Black Sea Fleet. The ship in the background is the pre-Revolutionary cruiser *Krasny Krim*.

BOTTOM LEFT: An M Class submarine of the Black Sea Fleet prepares for her next patrol.

BOTTOM RIGHT: The *Shchuka* Class submarine had a distinctive silhouette, with the 45 mm gun mounted on a step forward of the conning tower.

precision and skill with which Japanese carrier pilots disposed of Allied naval strength in December 1941 makes it unlikely that a Russian battle squadron would have been permitted much freedom to exert its influence. As matters turned out the policy of stationing a strong force of submarines in the Far East was the most realistic one. In any case, Japan had no wish to embark on a Pacific War with a hostile Russia at her back, and the 1941 neutrality pact negotiated by the Japanese Foreign Minister Matsuoka was sufficient to keep Russia neutral until the very last days of World War II.

The gigantic Soviet Navy which Stalin tried to create was unique in being designed without coherent thought or strategic doctrine. In purely industrial terms it was a great achievement, but in every other sense it entailed diplomatic effort, exertions and expenditure which could have been devoted to better purposes. So much that needed to be done was neglected to bolster the preposterous dream of a world-beating navy, and as a result the Soviet Navy was to pay dearly.

SOVIET AIR POWER

The Red Air Force came into being as the 'Workers and Peasants Air Fleet' during the days of the Revolution, a heterogenous collection of airplanes flown mostly by the same pilots who had flown them for the Tsar, converted either by revolutionary fervor or the threat of death. At the end of the Civil War this force consisted of about 325 aircraft, a motley collection of types acquired from every country which had produced aircraft during the First World War, and the re-organization of this force was given a high priority. As early as September 1920 an Aviation Research Institute was set up, staffed by such aeronautical experts and scientists left in the country, and in January 1921 an edict by Lenin authorized a Planning Commission to organize a ten-year program of aviation research and aircraft construction. That aviation was given such priority is less surprising than it might, at first glance, seem.

Committee decisions do not produce airplanes, and for the time being reliance had to be placed on making aircraft under license from foreign manufacturers until Russian designs could be developed. Nieuport and Spad fighters were built at GAZ-1 (State Aircraft Factory No. 1) near Moscow, while GAZ-3 at Leningrad, which occupied the plant of the old Russo-Baltic company, produced Gregorovitch seaplanes, a World War I design for which the drawings and tools had survived.

The Air Fleet itself consisted of some 67 units, including 13 seaplane detachments, of varying size and efficiency, and a most urgent need was to bring the service up to a basic standard of efficiency. In 1922, as a result of the Rapallo Agreement between Germany and Russia, 400 German aviation engineers and technicians arrived secretly in Russia and began the construction and organizing of a new aircraft factory at Fili, near Moscow. The man in charge was Prof. Hugo Junker who had been associated with Fokker and Germany and who was a respected figure in the aviation world.

At the same time, and in the same way, a military flying school was formed at Lipetsk, north of Voronezh, staffed by German instructors who had been officers in the wartime German Air Force. To this school came German and Russian aviation officers to receive instruction in technical and tactical subjects. By the end of 1922 there were several hundred German officer instructors, wearing Soviet uniforms, and the Russians had drawn up a training manual largely based on German experience and teaching.

The next few years were years of experiment; organizational ideas changed at frequent intervals, sometimes so rapidly that a new system would be promulgated before the previous one had been fully implemented, and it would merely confuse the issue to try and tabulate all the changes. Basically the Air Fleet reflected the Revolutionary Military Council's theories of 'revolutionary' or 'proletarian' principles of

BELOW: Soviet planes patrol the skies over Sebastopol in 1942.

BOTTOM: Shturmoviks over a Ukrainian forest in the winter of 1942–43, as the balance in the skies began to turn against the Luftwaffe.

RIGHT: The Ilyushin 11-2M3, a modernized version of the Shturmovik.

BELOW RIGHT: Shturmoviks on the assembly line in a factory east of the Volga, out of range of German aircraft.

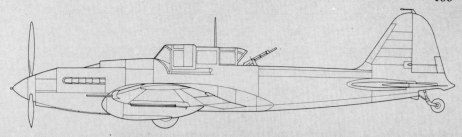

LEFT: The Petlyakov Pe-2 light bomber, introduced in 1940, which doubled as a dive bomber. Over 10,000 of this type were manufactured.

BELOW LEFT: A Poliakarpov I-16, an older, radial engined fighter, used extensively in the early stages of the war.

BOTTOM: A Russian city as seen from the bomb-sight of a German aircraft. The destruction which rained from the skies forced the Soviets to construct a modern air force capable of hurling back the Luftwaffe.

RIGHT: An LaGG 3 fighter of the Russian Army's air forces. Made entirely of wood, it could still take a lot of punishment, but was soon phased out in favor of more modern aircraft.

BELOW: A four-engined Soviet bomber which brought Foreign Minister V.M. Molotov to Scotland. RAF and Russian personnel are seen in the foreground.

BOTTOM LEFT: A radial engined I-16 fighter, which had a maximum speed of 270 mph and a retractable undercarriage.

BOTTOM RIGHT: A captured I-16 stands next to an Me-109. Despite its antiquated appearance in comparison with the German fighter, it was more reliable in sub-zero weather than the liquid-cooled Messerschmitt.

war, in which offensive action would be carried out in limited areas in order to further political aims, and in accordance with this idea the Fleet was composed of a number of semi-independent and autonomous detachments available to be attached to a military formation for a specific operation.

An early and fundamental question arose over the basic organization of regular and militia units, and some of this dispute rubbed off onto the Air Fleet. In 1923 it became the 'Military Air Force of the Workers and Peasants Red Army' and the squadrons were placed under the control of Red Army commands and districts, with their general administration the responsibility of a Chief Directorate of Air Forces. From now on the Air Force was

to be a subsidiary of the Red Army insofar as its combat employment was concerned, though it had autonomy in training and administration. An Air Force General Staff was formed in 1925, and in the same year the squadrons were organized into a systematic numbering system; until then they had retained irrelevant numbers inherited from pre-Revolutionary days or, in many cases, had abandoned any number they might have had and given themselves titles—the 'Lenin Squadron', the 'Worker's Squadron' and so forth. The organization was settled at five squadrons to an Air Brigade, each squadron to consist of three flights of three sections, the number of aircraft in the section varying with the size and purpose of the machines. Finally, in

1928, came another change when all the Air Brigades were brought under direct operational control of the Chief Directorate, though this did not alter the fact that for combat purposes the squadrons would be attached to Red Army units and would function under their immediate orders.

By this time the aircraft design bureaux and factories had begun to show results, though after a shaky start. The first demands from the Planning Commission had been for a fighter aircraft and for a tactical bomber. Prof. Junkers' factory produced a design for a fighter which was a resounding flop, so the contract was terminated, Junker left, and a Soviet engineer Andrei Tupolev was put in charge of GAZ-22 at Fili. Tupolev was to become Russia's

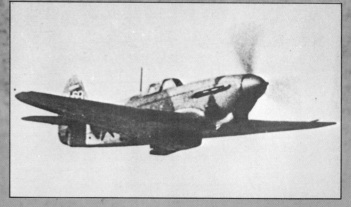

most outstanding designer. He had begun studying aircraft theory in 1908, worked in the aircraft industry during the war, helped to set up the TsAGI—the Central Aero and Hydro Dynamic Institute—in 1918; in 1922 he was made member of a commission charged with designing the first Soviet all-metal airplane. In later years he produced scores of brilliant designs, was imprisoned during the Purge years, rehabilitated, more designs, and finally died full of years and honors in 1972. Tupolev's first product from his new position was the ANT-3, a biplane fighter which was put into quantity production for the Air Force to replace the aging wartime models. He followed this by the ANT-4, a twin-engined bomber known by the Air Force as the TB-1, and then by the ANT-5, designed in cooperation with Pavel Sukhoi and Vladimir Petlyakov. The ANT-5 was the first all-metal fighter, built of duralumin and powered by a radial engine which was a license-built copy of the French Gnome-Rhône. Armed with two synchronized machine guns, it could reach 170 mph and was an extremely good machine, comparable with anything produced in the rest of the world at that time. It went into service in 1928 and remained the principal Soviet fighter for many years.

In the 1920s and 1930s the Soviets were afflicted with an urge toward 'giantism', equating 'bigger' with 'better'. For example, serious consideration was given to a 1000-ton tank armed with 6-inch guns in turrets, a real 'land battleship', and multi-turret tanks, too big to be practical, were built in some numbers. Tupolev appears to have caught this fever (and it remained with him all his life), developing bigger and bigger transport and bombing designs. He started with the ANT-9, a three-engined transport which made some spectacular publicity flights, went on to the ANT-6, a four-engined bomber of which over 800 were made, and eventually climaxed everything with the gigantic ANT-20, the 'Maxim Gorki', of 1934. This was the largest aircraft in the world at that time, an eight-engined monoplane with a wingspan of 206 feet and a speed of 135 mph. As a military design it was of no account, but it was a splendid pro-

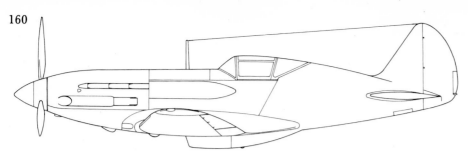

LEFT: The Mikoyan and Guryevitch MiG-3 fighter, one of the Red Air Force's most up-to-date models, had a top speed of 400 mph.

BELOW: The Ilyushin Shturmoviks over Germany. The 'flying tank' was not fast, but it was tough and maneuverable.

paganda machine which carried a printing press on board and would appear at air displays in the 1930s to shower the audience with leaflets extolling the achievements of the Soviet aviation industry.

Another designer making his name in the late 1920s was Nikolai N. Polikarpov, whose first employment in aviation had been under Igor Sikorsky at the Russo-Baltic factory. After the Revolution he superintended the manufacture of Spad 7 fighters under license and then went on to become highly successful; more aircraft of his design were built in Russia before 1939 than of all other designers put together. He specialized, in the early days, on pursuit planes, producing the I-3 fighter, the R-5 reconnaissance biplane, the DI-2 two-seater fighter and, in 1930, the I-5, a single-seat biplane with four guns and a high degree of maneuverability.

In spite of this spate of designs, the Air Force was still operating with a high proportion of elderly and foreign models; one authority has tabulated over fifty different kinds of aircraft in service prior to 1929, and it was obviously advantageous to cut this figure in order to simplify the supply and maintenance problem, but until the industry was able to start producing in quantity, the museum pieces had to fly. This was well seen in 1929 when there was a brief flare-up on the Manchurian border due to the Chinese Army evicting the Russian staff of the Chinese Eastern Railway. In the course of the subsequent 'incident' the Red Air Force bombed Manchouli, Hailar and other Manchurian towns and also flew missions in direct support of Blücher's Far East Army, bombing and machine-gunning ahead of the advancing troops. The aircraft used in this action were, almost

without exception, of foreign origin; the fighters were Fokker and the bombers Farman and De Havilland. In spite of a public statement by Stalin in 1925 that the Soviet Union was no longer dependent upon foreign aid for its aviation industry, the fact was that of the 1100 aircraft on the Red Air Force in 1929, 800 of them were of foreign origin, and as late as 1930 the USA were selling more aero-engines to Russia than to anyone else.

In 1928–29 there was more reorganization and change; the force was divided into reconnaissance, bombing, pursuit and attack squadrons, all of which were attached to Army formations in the Military Districts. Squadron strengths varied between 18 and 32 machines, depending upon the role and type of aircraft. These squadrons were then grouped into 'Aviation Brigades', an administrative aggregation which

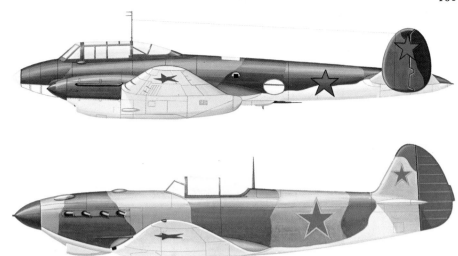

linked all the squadrons in a locality;
the number of squadrons in the brigade
varied with the geographical size of the
district covered. In addition, there were
numerous independent 'Corps Aviation'
or 'Troop Aviation' squadrons which
were directly assigned to specific infantry corps or artillery units for tactical
reconnaissance, liaison, artillery spot-
ting and close tactical support by
bombing. These specialized units were
administered by the local Aviation
Brigade, but were otherwise not under
the Brigade's orders.

By 1931 the Air Force strength was
some 1300 aircraft, divided roughly
into 40 per cent reconnaissance and
tactical support, 25 per cent fighter, 15
per cent bomber and 20 per cent reserve and training. The manpower was
in the region of 20,000 officers and
men, and there were about 16 brigades
in existence. Maneuvers were held with
ground forces, and these revealed
several weak spots: one fundamental
weakness was the low standard of the
pilots, which necessitated long hours of
repetitive elementary flying routines
before these basics were mastered.
Instrument flying, bomb-aiming,
photographic reconnaissance, communications and similar technical skills
were lacking, and most of this seems to
have been due to the preoccupation,
during the formative years, with per-
fecting the command structure and the
bureaucratic side of the organization at
the expense of more down-to-earth
training and practice.

The activities of Japan in Manchuria,
commencing in 1931, caused the Soviets
to set about expanding the Air Force.
By the end of 1932 the strength had
risen to 50,000 men; 21 aviation schools
were in operation, in which cadets were
to spend three years in basic and technical training before being sent to an
operational unit. The Osoaviakhim
para-military training organization
placed its principal accent on gliding
and flying training, and by 1932
claimed to have three million youths
undergoing instruction. Their facilities
included 20 schools, 14 glider fields, 40
airfields, five repair shops, and their
program covered powered flight and
airships, gliding and theoretical instruction. Younger children were encouraged in aero-modelling, while the
organization sponsored record flights
and air displays, including instruction
in parachuting which soon became a

national sport. This latter interest was
encouraged as a result of the formation
of the 1st Airborne Brigade by Tukhachevsky in 1932, one of the many
advanced ideas he put forward.

Another of Tukhachevsky's schemes
was the 'parasite fighter'. This had
been thought up by a technician named
Vakhmistrov, and it involved carrying a
fighter aircraft on top of a bomber, so
that the bomber could release it and
obtain fighter protection beyond the
normal operating range of the smaller

aircraft. The project worked successfully and was gradually embroidered
during the 1930s until it reached the
unlikely-sounding climax of a TB-3
bomber carrying no less than five
fighter aircraft; two I-5 biplanes above
the wing, two I-16 monoplanes below
the wing and an I-Z monoplane slung
on a 'trapeze' beneath the under-
carriage. But the whole project came to
a halt when Tukhachevsky and General
Alksnis, the C-in-C of the Air Force,
were arrested and shot during the 1937

LEFT: AN Me-109 is downed by a Yak above Tchernigov in 1943.

BELOW: A Russian fighter, probably a Yak-1, bites the dust in the summer of 1941.

Purge. It was later revived with the modified idea of carrying two dive-bombers to specific targets outside their normal range, and the one such combination to be built was actually used, in August 1941, to destroy a vital bridge at Chernavoda, on the Danube, in order to cut the German supply lines.

But before that time the Red Air Force had managed to see quite a useful and varied amount of combat, and their on-the-job training began in Spain. Air support was one of the first Soviet aids to make its appearance, 33 Air Force technicians arriving in Cartagena on 10 September 1936. On 15 October eighteen I-15 fighters arrived in crates, followed by a further twelve, followed by 150 aviators under the command of Colonel Yakov Shmushkievitch. By the end of October, Shmushkievitch (or 'General Douglas' as he was publicly known) had 200 pilots and 1500 ground crew in operation.

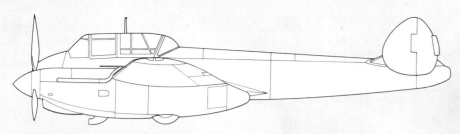

LEFT: Side view of a Yak-4. Note that in this more modern version the cockpit is placed further forward and the fuselage elongated to give greater speed.

The aircraft sent were Polikarpov I-15 and I-16 fighters and the Tupolev SB-2 bomber. The I-15 was a gull-winged biplane with fixed under-carriage, which had a 750 hp engine (a licence-built copy of the American Wright Cyclone). Capable of 220 mph it carried four machine guns and could also carry a light bomb load beneath its wings. The I-16 was a much more modern machine, a low-wing mono-plane with retractable undercarriage, a speed of 270 mph, two wing-mounted machine guns and armor-plating around the pilot. The SB-2 was the newest of the three; indeed it had only entered Red Air Force service a matter of weeks before its appearance in Spain. It was a fast (250 mph) twin-engined monoplane bomber, armed with three machine guns and with a 500 kilogram bomb load.

With these machines, and picked Soviet pilots to fly them, the Republicans had a run of success, since the Nationalist side had inferior Italian and French aircraft. Even the arrival of the German 'Condor Legion' on the Nationalist side failed to check the Soviet aircraft, since the German unit was using elderly aircraft. But once the quality of the Russian aircraft was appreciated, the Nationalists began to acquire better machines and the Con-dor Legion sent for some of the new Messerschmitt BF109s, after which the balance began to swing against the Republicans.

The initial successes by the Soviet pilots were, as much as anything else, a measure of the poor quality of their opponents. The Soviet tactics were based on out-of-date World War I ideas which had been enshrined in their first training manuals in the early 1920s and religiously followed thereafter: there may have been people with other ideas, but they didn't press them. Conformity was the rule in Russia, and initiative was tantamount to treason. Fighter aircraft were still going into action in massive formations derived from the 'Flying Circus' ideas of 1918, while bombers flew in broad daylight, convinced that their superior speed, altitude and armament would preserve them. While these ideas went unchallenged in the early days, the more imaginative flyers on the Nationalist side soon began to develop tactics to deal with them, and Soviet superiority in the air began to evaporate.

The Soviet 'volunteers' themselves were a headache to the Spanish. They were not amenable to discipline; like most of the International Brigades and hangers-on on the Republican side they considered themselves intellectually superior to the Spanish and they took little notice of what the Republican High Command wanted, frequently attacking targets which they wanted to attack instead of targets which the High Command wanted attacked in order to assist their ground operations. Perhaps the high point of Soviet indiscipline came with their deliberate bombing of the German warship *Deutschland*,

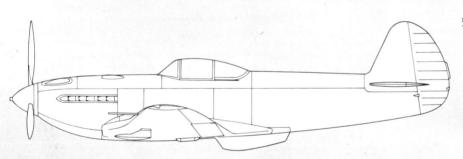

LEFT: Side view of a Yak-3 fighter.

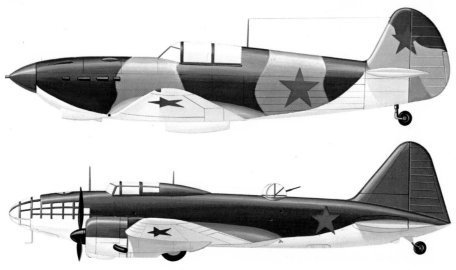

anchored off Ibiza, in May 1937, killing 22 German sailors and wounding a further 83. The Germans, in retaliation, sailed four warships into Almeria Bay and shelled the town of Almeria, an incident which placed Spanish-Soviet relations under considerable strain.

The Soviet pilots were originally sent out on a six-month tour of duty and then returned to Russia, but in the beginning of 1938 the Nationalists had gained air superiority and the Red Air Force was beginning to suffer a high rate of casualties. The Soviet Central Committee in Moscow could see that the Republican side was losing and decided to cut its losses; in June the decision was taken to pull out, and by October the Soviets had gone, handing over their aircraft to Spanish pilots. The efficiency of these men was not high, and their losses were enormous. Russia had supplied about 1200 aircraft to the Republicans; when the war ended there were less than a hundred left serviceable.

The results of the intervention in Spain were mixed; on the personnel side it gave a lot of pilots a taste of combat, and their experience, disseminated throughout the force, was a useful training feature. On the other hand many of those who survived the fighting in Spain, potential future commanders of the Air Force, fell victim to the in-fighting in Russia; Shmushkevich and many of the officers who served with him were arrested in the 1937–38 purge and were later shot. In the tactical field the fighters seem not to have unlearned their outdated maneuvers; there was absolutely no appreciation of the value of long range bombing, divorced from the immediate needs of the ground forces; but, on the credit side, the Soviets had developed an effective technique of low-level night intrusion operations by two or three fast bombers.

Meanwhile trouble had flared up in

Manchuria once more, and the Air Force had been prominently in action. In the 'border dispute' at Changkufeng the Soviet action there was assisted by four squadrons of Tupolev TB-3 heavy bombers escorted by Polikarpov I-152 fighters, which 'softened up' the Japanese positions prior to the Soviet attack. During the attack fighters and light bombers acted in support, strafing and bombing ahead of the advancing infantry and tanks, a tactic which the Japanese had not faced before and one which made a large contribution to the Soviet success.

A less-advertised Soviet air operation was the sending of 'advisers and technicians' to assist the Chinese against Japan in North China. Late in 1937 the first of these 'advisers' had arrived, and by the spring of 1938 they numbered some 350. This included 80 fighter pilots, ostensibly to instruct Chinese pilots in the operation of the Soviet aircraft supplied to China; but their actual task was to man four squadrons of I-152 fighters and two of SB-2 bombers in combat operations. The training task was done by other 'advisers', and 400 fighter aircraft were supplied to China. But the training was far too hasty and the Chinese pilots were cut to pieces by the more skilled Japanese, so that the Soviet flyers had to bear the main burden of the Chinese air operations.

In 1939 the Nomonhan Incident brought the Air Force into direct confrontation with the Japanese once more. The first phase of the fighting was relatively mild, both sides bombing and strafing with small numbers of aircraft, but as the confrontation escalated, so the number of aircraft increased, and in August there were some of the biggest air battles seen since the Western Front of 1918. Zhukov's forces had 580 aircraft, including 150 bombers and 350 fighters, while the Japanese had 475, including a high proportion of Mitsubishi and Nakajima fighters. The forces were fairly well

matched in their equipment; the Nakajima could beat the Polikarpov I-152 and I-153 fighters but was less effective against the I-16, for example. As a result, the honors were about even. No accurate figures have ever been quoted for the aircraft losses on either side, and the Soviet-published figures (145 Soviet to 600 Japanese) are too ridiculous to be worth considering — but the losses on both sides were certainly heavy. Reports from both sides during the action speak of 150 to 200 aircraft in the sky at a time in monstrous dogfights.

The combats in Spain and the Far East had shown that the Soviet aircraft were only just good enough and that they were in danger of falling behind; the German Messerschmitt 109 had run rings around them in Spain, and the Mitsubishis and Nakajimas had stretched them in China and Manchuria. A new fighter of modern specification was needed, and in 1939 work began by three new designers, names which had not been heard of before, but of which two have attained considerable fame since. The three aircraft were Aleksander Yakovlev's Yak-1, the Mikoyan and Guryevitch MiG-1, and the Lavochkin, Gorbunov & Gudkov LaGG-3.

Yakovlev had visited Britain in 1936 and had seen the Supermarine Spitfire. He had also been to Germany to see the Messerschmitt 109. His Yak-1 followed the same sort of lines as these, a low-wing monoplane, light in weight and high in power. The engine was a 1050 hp model, with a cannon between the cylinder banks, firing through the propellor shaft; two synchronized machine guns above the engine fired through the propellor arc; and six 82 mm rockets could be slung beneath the wings. Its maximum speed was 370 mph.

The MiG-1 was designed to meet an Air Force specification for an aircraft to use the new 4M-35 V-12 1350 hp engine, and it was said at the time that it was just about the smallest machine that it was possible to build around that engine and still leave room for a pilot. It was a low-wing monoplane with the pilot seated well back toward the fin, which didn't do much for his observation. Armament was a 12.7mm machine gun and two 7.62mm guns mounted above the engine. While it was the fastest Soviet machine at just over 400 mph, it had poor maneuverability

BELOW RIGHT: The Lavochkin La-7 fighter, developed later in the war, was produced in some numbers and saw service over Germany.

BOTTOM: Pe-2 bombers on the assembly line. Soviet aircraft factories were moved east of the Urals and worked 24 hours a day.

RIGHT: The MiG-1, though a fast aircraft, had poor maneuverability and required several modernizations before it was a match for the Me-109.

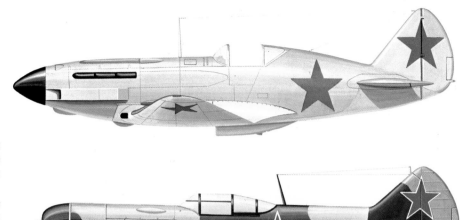

and flight characteristics and had to be modified before it was a good service machine, but it was a sound enough basis to work upon.

The LaGG-3 was similar to the others in form but was remarkable in being entirely of wood, an early form of resin-bonded plywood being the principal constructional material. With a 1100 hp engine, a 20mm cannon and two 12.7mm machine guns, it could also carry six 82mm rockets or 200 kilograms of bombs under the wings. It was never very popular with pilots, but it could soak up a lot of punishment; undoubtedly it would have been modified and improved during the war but for the fact that Lavochkin fell from favor and was virtually unemployed during the war.

The other important decision taken as a result of combat experience was to press for the development of a special-ized ground attack and tactical support aircraft. The Battle of Guadalajara in Spain, where a Nationalist column had been caught on a main road and wiped out by air power alone, and the use of fighters and light bombers ahead of the assaults in Manchuria had stressed the value of such close support, but the standard fighters and bombers, designed for other functions, were not at their best in such work and a special design was needed.

While the designers designed and the draftsmen drew, the war with Finland began and the Red Air Force was in action once more. Four bomber and two fighter brigades, about 900 aircraft in all, were made available to the four armies, and the Soviets confidently expected an easy victory. After all, the Finnish Air Force consisted of no more than 150 aircraft, the majority of which were obsolescent. But things turned out a little differently to what had been

166

BELOW: Major Rosskazov
greets pilots back from a
bombing mission in
Belorussia.

expected, and the reason for this was much the same as the reason for the ground forces having a hard time: the Soviets were adhering to their outdated tactical rulebook, while the Finns were allowing their initiative to triumph. The most effective section of the Finnish force was their 36 Fokker D-21 fighters, and these took their toll of the Soviets by charging head-on into their formations and scattering them, after which the individual aircraft could be easily picked off.

The weather, of course, affected operations; for days on end the snow prevented any air activity at all. Moreover, the Finns could not be everywhere at once, and so the Soviets, by sheer weight of numbers, were able to push through attacks which took some of the pressure off the Red Army and in one or two instances were also able to drop supplies to army units trapped and cut off by the Finns. Realizing that the Finnish Air Force was a tougher proposition than they had supposed, the Soviets then took to bombing the Finnish airfields, but this

was a waste of time since the Finns had long since dispersed their aircraft to camouflaged hides and airstrips.

For their February offensive the Red Air Force brought up additional aircraft, a total of 1500 being available for operations. The Finns had been reinforced by a Swedish volunteer squadron with 16 aircraft, and 30 Gloster Gladiator fighters had been sent from Britain. Although they fought valiantly, the Finns were hopelessly outnumbered, and within a week the Soviets had absolute air superiority over Finland. The Finns' final success was to stop the advance of the Red Army across the ice to Viipuri; relying on fog and snow flurries to prevent the Soviet Air Force intervening, the Finns mustered every available aircraft and bombed and machine-gunned the Red Army troops exposed on the ice, killing thousands.

In the Soviet analysis of the Finland affair, the Air Force did not make a good showing. In spite of repeated bombing of the major towns and targets selected for their importance to

Finnish supply and communications, the Finnish war effort or will to resist had not been diminished. The AON —Aviation of Special Assignments— which had been organized as the long-range bombing force in 1937, had proved inept. Their navigational ability was so poor that they had to fly in daylight and clear weather in order to find their targets and, having found them, their bombing was so inaccurate that the targets were often left unharmed. Much of this was due to the fact that the original commanders of the force had gone to the wall during the Purge and their replacements were useless. The AON was disbanded forthwith, the individual squadrons being dispersed to various Aviation Brigades, and Soviet interest in strategic bombing evaporated.

During 1940, while the Germans were rapidly gobbling up Europe, the Soviets looked to their aircraft industry. New factories were built, and the Yak-1, MiG-1 and LaGG-3 fighters went into volume production. A new light bomber, the Petlyakov Pe-2,

RIGHT: Soviet dive bomber carrying foodstuffs appears over the Crimea early in 1942.

BELOW RIGHT: Two I-16 fighters over the steppe. They carried a 500 kg bomb load.

appeared, a fast (375 mph) twin-engined machine would double as a level bomber or a dive-bomber and which was to become one of the main-stays of the force in the coming war, over 11,000 being made. But the most important new design was the Ilyushin Il-2, the 'Shturmovik', which was the answer to the demand for a specialist ground attack machine.

Sergei Ilyushin headed a 'design brigade' in the Soviet Central Design Bureau, and when the question of a close support machine came up, he reasoned that it would be required to carry a wide variety of weapons to suit different tasks; that it would need good low-altitude handling characteristics; and that it would need to be armored against ground fire. And around these ideas he designed the 'Shturmovik'. A low-wing monoplane with a 1600 hp engine, it was of mixed wood and metal construction with a 7mm armor-plate 'backbone' which protected the engine, pilot, fuel and cooling system and formed the foundation to which the rest of the aircraft was attached. On trial it reached a speed of 292 mph, but this was never repeated on production machines; speed was not its strong point. Firepower, maneuverability and toughness were the objects.

When the German invasion began in 1941, a high proportion of the combat strength of the Red Air Force was put out of action on the first day. A speci-ally-selected force of 30 bombers of the Luftwaffe crossed the German/Russian frontier in eastern Poland at maximum altitude shortly before the ground attack was scheduled to begin; they split up into twos and threes and at 0315 hours in the morning of 22 June, at the exact moment the German Army moved off, these raiders descended on the ten most important Soviet airfields in the forward zone, caught the Soviet aircraft parked in rows as if for inspec-tion, and destroyed the lot. As they returned to their bases, the main Luft-waffe striking force, 1250 aircraft, swept across Poland to deal with the minor airfields.

The Soviets were taken completely by surprise, and both these raiding opera-tions succeeded without loss to the Luftwaffe. It was not until later in the day that the Soviet Air Force recovered from its momentary paralysis and began to fight back; at 1100 a Soviet force of bombers attacked Luftwaffe

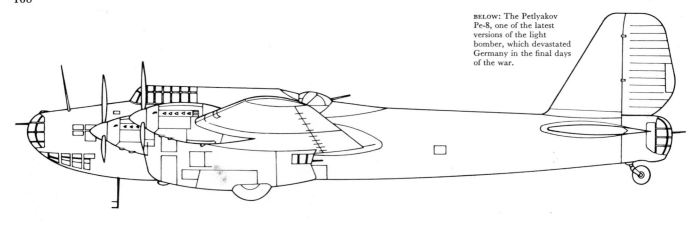

BELOW: The Petlyakov Pe-8, one of the latest versions of the light bomber, which devastated Germany in the final days of the war.

airfields in Poland, but they were almost entirely wiped out by German fighters. By sunset on the first day of the invasion the Red Air Force had lost 1489 aircraft; 322 shot down and the rest destroyed on the ground. In subsequent days the score mounted rapidly as the Luftwaffe shot down Soviet bombers by the score; they were less successful with the fighters, since although the Messerschmitts had the speed, the Yaks and MiGs were more maneuverable.

While the Air Force threw itself into battle, the aviation industry rapidly dismantled its western factories, shipped them off behind the Urals and out of range of the Luftwaffe, and rebuilt them. Over 600 factories and workshops were moved during the fall and winter of 1941. While these feats of

organization are remarkable—for example, the 'Shturmovik' factory near Moscow was uprooted in mid-September, moved two thousand miles, re-assembled, and had produced its first three 'Shturmoviks' by New Years' Day 1942—it obviously reduced aircraft output at an exceptionally critical time, but with the onset of winter (which, providentially, began early in 1941) the weather soon curtailed air activity. Another winter advantage was the high proportion of older radial-engined I-15 and I-16 fighters still in Soviet service; these were more reliable in sub-zero weather than were the liquid-cooled Luftwaffe machines.

Once the evacuated factories were functioning and new factories built and equipped, Soviet aircraft production leapt ahead. In 1941 15,735 machines had been built; in 1942, after a slow start due to the evacuation upheaval, the year's total was 25,400; in 1943, 35,000; in 1944, 40,300. Of these over half were fighters and 40,000 were 'Shturmoviks'. Not only was this surge of production due to the increase in factories and the constant exhortations to exceed the 'norm', it was due to a large degree in improvements in mass-production organization and the introduction of quantities of materials and machine tools from the USA. Russia obtained, under Lend-Lease facilities, 500 million dollars-worth of machine tools, a complete aluminum rolling factory, $2\frac{1}{4}$ million tons of steel, 400,000 tons of copper and 250,000 tons of aluminum, the equivalent of two years' production from their own sources.

Another piece of assistance which helped during these lean times was the first of the 20,000 aircraft supplied from Britain and the USA. These included such aircraft as the Bell P-39 Airacobra (4746 delivered); Bell P-63 Kingcobra (2400); Hawker Hurricane (2851); Supermarine Spitfire (1335); Curtiss P-40 Warhawk and Kittyhawk (2097); Douglas A-20 Havoc (2908) and Douglas C-47 Skytrain (707). It would be presumptuous to declare that these aircraft 'saved' Russia, but they certainly took some of the strain at a bad time.

Some changes in the organization of the Air Force took place in 1942. The events of 1941 had shown that tying squadrons tightly to low level field formations such as brigades or regiments was useless, since the military commanders had neither the time nor

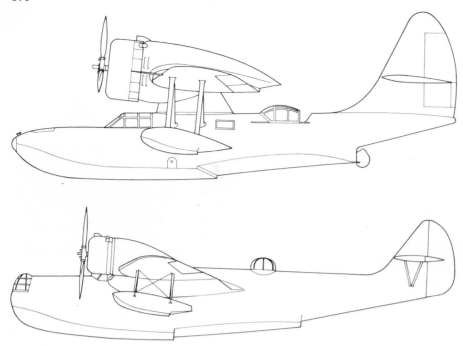

the inclination to see beyond their own immediate front, and the wide-ranging potential of the aviation arm had been curtailed. Authority over air operations was now given to Aviation Brigade Commanders, with the proviso that they were to consult with Army commanders when planning operations. Marshal Novikov was appointed Commander of the Soviet Air Force, with the prime task of organizing an overwhelming air support for the Army. The long range bomber force was once again removed from the Aviation Brigades and formed into the ADD (Long Range Aviation) under Marshal Golovanov. About 1000 fighters were organized under PVO, the Protective Air Defense organization, their task being the protection of cities and industries from bomber attack, in which they worked in close cooperation with the anti-aircraft artillery.

The Aviation Brigades themselves did not survive for much longer, since they were aligned to the peacetime Military Districts, and as these districts were stripped of troops for the front, so the Brigades were fragmented. The major unit now became the 'Air Army', anything from 60 to 2000 aircraft depending upon the demands of the particular front. Within these armies 'Aviation Corps' were formed, designated as Ground Attack, Fighter or Bomber Corps; the Corps were divided into 'Air Divisions' each with three or four 'Air Regiments'. This system, fluid as to numbers and constituent parts, fitted in with the Red Army's system of organization into Armies, Corps, Brigades and Regiments and allowed allocation of aviation to military units in a proportionate fashion while retaining overall command at Army or Corps level where the 'big picture' could best be seen.

Of actual combat during the war years there is little to be said. Gradually the Soviet pilots developed the individual skills necessary to stay alive; their navigation and bombing, communications and resourcefulness gradually improved with constant practice in actual warfare, always the best teacher assuming you survive. The 1920s tactical rulebook was finally thrown out and Soviet fighters adopted new methods, passed to them by British Royal Air Force instructors who arrived in 1941 to give the benefit of their experience in the Battle of Britain, absorbed from the Luftwaffe in actual combat, and polished and developed into their own system by their ace pilots. Instead of blundering across the front in massive formations, now the Soviet pilots flew in small groups, kept high in the air, and relied on their speed and maneuverability to be able to drop onto the German machines and shoot them down in a short engagement.

Probably the greatest Russian contribution to the science of aerial combat during the war was their high development of ground support. The Shturmoviks were the scourge of the battlefield, particularly successful in attacking German tanks. But their low speed and lack of rearward protection made them highly vulnerable to fighter attack, and in 1942 a conference of combat pilots and aircraft designers sat down to try and improve matters. The engine was boosted to give more speed and better maneuverability at low altitude, and, more important, the aircraft was completely changed into a two-seater, with an air gunner in a turret behind the pilot, armed with a 12.7mm machine gun. This new model went into action in October 1942 and gave a nasty shock to a lot of German pilots when they went in to the attack on

the Shturmovik's 'blind spot' and found it wasn't blind any more.

Stalingrad was as much the turning point for the Air Force as it was for the Red Army, and Soviet flyers shot down something like 900 German aircraft in the battle. They flew over 45,000 sorties over the area and dropped 15,000 tons of bombs, and ten Air Divisions of the 10th Air Army were nominated as 'Guards Air Divisions', a distinction given to units who had excelled in battle. One of the more remarkable features of the Stalingrad battle was the appearance of the 586th Fighter Air Regiment, equipped with the latest Yak-7b fighters; the notable thing about this regiment being that it was an all-female organization, from the CO to the mechanics, and none the worse for it. The ladies of this regiment claimed 20 enemy aircraft between them—and it must be pointed out that the Soviet scoring system was the toughest of all, which only credited a 'kill' if the victim fell within Soviet lines and could be positively confirmed. The 586th was part of the all-woman 122nd Air Group which included the 587th Bomber and 588th Night Bomber Regiments. These units functioned from 1942 until the end of the war and inflicted considerable losses on the Germans; by the end of the war 586th Fighter Regiment had flown 4419 sorties and had shot down 38 German aircraft.

In August 1943 the Red Army began its advance to recapture Kharkov and start on the road to Berlin. Accompanying the Army were 100 Air Divisions, 10,000 combat aircraft, and with a force like this at their throats the Luftwaffe had a thin time of it. They fought, and they fought well, but they were outnumbered by eight or ten to one. The aircraft situation was the same as the tank situation; the Soviets could make them faster than the Germans could shoot them down. And as the war progressed, so the odds lengthened. Although the Soviet pilots had improved their tactics, there was no longer, after 1944, much need to polish them; weight of numbers carried every engagement.

When the war came to an end the Soviet Air Force numbered a million and a quarter men and women, with 20,000 aircraft organized in 600 regiments. It had come a long way in 25 years; it was to go a great deal further in the next 25.

BELOW: The remains of
Soviet fighters caught on
the ground in June 1941.

SOVIET TANKS

BOTTOM: A German Panzer column advances in the summer of 1941. Russian tanks were no match for first armored assaults, but with the introduction of the T-34 the balance swung in favor of the Soviets.

RIGHT CENTER: A group of Soviet heavy tanks being examined by their German captors in 1941.

FAR RIGHT CENTER: A T-34 tank approaches a burning village.

By 1939 the tank development programs and experiments which had occupied most of the previous ten years had just about run their course. Such questions as armament, suspension, welding techniques, armor casting and engine design were fairly settled and a specification was put together to guide the designers of the next generation of tanks, those of the '1940–41 Program'.

The first item was the specifying of a high-powered diesel engine. This had been under development in the Kharkov Locomotive Works since 1934, and the end result was a 3.8 liter (231 cubic inches) V-12 liquid-cooled engine which developed 500 hp at 1800 rpm. The adoption of this type of engine was urged on the grounds of fuel economy, increased operational range, reduction in vehicle maintenance time and reduction of fire risk in combat. It was a wise move and a sound choice; one is inclined to wonder why the idea was not carried further and an air-cooled engine developed. Such an engine had been put in service by the Japanese in 1935, and air-cooling would have had undoubted advantages in the Russian winter. The answer probably is that more power could be delivered by a

liquid-cooled unit at that stage of development, and the Soviets were intent on obtaining a better-than-average power to weight ratio.

Armor was to be thick, sloped so as to deflect projectiles, and welded instead of riveted. Experience in the Spanish Civil War and Manchuria had shown that riveted armor tended to be more vulnerable to anti-tank shot strikes at the joints, and the rivets detached by otherwise harmless shot could enter the crew or engine compartments at high speed to become dangerous missiles.

Armament was to be a high velocity 76mm gun on the medium tank. In addition, work was to continue on developing a stabilizing device which would permit the gun to be fired while on the move. The track was to be wide in order to give low ground pressures and thus assist flotation in mud and snow. And the whole design was to be put together with an eye to simple mass production and easy replacement of components in the field.

In August 1939, faced with this specification, the Medium Tank Design Group sat down to synthesize all their past work and produce the ideal medium tank. Their design was com-

RIGHT: The BA-10 armored car, useful for reconnaissance, but soon found to be no match for the Panzers.

LEFT: The BT-7 medium tank, which was used with considerable success against the Japanese in Manchuria.

pleted by December and the Kharkov Factory immediately built two prototypes, completing them in the startlingly rapid time of two months. After a long traveling trial and firing trials at the Minsk test facility, these two prototypes, designated T-34, were sent to join the war in Finland to be tried in actual combat; but by the time they got there, in the middle of March 1940, the war was over and they were unable to show their paces. Nevertheless it was obvious that the design was sound, and production began in May at the Kirov Tank Factory in Leningrad, the first production model coming off the line in June. Within the next twelve months over 1200 had been produced, though there were some teething troubles which had to be overcome. The production of diesel engines could not keep pace with the production of chassis, and some early T-34s had to be fitted with older petrol engines, while transmission failure dogged many of the first year's batch, to such an extent that it was common to see a T-34 rolling into action with a spare transmission unit lashed to the engine deck.

The same program was responsible for the birth of the KV heavy tank. During 1938 a heavy tank specification had been approved, and three designs were drawn up; two models with twin

turrets and one model using a more conventional layout with a single turret. The twin-turret models, designated T-100 and SMK (Sergius Mironovitch Kirov—the designers and factory) were similar in layout, using a central turret with 76mm gun mounted on a raised armored pedestal, together with a forward turret mounting a 45mm gun. The suspension used torsion bars, small wheels and wide tracks, and both designs were powered by 400hp gasoline engines.

The more conventional design came from the same group of engineers at the Kirov factory; they used more or less the same hull and suspension but with a single large turret mounting a 76mm gun. This model was christened the 'KV' for Klimenti Voroshilov, People's Commissar for Defense, and prototypes of all three tanks were built and sent into action in the Finnish War. The twin-turret designs were a failure, largely because they demanded a seven-man crew, and the task of trying to control the activities of two independent turrets and the driver, look after communications and keep a grip of the battle situation was asking too much of any commander. The KV, on the other hand, was an immediate success, earning particular praise in its actions against the Mannerheim Line, and as a

result of this battlefield testing it went into full production in 1940. In that year 243 were built and another 393 before the German invasion in 1941.

When that invasion took place the Soviet tank strength was somewhere in the region of 20,000 vehicles—more tanks than the rest of the world's armies put together. But of this immense number only about 1100 were T-34s and 600 KVs; the remainder were BT5s and BT7s, T-26s and even older models retained for training. Moreover, the handful of new tanks were not concentrated into a single coherent force but were scattered piecemeal throughout the length and breadth of the country. More disastrous still, the crews and commanders of the armor were in an extremely poor state of training and morale as a result of the political upheavals of 1937–38.

The practical effect of Stalin's purges on the Army was to severely disrupt the armored force in particular. The old guard of cavalrymen who survived the purge, Budenny, Timoshenko, Voroshilov and their companions, had little faith in Tukhachevsky's theories of total war and massed armored striking forces, and one of their first moves on obtaining power was to break up the armored formations. Their natural inclination to do this was reinforced by

LEFT: The Red Square parade in 1938 demonstrated the quantity of Soviet armor which was available at that time. These light reconnaissance tanks were found to be far too vulnerable for combat when confronted by the Panzers.

BELOW: The T-28 multi-turret tank. Although formidable in appearance, this tank posed considerable problems in command and control, and was quickly phased out after 1941.
BOTTOM: A BT tank demonstrating the agility of the Christie suspension.

RIGHT: Marshal Chuikov, whose tank divisions smashed the German assaults at Kursk in the greatest tank battle in history.

the reports of General Pavlov, a tank specialist who had gone to Spain as an 'observer' during the Civil War. He reported that experience there showed that there was no room in modern warfare for independent tank formations, and that the tank's role was solely that of accompanying infantry. This, one of the innumerable false lessons which emerged from the Spanish Civil War, accorded well with what Stalin and Voroshilov believed, and was acted upon with alacrity. In 1939 the seven mechanized corps were disbanded and the tanks distributed in separate battalions to infantry divisions throughout the army. Such a radical split demoralized the tank troops. Their new commanders, fearful of showing too much enthusiasm for a form of tactics which was demonstrably not approved on high and, indeed, liable to cost them their heads if they espoused it, were content to let their new acquisitions stand idle, and little training was done. Armor lost its edge, the troops lost their keenness and became lax, and the infantry commanders completely neglected the potential of the tank battalions.

After seeing the results achieved by the Panzer divisions in Poland and France, the Soviet government had second thoughts, and, urged on by Zhukov (who had demonstrated what an independent tank force could do when he wiped out the 6th Japanese Army at Nomonhan) and Shaposhnikov (Chief of Staff), began to rebuild the dismantled mechanized divisions once again. This second upheaval was as unsettling to the soldiers as the first, and it was not helped by the shortage of officers fit to take commands in the new formations. Staffs had to be provided but the number of officers capable of filling the new posts was relatively small; in effect, a fresh generation of armored officers had to be educated. In the event, those who survived their first meeting with the German Panzers received their education in a hard school, but it was an effective one.

The initial German-Russian tank contacts were usually a walkover for the Panzers. For the most part the Soviets were using obsolescent BT and T-26 tanks which were no match for the PzKw IIIs and IVs; moreover the German crews and commanders were at a high pitch of training, and the Panzer division tanks were acting in concert, while the Soviet tanks were being com-

mitted to battle in penny packets and defeated in detail. But the initial German euphoria was soon to be leavened with some doubts and misgivings. Three days after the invasion had begun, the 1st Panzer Division, under Major General Kruger, met the KV for the first time. The existence of both the T-34 and the KV (or KV-1 as it was now known) had been kept a closely-guarded secret by the Soviets,

BELOW: The SU-152 self-propelled gun, a formidable close-support assault gun based on the chassis of the KV tank.

BELOW LEFT: The German Pzkw III was one of the most common tanks to face Russian armor throughout the early stages of the war in the East.

BELOW: A Panzer column using Czechoslovakian 38-T tanks moves through the dust of the steppe.

BELOW: The KV-1 heavy tank, which replaced the multi-turret models after experiences in Finland.

BELOW: A T-34/76, the standard medium tank of the Soviet Army and one which was described by the German generals as 'the best tank in the world'.

although they had allowed a party of visiting American press photographers to see the T-34 at the Stalin Tank School in May 1941, and the sudden appearance of the apparently invincible KV was a chastening experience:

'Our companies opened fire at about 800 yards but it was ineffective. We moved closer and closer to the enemy, who for his part continued to approach us unconcerned. Very soon we were facing each other at 50 to 100 yards. A fantastic exchange of fire took place without any visible German success. The Russian tanks continued to advance and all armor-piercing shells simply bounced off them. Thus we were soon faced with an alarming situation of the Russian tanks driving through the ranks of 1st Panzer Regiment towards our own infantry and rear areas. Our Panzer Regiment therefore turned about and drove back with the KVs, roughly in line with them. In the course of that manuver we succeeded in immobilizing some of them with special-purpose shells at very close range, 30 to 60 meters . . .'

As if that were not enough, a fortnight later the 17th Panzer Division, under Ritter von Thoma, discovered the T-34. One tank suddenly emerged from the undergrowth near the Dniepr River, 'a strange, low-slung tank of formidable appearance'. With German shot bouncing from its armor, it forged ahead, crushed a 37mm anti-tank gun beneath its tracks, shot up two PzKw IIIs, and sailed through the German

RIGHT: The T-34/85, a marriage of the T-34 tank and the 85 mm anti-aircraft gun, which not only was the most effective tank used in World War II, but it is still used extensively in combat today.

BELOW: A T-34/85 with its crew and one of the tank rider squad.

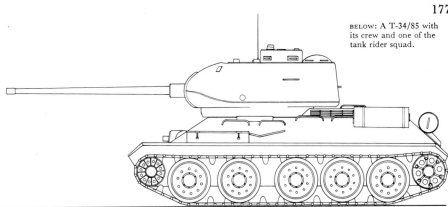

front. It left a nine-mile trail of death and destruction in its wake before it was stopped by being blasted from behind at short range by a 105mm field gun it had ignored and passed.

After their first invasion induced panic had died down, the Soviets began a hurried reorganization of the tank forces. While a tank division might look good on paper, it seemed that it was less effective on the ground, firstly because it demanded some high-class commanders, and secondly because it demanded a mass of tanks, and neither of these was readily available. This shortage of tanks is evidenced by just one example, the 14th Mechanized Corps. This should have had 420 T-34s, 126 KV-1s and 476 BT-7 and T-26 tanks. In fact when the Germans struck it had a total of 508 BT-5s and BT-7s. The commander of this unit was that same General Pavlov whose report from Spain had been instrumental in fragmenting the tank forces. Pavlov was acclaimed as one of the foremost tank experts of the Red Army, but with this scratch force at his disposal it needed more than theoretical expertise to stop the Panzers. Pavlov failed to stop them and was shot for incompetence.

At that time the handling of Soviet armor was, quite simply, non-existent. There were isolated instances of personal flair and bravery, but for the most part the tank crews had little notion of cooperation with each other or what to do when the battle was joined. General F. W. von Mellenthin, then an Oberstleutnant of the General Staff, later wrote of the Soviet tanks: 'They got in each other's way, they blundered against our anti-tank guns, or after penetrating the front line they did nothing to exploit their advantage and stood inactive and idle. Those were the days when isolated anti-tank guns had their heyday, and sometimes one gun would shoot up or knock out more than thirty tanks in an hour. We thought the Russians had created a tool they would never be able to handle expertly . . .' Self-delusion was not confined to tank commanders alone.

In order to rectify matters the idea of tank divisions was temporarily shelved, and independent tank brigades became the standard formation. These were supposed to consist of a tank regiment of three battalions, a motor machine-gun battalion, an anti-tank gun company and a mortar company, a peculiar

mixture, but in practice they usually became a two-battalion brigade of about 50 tanks, with the machine gun battalion and the anti-tank gun company attached. This produced a unit which was within the command capabilities of the officers, who were trying to learn their jobs as they went along; by the time they had mastered the handling of 50 tanks the production bottlenecks had eased, more tanks were becoming available, larger formations could be attempted once again, and the commanders could move up to try their hands with a larger formation.

But in late 1941 it was tank production which governed every consideration. It was little use to make splendid plans on paper unless the tanks were available, and this they certainly were not. The initial German advance had overrun the tank factories at Kharkov, Mariupol and Kirov, while the Leningrad factory was within artillery range of the Germans. The Kirov 185 plant was therefore removed from Leningrad and shipped, lock, stock and barrel, to a new site at Chelyabinsk, while what had been saved of the Kharkov plant was also sent there. The two evacuees

LEFT: The SU-122 self-propelled howitzer, which was based on the chassis of the T-34 tank.

BELOW: The T-34 tank, whose 76mm gun was able to pierce the armor of all but the Tiger and Panther tanks, Germany's latest and most sophisticated models.

RIGHT: KV tanks being presented to their crews by a farmers' commune, who raised the funds for its construction.

RIGHT: KV tanks being presented to their crews by a farmers' commune, who raised the funds for its construction.

were then combined with the Chelyabinsk Tractor Factory to form a new combine called 'Tankograd', and within two months of beginning the move, this new plant produced its first KV-1. It went on to turn out some 18,000 KV-1 tanks and chassis, plus about 48,000 tank engines before the war ended. A similar combination of evacuated factories formed the 'Uralmashzavod' at Nizhni-Tagil, which became one of the principal producers of T-34 tanks. In all, by 1943 there were 42 factories spread across Russia solely concerned with turning out T-34s and KVs. The Soviet tank designers had got it right; they had produced a brace of tanks of such sound basic design that it was possible to ignore every other idea and concentrate on these two, a logistic ideal which no other combatant achieved. And once the factories got into their stride, the flow of tanks to the Army began to assume proportions which virtually guaranteed that the Russians could make tanks faster than the Germans could destroy them. In 1941 the total tank and self-propelled gun production was 6590 units; in 1942, 24,668; in 1943, 24,000; in 1944, 29,000 and in 1945, 25,450, a grand wartime total of 109,708 vehicles. By comparison, the total US tank output in the same period was 88,000 and the German 23,000.

In the meantime the Soviets made do with what they had, hoarding their precious T-34s and keeping them for the toughest spots. By the end of 1941 the Panzers had reached the limit of their tenuous supply line and the conditions of early winter began to slow them

Russian Tank Details

Type	Weight/ tons	Length	Width	Height	Engine BHP/rpm	HP/ton	Max speed mph	Radius of action in miles	Armament/No. of Rds mm		Armor Max/ min mm	Crew
									Main	MGs		
Tanks 1920—39 Light Tanks												
M17 "Russian Renault" 1920	7	16′8″	5′10″	7′6″	Fiat 6 cyl 33·5	4·8	5	37½	37/250	1—7·62/3000	16/8	2
T23 1929	3·5	16′*	6′*	7′*			22			1—7·62	16/8	2
T17 1926	3·6		•		Petrol engine 2 cyl 18	5				1—7·62		1
T18 (MS1) 1927[1]	5·5 to 7·5	14′7″	5′10″	7′1″	Petrol 4 cyl 35	6·3	10	37½	1—37/250	1—7·62/3000	16/6	2
T27 1930	2·7	8′8″	5′4″	4′5″	GAZ. AA 4 cyl 40/2200	14·7	25	125		1—7·62/2520	10/4	2
T37 1933	3·9	12′6″	6′8″	6′1″	GAZ. AA 40/2200		22	125		1—7·62/585	9/4	2
T37A 1934	3·2	12′6″	6′8″	6′1″	GAZ. AA 40/2200	12·5	22	125		1—7·62/585	9/4	2
T38 1936	3·3	12′7″	7′9″	5′5″	GAZ. AA 40/2200	12·1	25	143		1—7·62/1512	9/4	2
T26 Series 1928	The Vickers-Armstrong 6 ton tank, of which 15 were purchased from UK in 1928.											
T26A 1931	8·6	16′3″	8′0″	6′10″	T26 4 cyl 91/2200	10·4	18	100		2—7·62/6000	15/6	3
T26B 1933	9·4	16′3″	8′0″	8′0″	T26 4 cyl 91/2200	9·2	17·5	187	1—45/100	2—7·62/4000	15/6	3
T26C 1937	10·3	15′4″	8′1″	7′9″	T26 4 cyl 91/2200	8·7	17	125	1—45/100	2—7·62/3600	15/6	3
T46 1935	The first Christie tank series, based on two machines purchased from USA.											
BT2 1931	10·2	19′2″	7′2″	7′6″	Liberty V12 343/2000	33·6	28	112	1—37/90	1—7·62/2700	13/6	3
BT5 1933	11·5	19′2″	7′2″	7′8″	M5 V12 350/—	30·4	38	112	1—45/115	1 or 2— 7·62/2500	13/6	3
BT7 1935	13·8	18′10″	7′8″	8′0″	M17T V12 450/1750	32·6	33	220	1—45/188	2 or 3— 7·62/2394	22/6	3
BT-IS 1936	Experimental machine showing pronounced pyramidal form. Produced only as trials vehicle. Never in production.											
Medium Tanks												
T24 1927	18·5	21′8″	10′0″	9′4″	M5 V12 250/—	13·4	13		1—45	4—7·62	20/8·5	5
TG 1929	25				M5 V12 300/—	12	22		1—7·62	4—7·62		5
T28A 1932	27·5	24′9″	9′4″	9′4″	M17 V12 500/1450	17·9	25	100	1—76·2 howitzer/ 64—70	4—7·62/7938	30/20	6
Heavy Tanks												
T35 1932	45	32′4″	10′8″	11′4″	M17 V12 500/1450	11·1	18	93	1—76·2/100 2—45/226	5—7·62 10000	30/11	10
SMK 1937	56				500	8·9			1—76·2— 1—45/—	3—7·62	60/—	6—7
T100 1938	56				500	8·9						
T46-5 (T111) 1937	28				300	10·7	18		1—45/—	2—7·62	60/10	4—5
Tanks 1939—45 Light Tanks												
T40 1940	5·5	13′8″	7′8″	6′6″	GAZ. 202 6 cyl 85/3600	15·4	28	175	1—12·7/550	1—7·62/2016	13/6	2
T50 1940	13·5	17′4″	8′3″	7′2″	W4 6 cyl 300/2000	21·4	32	200	1—45/150	1—7·62/4000	37/15	4
T60 1941	5·8	13′8″	7′10″	5′10″	GAZ. 202 6 cyl 70/3400	12	27		1—20/750	1—7·62/1000	20/7	2
T70 1942	9·2	14′4″	8′0″	6′10″	GAZ. 70 6 cyl 2 x 70/3400	15·2	27		1—45	1—7·62	45/10	2
T80 1942	11·6	14′8″	8′4″	7′3″	GAZ. 203 6 cyl 2 x 85/3600	13·7	27	200	1—45/94	2—7·62/1008	60/16	3
Medium Tanks												
T34/76A	26·3	19′9″	10′0″	8′2″	W-2-34 V12 500/1800	19	33	250	1—76·2/76	3—7·62/2898	45/16	4
T34/76B	28	19′9″	10′0″	8′2″	W-2-34 V12 500/1800	18	33	250	1—76·2/100	3—7·62/2898	60/16	4
T34/76C	30	20′3″	9′10″	8′10″	W-2-34 V12 500/18000	16·6	33	250	1—76·2/100	2—7·62/3150	75/16	4
34/85	32	20′3″	9′10″	9′1″	W-2-34 V12 500/1800	15·6	31	185	1—85/76	2—7·62/3150	75/16	4
T43 1943	30	20′3″	9′10″	8′10″	W-2-34 V12 500/1800	16·6	33	250	110/—	2 x 7·62/3150	75/16	4
T44 1944	31·9	20′3″	10′6″	8′0″	W44 V12 520/2000	16·6	32	150	85/—	2 x 7·62/3150	90/15	4
Heavy Tanks												
KW1 1938/9	43·5	22′6″	11′0″	9′0″	W-2-K V12 600/2000	13·8	21	210	76·2/111	3 x 7·62/3000	90 & 75/30	5
KW1A 1940	43·5	22′6″	11′0″	9′0″	W-2-K V12 600/2000	13·8	21	210	76·2/111	3 x 7·62/3000	90 & 75/30	5
KW1B 1941	47·5	22′6″	11′0″	9′0″	W-2-K V12 600/2000	12·5	21	210	76·2/111	3 x 7·62/3000	110/40	5
KW1C 1942	48	22′6″	11′0″	9′0″	W-2-K V12 600/2000	12·4	21	210	76·2/111	3 x 7·62/3000	130/40	5
KW1S 1942	42·5	22′6″	11′0″	9′0″	W-2-K V12 600/2000	14·1	27·5	210	76·2/111	3 x 7·62/3000	82/30	5
KW85 1943	46	22′6″	11′0″	9′0″	W-2-K V12 600/2000	13			85/70	3 x 7·62/3276	76/30	5
KW2	52	22′8″	10′10″	10′10″	W-2-K V12 600/2000	11·5	15·25	210	152 howitzer/36	3—7·62/3000	110/35	6
Joseph Stalin IA 1943	44	22′6″	10′2″	9′1″	W-2-IS V12 600/2200	14·1	22	100	85/59	3 x 7·62/2520	160/20	4
JS2 1944	46	22′6″	10′2″	9′1″	W-2-IS V12 600/2200	13	22	100	122/28	3 x 7·62/2330	160/20	4
JS3 1944-45	45·8	22′2″	10′8″	8′1″	W-2-IS V12 600/2200	13	25	118	122/28	1 x 12·7 1 x 7·62	200/230/30	4
Post-1945 Tanks Light Tanks												
PT76 1952	14	22′0″	10′3″	7′4″		31			76·2/—	1 x 7·62	20—30	4
Medium Tanks												
T54A 1954	36	20′4″	10′6″	8′0″	V12 CI 520/?	14·5	31	150	100/42	1 x 12·7 1 x 7·62	75/30	4
T54B 1955	36	20′4″	10′6″	8′0″	V12 CI 520/?	14·5	31	150	100/42	1 x 12·7 1 x 7·62	75/30	4
T54C 1961 (alias T55)	36	20′4″	10′6″	8′0″	V12 CI 520/?	14·5	31	150	100/42	1 x 7·62	75/30	4
T54D 1961	36	20′4″	10′6″	8′0″	V12 CI 520/?	14·5	31	150	100/42	1 x 7·62	75/30	4
T54E 1963	36	20′4″	10′6″	8′0″	V12 CI 520/?	14·5	31	150	100/42	1 x 7·62	75/30	4
T62 1963	37	23′5″	11′2″	10′2″					1 x 115/—	1 x 12·7 1 x 7·62		
Heavy Tanks												
T10 1957	50	25′7″	11′2″	8′4″	V12 700/—	14	28	100	122/—	2 x 12·7	200/30	4

[1]Also T19. A small vehicle without a turret, mounting one MG. In shape a little like a Bren carrier, with higher sides and the small rollers and springs of the T18.

*Approximate

LEFT: The T-60 light tank, which saw little use after the first few weeks of war due to its light armor and vulnerability.

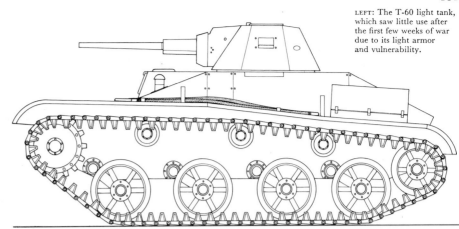

BELOW: The Finnish war demonstrated that elderly designs such as this could not survive in modern warfare.

BOTTOM: T-34s move up to attack in Belorussia in 1944.

LEFT: The T-60 light tank, which saw little use after the first few weeks of war due to its light armor and vulnerability.

down. Temperatures fluctuated widely, and a stretch of ground which was frozen hard at dawn and gave a good surface for tank maneuvers could thaw by late afternoon into an impassable quagmire which bogged the Panzers into immobility. In these conditions the wide tracks and low ground pressure of the T-34 showed to advantage, and the Soviet tanks could swoop across country which the Germans regarded as being impassable for armor.

During 1942 the Soviet tank strength gradually increased until there were 138 tank brigades available, although the level of ability of the crews had not increased in proportion. But Stalin was sufficiently impressed by sheer numbers to imagine that the mere possession of tanks equated with success, and as early as March he ordered an armored thrust to recapture Kharkov, a task to which he allotted almost all the T-34 and KV-1 tanks available. In spite of objections by Zhukov and Shaposhnikov, the plan went forward, and in May Marshal Timoshenko launched the attack. By sheer weight it punched through von Paulus' 6th Army and tore ahead, confident of arriving in Kharkov in a matter of hours. Unfortunately for Timoshenko's military

LEFT: Russian BT tanks
with guns and transport
in the background move
out on maneuvers in the
spring of 1941.

BELOW LEFT: Two T-34s
knocked out in the
Crimea being examined
by German troops.

BELOW RIGHT: A German
75 mm assault gun
supporting the attack on
Voronezh in January
1943.

BOTTOM: KV-1 tanks
lead an infantry attack
into the forests on
maneuvers.

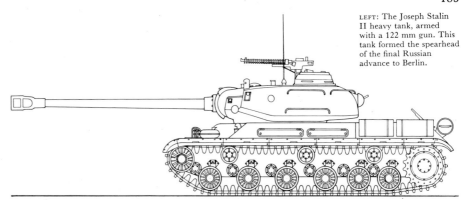

LEFT: The Joseph Stalin
II heavy tank, armed
with a 122 mm gun. This
tank formed the spearhead
of the final Russian
advance to Berlin.

reputation, General von Kleist's 1st Panzer Army was in the process of concentrating close by for a future operation. Timoshenko had been told of this but, in concert with his Political Commissar, Nikita Khrushchev, dismissed it as of no account. Von Kleist waited until Timoshenko was thoroughly embroiled and stretched out across his front, and then tore into his flank, carved his armies up and decimated them. In one swoop much of the Soviet stock of first-class tanks was smashed or captured. And as a result, the German Army managed another summer of successful campaigning before the Soviet armored strength could be built up sufficiently to counter it.

The arrival of the T-34 and KV caused the Germans to devote energy to the provision of better anti-tank guns and better tanks in order to redress the

BELOW: T-34 tanks knocked out in battle south of Lake Ladoga during the defense of Leningrad.

BELOW RIGHT: A knocked out T-34 near Orel provides overhead cover for a German dugout.

BOTTOM: A German assault gun passes two disabled T-34 tanks.

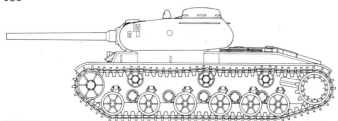

LEFT: The KV-85, a combination of the KV chassis and the T-34/85 turret, which provided the KV with a better armor-defeating firepower.

BELOW: Panzers advance through the wheat fields near Belgorod in 1943.

balance. In response the Russians began to make improvements in their designs; they were helped in this by the sound basic elements which left room for future improvement. The first change to the T-34 was the fitting of a more powerful 41-caliber 76mm gun to replace the original 30-caliber model, which gave a higher muzzle velocity and a small increase in its capability to pierce armor. Then came a protective change with a new design of turret. The original T-34 turret had a conspicuous overhang at the rear, and this was a weakness soon exploited by the Germans. One of their most effective infantry measures against the T-34 was to run behind and throw a time-fused Tellermine so as to wedge it beneath the overhang. The subsequent blast (for the Tellermine contained ten pounds of TNT) invariably wrecked the turret and killed the occupants, frequently lifting the turret completely off the tank. This overhang was also dangerous

under fire, since it could easily deflect shot downward to strike the traversing ring and thus jam the turret. These defects were overcome by a new design of turret without the overhang, which appeared early in 1942. Other minor improvements included increased fuel capacity and improved welding techniques in the armor.

The prime demand, though, was for more powerful armament, and this was achieved by adopting a fresh design of turret which had been drawn up for the KV tank and fitting it with an 85mm gun derived from an existing anti-aircraft gun. This new weapon fired a $20\frac{1}{2}$ pound armor-piercing shell at 2600 ft/sec to pierce 100mm of plate at 1000 yards range. This was by no means outstanding, since the German 88mm PAK 43 fired a 23-pound shell at 3280 ft/sec to defeat 190mm at the same range. So the Soviets took a leaf from the German book and developed a high velocity 'Arrowhead' shot, a lightweight

steel projectile carrying a core of tungsten. This weighed eleven pounds and with a velocity of 3375 ft/sec could defeat 130mm at 1000 yards. But the 88mm tungsten-cored shot could travel at 3700 ft/sec to pierce 240mm at this range, so the 85mm Soviet gun was left a long way behind. What saved the Soviet tanks was the desperate shortage of tungsten in Germany, a shortage so severe that after 1942 all available supplies were earmarked for machine tool use, and once the available stocks of special ammunition were used up, the performance gap between the 85 and the 88 was considerably reduced.

The new T-34/85 had other improvements; the new turret allowed three men to occupy it, which eased the tank commander's life, since on the T-34/76 models he had to double as gunner at times. The armor thickness was increased to 110mm on the front and 90mm on the turret, and a new five-speed gearbox was installed. The first of

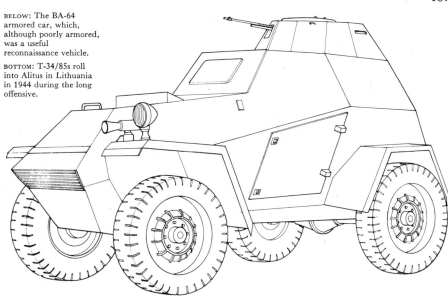

BELOW: The BA-64
armored car, which,
although poorly armored,
was a useful
reconnaissance vehicle.

BOTTOM: T-34/85s roll
into Alitus in Lithuania
in 1944 during the long
offensive.

this new design were made during the winter of 1943–44 and issued to Guards Armored Divisions in the spring of 1944, and it gradually replaced the 76mm gun model as the war continued.

The KV-1 was similarly improved; the first change was to a thicker turret, using 120mm of cast armor, but on consideration it was felt that better immunity to enemy attack would be achieved by improving the tank's performance rather than simply thickening the plating. Sheer thickness would always be defeated in the long run, but a more agile tank was a more difficult target to hit; moreover, when T-34s and KV-1s worked together, the lesser speed of the KV was a drag on the T-34s. To achieve this desired agility the armor was now reduced in thickness so as to cut the weight from 47 tons to 42½ tons; the engine was improved; and a new transmission fitted. The result was an increase in speed from 18 mph to 25 mph, at which it could keep up with the T-34.

While this model was being developed and put into production, the Battle of Kursk was fought, and the result of this slogging match went a long way to convincing the Russians that heavier guns were going to be needed in future tanks. The refitting of the T-34 to take the 85mm gun was already being discussed, and this program was now expanded to bring in the KV-1 as well. A new turret was designed which could be fitted to both tanks, so that in effect the T-34/85 was a T-34 with a KV-1/85 turret on it. The KV-1/85 went into production late in 1943, while existing KV-1s were withdrawn from service to be fitted with the new turret. But in the course of this modification the weight went back up to 47 tons and the speed dropped abysmally to 15 mph. Obviously, it wasn't the proper answer.

During 1943 the Commissariat for Tank Industry had foreseen the need for a new heavy tank and had ordered a number of designs to be prepared. Among these was a thorough-going reworking of the KV design. A new 513hp engine, new transmission and new steering gear were used, the suspension altered, and a new cast turret designed using the 85mm gun. The weight was reduced to 44 tons and the speed increased to 23 mph, with an enormous improvement in maneuverability because of the new transmission

and steering systems. This model was approved as the 'Josef Stalin' (JS) tank, and a small number were made during the winter of 1943–44; mass production was deferred until it was certain that the new design was one which worked on the battlefield. Another version was produced at the same time, mounting the 100mm anti-tank gun, a weapon with a useful performance (3350 ft/sec and 180mm of plate at 500 yards with a 20 pound arrowhead shot), but even this didn't seem to be quite the right solution.

Finally, in the spring of 1944, the designers hit the bullseye. They designed a completely new turret and into it they managed to stuff a highly-modified 122mm Corps Artillery Gun barrel and breech. This, in its normal role, had fired a 55-pound shell at 2400 ft/sec, but the tank version used a 40-pound shot at 3000 ft/sec. The breech mechanism was changed from the cumbersome screw type to a semi-automatic sliding wedge, which was much easier to use inside the confined space of a tank

turret and which allowed a rate of fire of six rounds a minute, but the price of all this was a reduction in the quantity of ammunition which could be carried due to the much greater size of each round. Nevertheless, this was the tank with the big punch that the Army wanted, and the JS went into production late in 1943, first appearing in action in the spring campaigns of 1944. Its designer was not satisfied, and in 1944 he produced the JS-2, which had a re-designed hull and some other improvements. This was immediately approved to replace the earlier JS and was in action by the end of the summer. Finally the designer, Z. A. Kotkin, made some more small improvements in hull contours and turret shape, and produced the JS-3, but since this model did not go into mass production until January 1945 it was never used in combat. It gave the Americans and British something to think about when it was first disclosed at the Victory Parade in Berlin.

But before they could take part in that parade, the Soviet tankmen had to

BELOW: A T-50 light
tank, captured by the
Finns during the Winter
War.

BELOW RIGHT: A T-28
heavy tank with winter
camouflage captured by
Finns.

BELOW: A Russian armored train, typical of many such trains used to control vast areas of the countryside to defend the Soviet lines of communication.

BELOW: T-34 tanks being examined by their German captors.

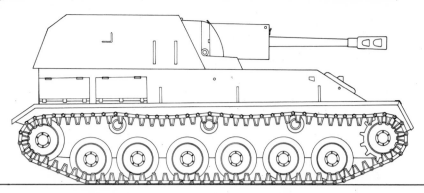

LEFT: The SU-76
self-propelled gun. This
modification of a light
tank chassis mounted a
high velocity 76 mm gun
and doubled as an
infantry support weapon
or tank destroyer.

get to Berlin, and the state of training and equipment in early 1943 was unlikely to achieve such a result. Constant combat against the Panzers soon rubbed off the awkward corners, and by early 1944 the elementary tactics of tank handling were understood from the top to the bottom of the force. No longer did they get in each other's way; no longer did they sit around wondering what to do next. And this improvement had been helped by a material addition to the tank force, the assault gun. One of the defects of early Soviet tank tactics was the paucity of artillery support once the tanks were on the move. The normal field and heavy artillery, in indirect fire support positions, could do little once battle was joined; the communication network was not sufficient to allow the artillery to have forward observers in tanks, a system used by the British and US Armies, and ground observers in observation posts behind the battle could not see what was going on with enough accuracy to call for fire. The direct-fire artillery in the front line was equally helpless, since in the vastness of the steppes the battle often got out of their immediate purview, and in any case they were usually screened from their targets by the activities of their own tanks and troops. Trying to bring ordinary artillery into the thick of a tank battle was out of the question, though the Soviets, careless of casualties, frequently tried it.

The answer was, of course, to armor the artillery and take it along with the tanks. This would allow the Soviet tanks to concentrate on fighting German tanks, safe in the knowledge that there was artillery on hand to deal with strongpoints and anti-tank guns. The Soviets had been experimenting with self-propelled gun designs since the 1930s, so they had some experience to guide them. But a more significant factor was the appearance of numbers of German assault guns on the front, basically turretless tanks with heavier guns aboard. The point was taken, but the precarious manufacturing position meant that it was not until late in 1942 that any capacity could be allocated to producing self-propelled guns at the expense of tanks. Once the tank pro-

gram was running well, then the SP gun proposals were brought forward. Since the production of light tanks was being gradually run down—since light tanks were now known to be virtually useless except as reconnaissance vehicles—light tank production facilities were turned over to SP gun manufacture, and the first model to appear, the SU-76, was a reworked and lengthened light tank chassis with a 76mm field gun mounted in an armored superstructure. This went into production in December 1942, and it appears to have been 'sold' to the Army as a potential tank destroyer. But in truth, the gun wasn't good enough and the vehicle itself insufficiently well armored to go mixing it with tanks, so that it finished up as an infantry support assault gun, moving forward with the foot soldiers to blast any obstacles which appeared in front of them after the tanks had made the first assault.

Which was very nice for the foot soldiers but hadn't been much help to the tanks, so early in 1943 the Chelyabinsk factory produced a prototype SP gun which was the chassis of the KV tank carrying an armored box on top, with a 152mm Corps Gun/Howitzer mounted in the front plate of the box. Reputedly, the prototype was designed and built in 25 days; it was immediately accepted and went into production in February 1943. It first saw action at Kursk, was called the SU-152, and its covering fire and massive construction was a significant factor in the Soviet victory there. The gun fired a 95lb shell, or a 107lb piercing shell, and also used a highly effective incendiary shell which was fatal to tanks.

One slight disadvantage was that it could only carry 20 rounds of ammunition, and after firing these—which didn't take long in a hectic action—it had to drive off the battlefield to replenish. In order to provide a weapon with a greater capacity, some similar vehicles were produced which used a 122mm gun, but the increase in ammunition did not compensate for the reduced power of the gun, and few of the SU-122 were built.

This provided the heavy support for the tank advances. All that remained now was to take some of the pressure off

the tanks by providing tank destroyers, limited-traverse, high-velocity self-propelled guns specifically designated to hunt down Panzers while the battle tanks maintained the forward momentum of the attack. The first of these was the SU-85, a modified T-34 chassis with a fixed superstructure instead of a turret and the gun in the front plate. This offered the same performance as the T-34/85, and something better was required. Since arming a chassis with a fixed gun allowed a heavier gun to be used than was possible inside a turret on the same chassis, the T-34 in its SP version could tolerate a more powerful weapon, and this was provided by fitting in the 100mm anti-tank gun M44 to make the SU-100. This had an ex-

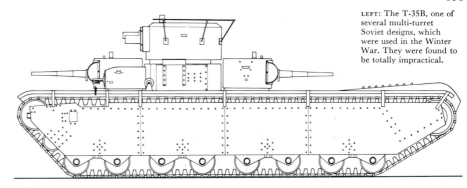

tremely good anti-tank capability, and as a tank destroyer it became one of the foremost threats to the German Army.

By the late spring of 1944 Soviet armor was completed; the KV, JS and T-34/85 tanks formed the striking force, while the SUs acted as artillery support and anti-tank screen. With all these pouring from the factories in an increasing stream, minor deficiencies in training and tactics were concealed and mitigated by the sheer weight of numbers which could be put into the field. By this time the commanders had learned their business, the armored division was resuscitated, and tank corps and even armies were formed. From now on Soviet armored operations relied less on finesse and cunning than on swamping the enemy with more tanks than he could hope to beat off. With battalions of tank-riding infantry clinging to the turrets, the tank armies rolled forward irresistibly, smothering the German Army with sheer weight of metal. Even so, if the metal itself had not been of the right type, the battle could still have gone the wrong way. But there was little danger of that; the Russian tank designers had done their work superlatively well. Russian tanks were without doubt among the best in the world by 1945. The T-34/85 is still used today.

THE LONG OFFENSIVE

February 1943 seemed to be the pinnacle of the triangle in the conflict on the Eastern Front. What had been an uphill struggle for the Russian war effort was at its peak; ahead lay the road to victory. There would be times yet in 1943 when it seemed feasible that the Germans still had the possibility of destroying the Russians 'en masse' along certain sectors, but Russian war industries, technology, and manpower, combined with the strategy and sound judgement of the new war leaders such as Chuikov, Zhukov, Rudenko, Voronov and others tipped the balance of power along the front in favor of the Russians. The initiative would never again be grasped by the Germans.

By the end of February the German II Army, near Voronezh, was soundly defeated and through the 200-mile gap left by that army Russian troops poured in, creating what would come to be known as the Kursk salient. Although fighting continued throughout February and March in this area. German defenses in the south remained along the Donets and Mius Rivers. February also saw Russian armies push the Germans out of the Rzhev-Vyazma salient. Breaches were made against the German Army Group North, and from February through July 1943 Russian troops under Govorov and Meretskov kept the people of Leningrad going and effectively opened the encirclement around

BELOW: The battle over, the Red Flag waves once again over the main square in Stalingrad as Soviet forces re-occupy the city in February 1943. The Long Offensive had begun.

RIGHT: Soviet troops pass a dead German in the Caucasus in January 1943 as the hot pursuit of the retreating enemy begins.

that city. Although Leningrad still had much to face in the coming year, the Russian people of that city knew that the blood and sacrifice of the previous years had not been in vain.

Winter, as before, had been harsh on the Germans, but their troops had managed to stop the Russian heavy advance, though not without severe loss of lives and equipment. Once more spring became a time for both armies to slow down their assaults and prepare again for the better weather.

The Russians knew the taste of vic-

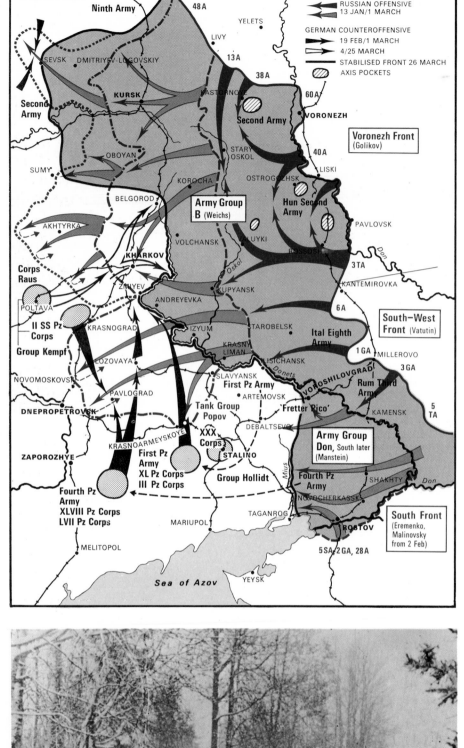

Army Group Centre (Kluge)

OREL · NOVOSIL

Ninth Army

48 A

Bryansk Front (Reiter)

YELETS

LIVY

13 A

SEVSK · DMITRIYEV-LOGOVSKIY

KURSK

38 A

LASTORNOE

60 A

Second Army

Second Army

VORONEZH

OBOYAN

STARY OSKOL

Voronezh Front (Golikov)

40 A

SUMY

KOROCHA

OSTROGOZHSK

LISKI

BELGOROD

Army Group B (Weichs)

VOLCHANSK

Hun Second Army

PAVLOVSK

AKHTYRKA

UYKI

ROSSOSH

Don

KHARKOV

Oskol

KUPYANSK

3 TA

KANTEMIROVKA

Corps Raus

ZMIYEV

ANDREYEVKA

6 A

POLTAVA

IZYUM

STAROBELSK

South-West Front (Vatutin)

II SS Pz Corps

KRASNOGRAD

Ital Eighth Army

1 GA · MILLEROVO

Group Kempf

LOZOVAYA

KRASNY LIMAN

3 GA

NOVOMOSKOVSK

LISICHANSK

Donets

PAVLOGRAD

SLAVYANSK

VOROSHILOVGRAD

First Pz Army

ARTEMOVSK

Rum Third Army

DNEPROPETROVSK

Tank Group Popov

'Fretter Pico'

KAMENSK

5 TA

'Fretter Pico'

DEBALTSEVO

KRASNOARMEYSKOYE

XXX Corps

Army Group Don, South later (Manstein)

ZAPOROZHYE

First Pz Army XL Pz Corps III Pz Corps

STALINO

Group Hollidt

Fourth Pz Army

SHAKHTY · Don

Fourth Pz Army XLVIII Pz Corps LVII Pz Corps

Mius

NOVOCHERKASSK

TAGANROG

MARIUPOL

ROSTOV

South Front (Eremenko, Malinovsky from 2 Feb)

MELITOPOL

YEYSK

5 SA, 2 GA, 28 A

Sea of Azov

FRONT LINES, 1943
— 12 JAN
— 19 FEB
········ 2/4 FEB
········ 1 MARCH
← RUSSIAN OFFENSIVE
13 JAN/1 MARCH
GERMAN COUNTEROFFENSIVE
➤ 19 FEB/1 MARCH
▷ 4/25 MARCH
— STABILISED FRONT 26 MARCH
▨ AXIS POCKETS

tory. Yet as the German Army sat back licking its wounds, the Soviets knew that their conventional forces were still to some degree incapable of carrying out the true death blow that was needed. Although Russian troops were not continuing their aggressive efforts along the front, they still had two aces in the deck which they could constantly count on. The first card was dealt through the cruelty on the part of the Germans toward the conquered peoples of Russia, and the second was the strength of the Soviet partisan groups. These two elements fed each other in a perpetual circle of hate, fear and destruction. German cruelty incited the people to rebel; whereby the partisans' destructive actions behind the lines spurred the Germans to continue their barbarity.

Since the first days of the war, Soviet leaders had seen the need to conduct partisan or guerrilla warfare behind the German lines, disrupting the lines of communication and supply so vital to the flow of the German war machine. One week after the invasion had taken place the Central Committee of the Communist Party issued a directive calling for troops cut off behind the German advance and the loyal people of Russia to conduct sabotage activities and destroy the Fascist invader at every opportunity, regardless of the consequences. Stalin's famous speech on 3 July 1941 amplified this directive by saying that the partisans' role was 'to create unbearable conditions in the occupied areas for the enemy and all who help him, to pursue and destroy them at every step, to disrupt everything they do'. Although partisan activity continued until autumn of that first year, it was very disorganized and the massive Soviet defeats led many to avoid the partisan movement. By the end of autumn the Central Committee had organized the various partisan groups under a loose control, and tried as best they could to coordinate partisan activities with those of the Army, and in so doing destroy the German effort from both front and rear. During Zhukov's great counter-offensive which stopped the Germans at Moscow, no less than 10,000 Russian partisans took part both in sabotage and actual front line fighting in support of his efforts. It was actually this turning point in the war which brought about a feeling of hope and rekindled the fire of resistance. The Russian people had begun

BELOW: Female volunteers join the forces in Moscow.

BOTTOM: A Ukrainian captain and his men celebrate the receipt of chocolates and cigarettes from Britain. Regular supplies of more vital material were flowing regularly through the Arctic to Archangel and Murmansk.

to view the Germans not as the 'all conquering', but as an enemy to be defeated. Throughout 1941 and 1942 thousands of German troops which could have been stationed along the Front had to be used for security duty in suppressing the partisans. This fact showed that the behind the lines 'soldiers' were doing their job, as the more German troops they could tie up meant less Germans for the Soviet troops to meet on the front lines.

Partisan groups in late 1942 were in part responsible for German troops' failure to relieve the forces trapped in Stalingrad. They fought what was called the 'war of the rails' which kept German resupply trains from reaching their destinations. By 1943 hundreds of thousands of partisans, huge invisible armies, fought and harassed the German soldiers in Belorussia and the Ukraine. In the Belorussia area alone, between August and November 1943, nearly 200,000 rails were blown, over 100 trains were wrecked, and more than 70 rail bridges destroyed. These sabotaged rail lines accounted for nearly two-thirds of the total German rail commitment in that area. By the end of 1943, Russian armies were truly on the path to victory, never again to be turned back. Ahead of that advance the partisans continued their covert activities. It is therefore to the masses of faceless 'heroes' that the Russians owed much of their success.

On the front spring 1943 was almost over. The combined efforts of Albert Speer, the head of the German war production, and General Guderian brought about the first real reforms in the German Panzer divisions since the beginning of the war. It was in those spring months that the wheels of German industry began to once again move and turn out more modern, up-to-date weapons with which to continue the war effort. Germany began to produce its new tanks in large quantities. It was true that the Tiger tank was first built in 1942, but only 78 of this model were produced. Not until 1943, however, was a truly modernized production scheme organized, which resulted in the production of 650 Tiger Is and 1800 Panthers—or PzKpfw Vs. Also during this time the PzKpfw IV, F2H models, which were the up-dated main line battle tank of the German Army, jumped from a 1942 production level of 827 to well over 2000 in 1943. In spite of this great improvement and a large increase in the production of self-propelled guns, German armor pro-

LEFT: German soldiers cover their retreat under Russian fire as they cross a stream in rafts.

BELOW: Cavalry units still played an important role on both sides of the front. Both the Germans and Russians used Cossacks on horseback for reconnaissance.

RIGHT: Anti-aircraft guns being manufactured across the Urals, well out of range of the Luftwaffe.

BELOW RIGHT: German troops on skis maneuver on the Finnish front, emulating the example shown by their allies in both the Winter War and after Barbarossa.

duction remained one year behind that of the Russians. Although these new tanks were rolling off the assembly lines, large quantities of old PzKpfw III Js still had to remain in production as a major front line tank until well after the Battle of Kursk. On the Russian side, even before the invasion took place, the industries had been working on and producing their two new main tanks—the T-34 and KV-1. By 1943 those tanks made up almost the total armor force of the Russian armored corps, and new tanks such as the KV-85 and the SU-85 and SU-52 self-propelled guns were being built to further increase Soviet superiority. The tank of the hour in 1943 was the T-34c. This tank, though not built for comfort as were much of the German armor, had a reliability and cross-country speed which could not be disputed. It is in the light of these two growing armored forces that the next step was taken on the Eastern Front.

Hitler and his generals realized that another major front attack using any of the Army Groups was almost impossible. Their dilemma was magnified by the German inability to mass enough troops along the front to create a static defense against the Soviet armies.

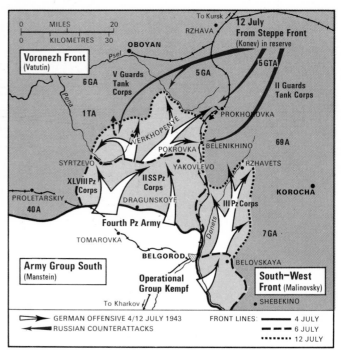

Along the whole of the Russian Front, both the German and Russian troops manned easily defensible positions, which could effectively turn back any major assault. One place, however, did present itself to the Germans as a point where they might once again gain the initiative; the area where in early 1943 the German II Army's retreat had opened the way to the creating of the Kursk Salient. This salient was viewed by Hitler as a place where German forces could attack, cut off and isolate approximately five to seven Russian armies. In so doing he thought to gain enough impetus—a victory—that would succeed in throwing the Russians into such a chaotic state that a drive could be made from the south, taking Moscow from its southern and rear flanks. The Germans massed troops, especially Panzer units, facing the salient. The plan of attack was very simplistic: Schmidt's II Panzer Army in the North was to attack southward toward Kursk, while Hoth's IV Panzer Army in the south attacked northward at the base of the projecting Russian line, meeting with the II Army somewhere in or around the city of Kursk. This attack was scheduled for May, a time when the Germans thought the ground would be significantly dry enough for the tanks to move unimpeded. Due to snags in German tank production, Hitler was forced to postpone the attack until July. That three-month period of delay afforded the Russians the critical time needed to bring about the beginning of the end of German dominance.

Once again Zhukov was chosen to perform the tasks of Commander of the Kursk front. He divided the Kursk salient into two fronts: the northern half was called the 'Central Front' and placed under the adept General Rokossovsky, while the southern half, the Voronezh Front, fell under the command of Vatutin. From May through July Soviet forces in the areas built no less than six main defensive zones, which had a width of at least 150 kilometers along the front. These zones consisted of anti-tank implacements, bunkers, communication ditches and every type of fortification deemed necessary to stop the Germans. The Russians knew that a German attack was imminent; Zhukov was taking no chances.

Martin Caidin points out in his book *The Tigers are Burning* that 'between April and June the front troops dug about 5000 km of trenches, laid about 400,000 mines and land charges. On the sector of the 13th and 17th Armies alone, 112 km of wire entanglements, with 10·7 km of live wire entanglements were built and over 170,000 mines laid'. The two Russian armies, although deployed along the north sector of the salient, were more than indicative of what the Germans would run into along the entire Kursk Front, Another interesting aspect of the defense of the salient is found in what the Russians called 'Pakfronts'. These fronts were interlocking defense zones, created to make every sector of that Russian front—and the six deep defense lines—independent and self-sufficient. These fronts had the ability to concentrate all of their anti-tank capabilities at any point along the front and had complete coverage and interlocking machine gun zones to protect themselves from infantry assault. Personnel trenches were also dug for use by the Russian soldiers in getting

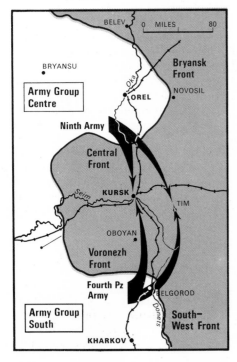

behind the German armor when and if a section was overrun. The basic Soviet principle was to separate the infantry from the armor and destroy the two independently. Without the infantry a tank can become extremely vulnerable, and a determined group of troops, trained as 'tank killers' can wreak havoc on even the heaviest armor units.

Using these tactics the Soviets still had two major factors in their favor. First of all, the Soviets had gained air superiority of numbers along the front, and although the German Air Force could hardly be ruled out, the Russian Air Force with the right opportunities would be able to dominate the skies. The second and by far the greatest advantage the Russians had in the Battle of Kursk was the fact that the German Army was to attack them. The Russians could stay secure in their defensive positions until the backbone of the German attack was snapped by the powerful Soviet defense. From the chaos and destruction which he hoped would ensue, Zhukov could launch another of his major counter-offensives.

On 5 July 1943, as the morning light first broke across the Kursk Salient, German armor and troops emerged from their positions. As the first Germans took their first steps, the Army seemed destined to failure. Once again the Russians knew from the intelligence of deserters, prisoners and spies the exact time and date of the attack. As the German artillery barrage opened the prelude of fire, Zhukov ordered his own batteries to counter-fire, which threw many of the German troops into disarray only minutes before they were due to attack. The Soviet barrage, which turned into a sort of artillery duel, so shocked many of the German

units that in some sectors it took the Germans almost all day to reorganize themselves. At approximately the same time on that morning, Russian and German aircraft dueled over airfields near the Kharkov region, and German fighters barely staved off an early disaster which could have been inflicted by the Soviet bombers.

By 0530 hours on the Kursk Front the German Army advanced in full strength against the Soviets' 13th Army. The Germans attacked along a 28-mile front. It was only after the battle that Zhukov learned that the northern attack was merely a diversion from the main attack—a drive from the south by the German IX Army and IV Panzer Army against the Voronezh Front.

The German attack met with great success in the early hours of attack. The new German Tiger tanks and the Ferdinand self-propelled guns cracked open the Russian lines and ripped through the Soviet 15th and 18th Rifle Divisions. In those first anxious hours Russian commanders in the area pushed forward Soviet armor in an attempt to engage and halt the powerful new tanks. As quickly as the Soviet armor appeared the German Tigers destroyed them at distance. Soviet crews, unable to get within firing range of the Tigers, found their tanks becoming flaming metal coffins. As the Soviet line seemed doomed and collapsing in front of the huge Tigers as they crawled out of the morning, a 'miracle' or as it is better known a 'fluke of war' graced the Soviet troops. Soviet infantrymen, who had been scattered by the assault realized an odd sensation of something being 'wrong'. Why was no one being cut down as they fled the Tiger advance? The word spread through the Soviet

ranks as it became unbelievably apparent that in Hitler's obsession to produce and employ the new German tank, no secondary armament—machine guns—had been equipped on the monstrous Tigers to protect them against infantry assault. Separated from their own infantry cover, the Tigers were at the mercy of the Soviet line troops. Had they been considered too powerful to need the anti-infantry protection, or was it a war production blunder? It matters very little. The lack of machine gun cover was an open invitation to the Russian infantry, which reversed the flow of the battle. With wild cries Russian troops fired flame throwers down the ventilator systems, threw grenades down the hatches, and fired into the driving slots of the German tanks, killing or burning alive the German crews within. Those mechanical giants were destroyed in a modern enactment of the fight between David and Goliath. For the next five days the German advance in the north made very little headway, and by 10 July, through heavy loss of tanks and troops, the onslaught finally ground to a complete halt.

Although the Germans had pushed heavily in the northern front, the true attack lay, and the great battles were fought along the Voronezh Front. Coinciding with the northern attack, on 5 July German troops attacked along the Voronezh Front and launched an opening blow of no less than 1300 tanks. By night the Russians were forced to bring up heavy re-enforcements and were massing behind the second of their six defense lines. On 6 July the German IV Panzer Army was headed toward Oboyan, and making great progress. Just south of Oboyan a large tank battle

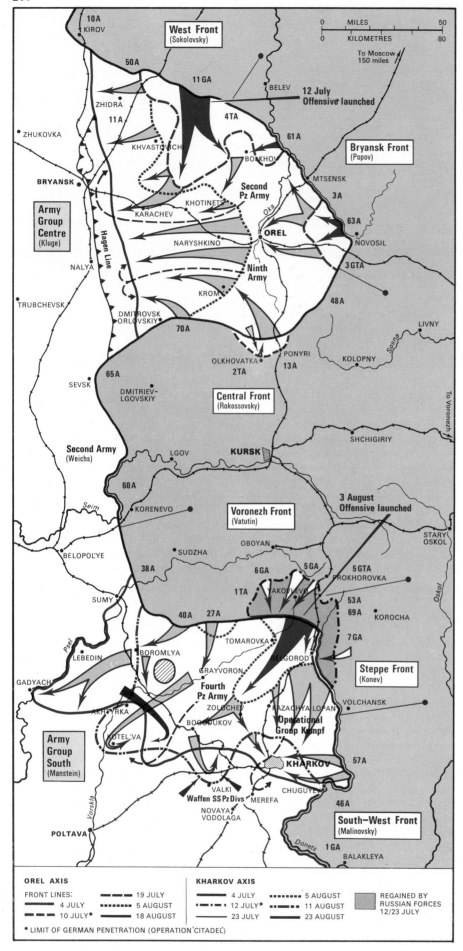

West Front
(Sokolovsky)

10A
KIROV

50A

11GA

To Moscow
150 miles

0 — MILES — 50
0 — KILOMETRES — 80

ZHIDRA

11A

BELEV

4TA

12 July
Offensive launched

ZHUKOVKA

KHVASTOVICHI

61A

BOLKHOV

Bryansk Front
(Popov)

BRYANSK

KARACHEV

KHOTINETS

Second
Pz Army

MTSENSK

3A

Army
Group
Centre
(Kluge)

NARYSHKINO

Oka

 OREL

63A

NOVOSIL

NALYA

Ninth
Army

3GTA

Hagen Line

KROM

48A

TRUBCHEVSK

DMITROVSK
ORLOVSKIY

70A

PONYRI

LIVNY

Sosna

To Voronezh

OLKHOVATKA

13A

KOLOPNY

2TA

SEVSK

65A

DMITRIEV-
LGOVSKIY

Central Front
(Rokossovsky)

Second Army
(Weichs)

LGOV

KURSK

SHCHIGIRIY

60A

Seim

KORENEVO

Voronezh Front
(Vatutin)

3 August
Offensive launched

BELOPOL'YE

38A

SUDZHA

OBOYAN

STARY
OSKOL

SUMY

40A

27A

6GA

5GA

5GTA
PROKHOROVKA

Oskol

1TA

YAKOVLEVO

53A
69A

KOROCHA

TOMAROVKA

7GA

Psel

LEBEDIN

BOROMLYA

GRAYVORON

BELGOROD

Steppe Front
(Konev)

GADYACH

Fourth
Pz Army

ZOLOCHEV

KAZACHYA LOPAN

VOLCHANSK

AKHTYRKA

KOTEL'VA

BOGODUKHOV

Operational
Group Kempf

Army
Group
South
(Manstein)

KHARKOV

57A

Vorskla

VALKI

CHUGUYEV

Waffen SS Pz Divs

MEREFA

NOVAYA
VODOLAGA

46A

POLTAVA

South-West Front
(Malinovsky)

Donets

1GA

BALAKLEYA

 OREL AXIS

FRONT LINES:

4 JULY
10 JULY*

19 JULY
5 AUGUST
18 AUGUST

KHARKOV AXIS

4 JULY
12 JULY*
23 JULY

5 AUGUST
11 AUGUST
23 AUGUST

REGAINED BY
RUSSIAN FORCES
12/23 JULY

* LIMIT OF GERMAN PENETRATION (OPERATION 'CITADEL')

LEFT: Final stages of the Battle for Kursk, from which the Nazis never recovered.

BOTTOM RIGHT: Russian troops are greeted with garlands of flowers after the liberation of Smolensk.

RIGHT: Finnish infantrymen advance under a smoke-screen in one final effort to take Leningrad.

FAR RIGHT: A Russian Jewish woman trudges through the winter snows. As the Nazis retreated millions of Russian Jews were transported to extermination camps in Eastern Europe.

change things seemed to be going in German favor. But these conditions did not last long.

By 9 July fierce fighting along the front and heavy loss of German armor, with no replacements available, began to slow the German advance. In the next two days, the 10th and 11th, the Germans managed to do no more than push a gap less than nine miles deep and fifteen miles wide for their attack on the southern Kursk Front. The III Panzers and the Gross Deutschland Divisions had run completely out of steam and Germany's hopes for victory stagnated and died at the end of the day—11 July. The next morning Zhukov's counter-offensive would destroy not only the German advance, but Germany's ability to successfully strike at the Soviet armies ever again.

12 July 1943 was truly a day of reckoning which saw the 'greatest tank battle of history' fought in the area of Prokhorovka. That morning the two mighty armies struck each other with a total of more than 1500 tanks. General Rotmistrov sent the Soviet 5th Guard Tank Army forward to cut through the German lines. What followed was almost unbelievable. Total chaos overtook the battlefield, and the commanding staffs of both sides were reduced to waiting for an outcome. The battle was no longer in their hands, but rested with the grim determination and fighting ability of their troops. Both German and Russian tank crews fought valiantly throughout the day. The running tank battles were not the unusual 'maneuver and fire' that both forces knew so well, but deteriorated to suicidal charges. Like ancient knights they thundered across the battlefields exchanging blows, not with lances, but with powerful, high velocity guns which in most cases fired at opponents while only a few feet apart. By evening of the 12th the entire battlefield glowed with the flames of destroyed tanks . . . the embers of a dying fire. In that one day Germany lost more than 300 tanks and well over 10,000 men. The German offensive was over, and their retreat began which lasted for two years until supreme domination by the Russians was won along a broad front over a thousand miles long.

In the north on 12 July Soviet troops of the Western, Bryansk and Central Fronts struck at the Germans in the Orel Salient. With three major drives,

took place. Hoth's IV Panzers suffered severe losses, but had smashed the Russian armor in a running tank battle, forcing Zhukov to commit his armor reserves almost immediately to stem the flow of the German advance. On 7 and

8 July German armored units continued to advance, forcing the Russians to withdraw to Syrtzevo and Gremutshy. During those two days both German and Russian armor units battled for the hills around those towns and for a

which lasted through the rest of July and until 18 August, Soviet forces drove the German troops out of that northern position. Russian troops cleared more than 60 miles on the northern flanks, and finally pushed the Germans back to the Hagen Defense Line. In the south the counter-offensive did not begin until 3 August when elements of the Southwest, Steppe and Voronezh Fronts not only pushed the Germans out of their recently conquered territory, but

pressed the German IV Panzer Army back, managing to recapture Kharkov by 23 August. With this maneuver alone, the entire southern wing of the German front was on the verge of collapse. Many historians feel that Hitler's decision on 13 July to transfer armored divisions — several of which went to his Western Front to counter the Anglo-Allied invasion of Sicily — was one of the main reasons for the Kursk failure. But it mattered little what the

Germans prepared in that third, and last, offensive in Russia; they were doomed from the start. Hitler's enthusiasm for pressing the attack, even though it was recommended by his senior Staff Officers to abandon the operation, helped shorten the war by at least one year and enabled the Russians to gain the upper hand.

Zhukov's offensive took not only the form of halting and turning back the Germans around Kursk, but soon

became the springboard for the Russian offensives facing Army Group Center and Army Group South. Between August and December 1943 nine Soviet fronts rolled across the Ukraine and Central Russia. On 26 August the Red Army began its campaign to liberate the Ukraine, and the STAVKA invoked such ploys as the Soviets' highest decoration as a reward for the first soldiers to cross the Dniepr. Within the next four months Soviet troops would push the German Army well over 200 miles in some areas, and recapture the majority of the key towns in the Ukraine. including Kiev, which was finally retaken by 6 November.

ted Smolensk on 25 September. Although troops in the south continued fighting in skirmishes until December, the attacks and major battles in the central area were basically over by the coming of October. The Smolensk operation had given the Red Army approximately 120 to 150 miles of liberated territory in Belorussia. The operation had heavily defeated three German armies, and destroyed no less than six fortified belts of German defenses. Though German troops could still manage a somewhat dogged defense in 1944, the situation was clear. It was becoming merely a matter of time once again before Russian troops would expel the Germans from Russian soil and begin their drive into the heartland of Germany.

In the Central Front the battle for Smolensk was the major combat in the area, and units of the Western Front combined with the Kalinin Front for a total of no less than twelve Soviet armies pushing against 50 per cent—or 40 divisions of Army Group Center. The opposing fronts had well over $1\frac{1}{4}$ million men, 20,000 guns and 14,000 tanks. The Soviets had achieved air superiority, which they would retain until the end of the war, as well as more than 200 other combat aircraft poised on the front against the Germans. The Russians managed to break the German Front in seven sectors, and elements of General Sokolovsky's Western Front and the 5th Mechanized Corps, with General Yeremenko's Kalinin front, breached the German Line and liberated

Throughout 1943 Soviet forces made great advances in all areas but one. The Leningrad battle lines had not altered since 18 January of that year.

BELOW: German tanks pause before a burning house near Smolensk during the retreat in 1943.

BOTTOM: The relief of Leningrad, the end of the 900-day siege.

BELOW LEFT: An American Lend-Lease locomotive arrives at an Iranian port for trans-shipment to the Soviet Union. US aid increased dramatically in 1943.

BELOW RIGHT: Marshal Chuikov, whose tanks repelled the German assault at Kursk and won the battle for Russia.

RIGHT: German troops take two Russian prisoners into captivity in the Crimea. As the Nazis retreated Russian prisoners were sent to labor camps or merely shot.

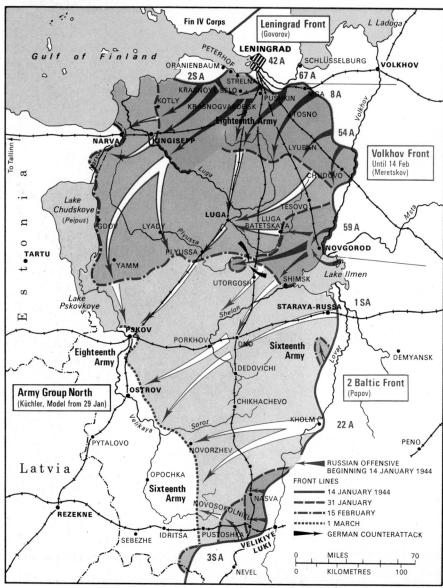

The Soviet High Command seemed to tolerate the siege in order to make strategic gains elsewhere. Of the three major contested areas, this northern-most flank of Leningrad took the lowest of priorities. However, in January 1944 the Russian Command managed to assemble eight Soviet armies along the Leningrad Front. General Govorov's forces then swept across the frozen Gulf of Finland while simultaneously General Meretskov's Volkhov Front attacked from across the frozen Lake Ilmen, completely surprising the German units and quickly penetrating their defenses. Although the German troops reacted fairly quickly to the attack, and managed a flexible, mobile defense, Soviet numbers were taking their inevitable toll. The Soviet armies outnumbered the Germans by 2.5:1, they had 3.5 times the artillery, and six times as many tanks. The Germans were virtually overwhelmed. By 19 January 1944 two German divisions had been completely wiped out, and five more severely crippled. Over 1000 men were captured and large quantities of artillery pieces and small arms fell into Russian hands. Many of the artillery pieces captured were those which had been used in the initial bombardment of the city.

Fearing encirclement in many areas, the Germans, while suffering heavy losses, pulled back to a defense line which was equal to that they had held in the early days of 1941. They had been hurled back more than 170 miles by 26 February. The last German threat to any major Russian city was broken with 7000 German prisoners taken. The Leningrad blockade and siege was ended after 900 days.

At the same time the Leningrad offensive was in full swing, the Russians concentrated a major effort in the south. Although those offensives did not gain as much ground as previous drives, Russian troops managed to push south of the Pripet Marshes and in January 1944 crossed the old 1939 German-Russian border. By the early March thaws Russian troops found themselves as far west at Lutsk in Poland, placing the left flank of Army Group South in an extremely vulnerable position. In April the Russians, through air superiority, assaulted German troops in both the Crimea and what remained of the unconquered territory of the Ukraine. By 7 May the Sebastopol fortifications

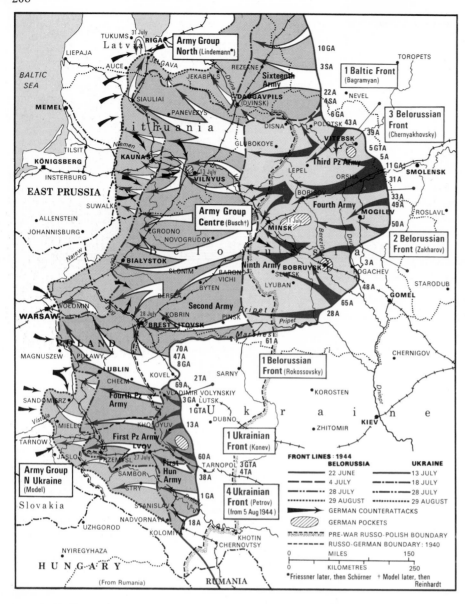

Hitler's satellite allies, who were consistently the weak link, were the object of the Russian assaults.

The first of these countries to be 'eliminated' was Finland, with hostilities finally ending on 4 September. Those German troops stationed in Finland either surrendered or escaped into Norway. The Finnish Front fell along relatively the same lines as the old borders before the war. Rumania, Hungary, and the Baltic States of Latvia, Lithuania, and Estonia were all to fall within the coming year; not only as invaded, conquered countries, but to become satellite nations under the military and economic influence of Russia.

On 23 June 1944 Soviet artillery once more began to pound mercilessly at the German troops. For Army Group Center, located in Belorussia and the Pripet Marshes areas, the Soviet planned attack was an uncomplicated one. Vasilevsky commanded the Ist Baltic and 3rd Belorussia Fronts, while Zhukov took command of the 1st and 2nd Belorussia Fronts, 'White Russian Fronts'. In the north, under Vasilevsky, the Armies were to strike at the German III Panzer and IV Armies and attempt to encircle the marsh area, striking toward East Prussia. On the south Zhukov's two fronts were to swing northward through the swamps at the German IX Army, trying to force an encirclement or a hammer and anvil effect against the German troops. Guerrilla activity had begun on 22 June with the harassment of German communications, which actually cut off German troops from their senior command headquarters. In the Russians' opinion the 22nd was an ideal psychological date, as it was the third anniversary of the German invasion. Soviet commanders were confident that this attack against Army Group Center would take the Russian troops from fighting on Russian soil and be the beginning of their thrust across Poland straight toward Berlin.

One other startling fact must be realized when discussing the Soviet command during that summer offensive. Since Kursk Soviet officers down to the division level were filled with such confidence that the planning for the major offensives were delegated not only by the front commanders, but young officers possessed the skill and knowledge to add their own ideas to the planning. The black clouds and grim

were retaken. However, much of the German force managed to escape from the garrison due to Russian inability to engage the evacuating Germans with their Black Sea Fleet. By the end of May the Ukraine had been retaken, Russian troops were pushing into Poland and Rumania, and once again Russian troops were poised along the front for the great Soviet summer offensive of 1944.

During the Russian offensive of 1943, one of the major factors which helped the Soviets maintain momentum was the Lend-Lease goods from the US which were rushed to the Russians. More than $2\frac{1}{2}$ million tons of petroleum products, industrial equipment, and enough food to feed every Russian soldier more than $1\frac{1}{2}$ times the amount of concentrated food nutrients needed per day. Along with the food, Russian troops received hundreds of thousands of planes and trucks, and approximately 7000 tanks, which, although not as good as the Russian T-34, still could be used in offensive and defensive areas on minor fronts. In the beginning the US had problems delivering Lend-Lease goods, but by 1944 supplies flowed

from the Atlantic into the Arctic Ocean to the Soviet port of Archangel; in the south through the Persian Gulf via Iran, which had been invaded and secured since 1941 by the British and Russians; and through Siberia from Alaska across the whole of Russia. These Lend-Lease goods must be looked at in the sense that America understood that Russia was at that time the deciding force in the war against Germany. By the time the Allied forces were ready to step back onto the Continent they could easily defeat the Nazi forces whose backbone had been broken under the weight of the Russian onslaught. Though Stalin screamed constantly for the invasion, it would not be until mid-1944 that Capitalism could supply Communism with much more than 'goods and commodities' to help defeat the Fascists.

Throughout all of 1944 Stalin, the STAVKA and all the Army commanders realized that this would be their year of conquest, in spite of the fact that the German Army was not really defeated, nor made ineffective as a force until the summer of 1944 with the destruction of Army Group Center.

seriousness which surrounded battles such as Moscow and Stalingrad were replaced by an exuberant confidence formerly monopolized by the German Army. This confidence and success had its roots in three major factors. First of all, the Soviet soldier possessed the confidence that he was the best fighting man in Europe. Secondly, like the American soldier he had material superiority over his German counterparts in ammunition, food supplies, equipment and other basic necessities for the destruction of the enemy. Thirdly and most importantly, the Soviet Army was riding the wave of initiative which has never receded and remains poised behind the Iron Curtain today.

On 24 June the Soviet troops launched their attacks. One from the north and south, and in a single day pushed 10 km into the German front. Three days later the Soviets were 80 km deep into the Bobruisk area, and two full German Corps were completely isolated. On the 29th with the city of Bobruisk falling and incredible losses on both sides mounting, as the smoke cleared eight German Divisions no

longer existed. Within that week more than 100,000 German troops were killed and nearly 40,000 taken prisoner. One of the 'casualties' was Marshal Busch, sacked by Hitler and replaced by Model.

By that time the German IV Army was almost annihilated. The IX Army and the IV Panzers were seriously mauled, and German reinforcements were rushed in piecemeal to try to brace up the crumbling front. In the next week a Russian blitz took place. Soviet forces penetrated almost 500 km on a front almost 400 km wide. Ger-

man losses were incredible as Hitler once more ordered his troops to stand fast, which only added to the casualties. Belorussia was ripped from the grasp of the Germans, and by 23 July with the Soviet attack exhausting itself more in its rapid movement than by the Germans, the front line of Army Group Center area was pushed back to that of the original border of 1941. The demon of war no longer smiled upon the Germans, but looked upon the hearty, brown-clad, determined Soviet soldiers, who, confident of victory, prepared for their now-inevitable triumph.

With the destruction of Army Group Center Germany had suffered nearly a half-million dead and more than 150,000 prisoners were taken, Thirty divisions were completely destroyed along with 25,000 tanks and tens of thousands of vehicles and artillery. Not only had the Soviets crushed German hopes of winning the war, but this whole disaster must be viewed with several other points in mind. First of all, before the campaign started, on 6 June 1944 American and British troops assaulted the beaches of Normandy and France, making Stalin's two-front war a reality. Throughout June and July limited Soviet offenses took place in the Ukraine, Finland and the Baltic States. In this way the Russians proved that they had the ability to conduct war on all fronts at all times, something Germany was never able to do after the first months of the invasion, and during those dark German days of July 1944, although morale had not broken down among the soldiers or population, a conspiracy took place to assassinate Hitler. Although the July plot failed, it showed that the Army's commanders knew at the time that the war was lost and saw more clearly what lay in the future than their Führer.

By August 1944 the Allies had something to cheer about. The breakout in France was in full swing. Florence was liberated on the Italian Front. On 20 August Soviet forces launched a general offensive into Rumania. At the height of that campaign the Rumanians saw that their position was hopeless and defected totally to the Russians. Sixteen German divisions of the reconstituted German VI and VIII Armies were trapped. With the arrival of September the new Bulgarian government, set up by the Soviets, declared war on Germany while Rumania had been almost totally overrun.

The war took a different turn on the Eastern Front. Hitler and Guderian, who was then Chief of the German General Staff, knew that the only way the Eastern Front could be stabilized was by a mass shortening effort. Army Group North's hopes lay in evacuating Estonia and Latvia, but at the last moment Hitler suspended the order, and once again told the troops to stand fast. Army Group Center under Reinhardt was to defend in Poland and East Prussia. In the south three new Army Groups were formed: the North Ukraine Front, the South Ukraine Front and Army Group F—which was located in Greece and Yugoslavia. All along the front German forces were in a suspended state of retreat facing defeat in the path of the Russian Army. Guerrillas such as Tito's partisans in Yugo-

slavia were now openly fighting the Germans in force. The Poles who had staged a tragic and unsuccessful uprising in Warsaw still wanted to support Soviet forces located just outside Warsaw.

In those fall and winter months that followed a situation began to develop which began a struggle of the democracies against Communism. On 4 October, with Churchill's decision to send British troops into Greece, the Soviet offensive of 1944 was only the curtain raiser to the land grab between the Allies and the Soviet Union which would come in the new year. It was no longer a question of whether or not Germany would win the war. It was now a question of whether the Western Allies could overrun Western Europe before the Soviet steamroller reached Berlin.

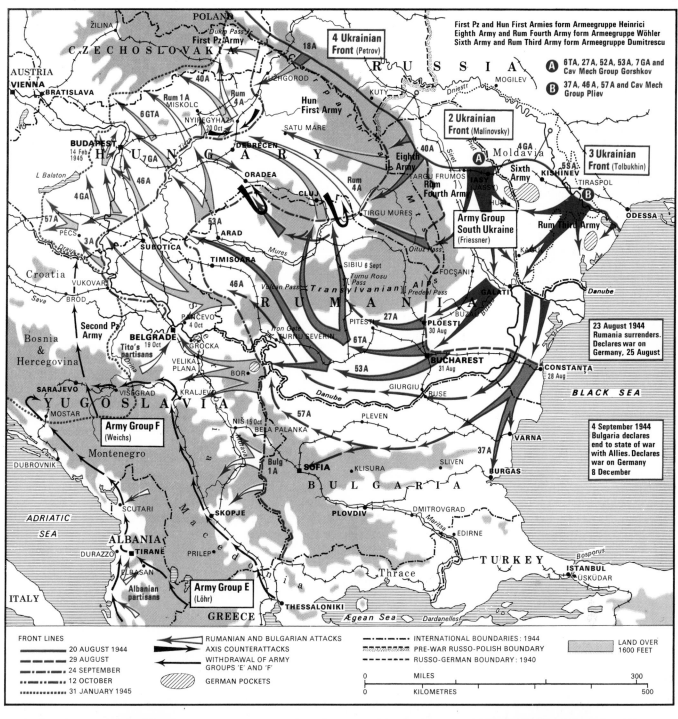

INTO THE REICH

LEFT: A Red Army infantryman on patrol along a canal in eastern Germany in 1945.

BELOW: Cossacks of the 4th Cavalry Corps mass in Poland for another assault during the Long Offensive.

During the last three months of 1944 Russian forces continued their thrust through the Baltic States, and although slowed at several points along the way, by the beginning of the new year they had engulfed most of Hungary and all of Rumania, lay outside the city of Warsaw, and were poised along the borders of East Prussia. Army Group North was totally cut off in the Latvian Peninsula on the Baltic Sea, with 20 veteran German Divisions isolated in that area. In the South, Tito's guerrillas in Yugoslavia were receiving large amounts of Russian aid. What little jostling of the front took place in those months occurred in the Carpathians or the Danube Valley, around the city of Budapest, in preparation for the Russian drive into Austria.

On the day before Christmas 1944, Russian troops managed to encircle Budapest, and with the arrival of the new year the beleaguered city fell. During that same time period, although German troops were still putting up stubborn resistance along the front, Germany was locked in a commitment against the Allies on the Western Front—The Battle of the Bulge. That battle, despite initial German success, was finally lost. In effect it did nothing more than prolong the fighting of the Western Front while eating up the small reserves that the German General Staff had saved to support their sagging forces. Allied bombing raids at that time had not only disrupted German communications but had seriously damaged the petroleum industry, creating a

BELOW: Russian troops enter the outskirts of Vienna in 1945.

BELOW: Dancing with Russian soldiers in the streets of Lvov after its liberation in 1944.

BELOW: Russian troops enter the outskirts of Vienna in 1945.

BELOW: Dancing with Russian soldiers in the streets of Lvov after its liberation in 1944.

critical gas and oil shortage on all fronts, particularly the Eastern. With Germany sinking to its knees, all indications predicted that the next Russian offensive would take place in Poland, undoubtedly aiming itself directly at Berlin. At the same time continuing pressure would be applied to German forces still in Hungary. Russia's primary target in that area was Vienna. At this point Russia had a clear 11:1 superiority in infantry, 20:1 in both aircraft and heavy guns, and most important, 7:1 superiority in tanks.

By 12 January 1945 the long delayed Russian offensive in the area of Poland had begun, with Marshal Koniev's 1st Ukraineans punching through and making a bridgehead in the Baranow region. The Germans were completely outnumbered and with no secondary defense line were pushed back to Kielce. In the next 14 days the 1st and 2nd Belorussian Armies moved rapidly into Poland and East Prussia. Zhukov, in a brilliant drive managed to swing his troops across the Oder River. Zhukov's own forces then halted just outside the city of Kustrin. This maneuver placed the Russians only 40 miles east of Berlin, but Zhukov was forced to wait and consolidate his position.

In that drive Zhukov had outrun his supplies and had bypassed two heavily fortified cities, Torun and Poznan. These had to be captured and destroyed in his rear area. While these consolidations and sieges took place the front stabilized itself with the 1st Armies of the Ukraineans and Belorussians actually within German borders

Fronts pushed rapidly forward. By 7 April Vienna was surrounded, with Soviet forces as far west as St. Polten. The next six days saw bitter fighting in and around Vienna, but Russian troops finally captured the old Hapsburg city on the afternoon of 13 April. In the second half of the month the weight of the Soviet offensive shifted north of the Danube, supporting attacks against the right flank of Army Group Center. Through the maneuvering of Soviet forces Army Group South was finally isolated, and in the process of being destroyed, when on 7 May after being hard-pressed by the Soviets the Army Group surrendered to General George Patton's 3rd Army, which had swung out of southern Germany into Austria in the direction of Czechoslovakia.

Before continuing with the final episode of the war on the Eastern Front, a look at the 'cause and effect' of Russian policy is needed. By June 1944 the Anglo-American lines were taking the final steps in the collapse and conquest of Germany. Later on in that year at the Quebec Conference, Churchill and Roosevelt discussed not only the ending of the war, but the throwing of their total weight behind 'stage two'—the war against Japan. Primarily there were reluctantly grim discussions as to the possible problems of winning the 'total war'. In October 1944 Churchill journeyed to Moscow to confer with Stalin on what amounted to the old problem of military operations and political influence in the Baltic region. It was at this time that Churchill and Stalin decided how the 'pie' of their interests in Europe would be cut. It is said that on a scrap of paper Churchill wrote that Rumania and Bulgaria would be 'overseen' by Russia, Greece by the British; Hungary and Yugoslavia would be a 50/50 division with both Britain and the Soviet Union equally influencing the military and political policies in the two countries. It was also during this conference that Stalin decided the fate of Poland. Stalin realized that it was his for the taking. By late 1944 almost all of Poland had been gobbled up by the Russian armies and there was little the West could do to reinstate the exiled Polish government.

It was through this agreement that England was able to crush the Greek Communists. By not openly interfering

and along the Oder River. Tobrun and Poznan fell on 23 February, and elements of the 1st, 2nd and 3rd Belorussian Fronts turned north to overrun East Prussia. With great success Russian troops managed to take the area, but once again the Russian Navy failed to halt the troop evacuations by the Germans through the Baltic Sea to ports within northern Germany. The amateurish display by the Russian Navy once more showed that even though the Russian Army commanders could manage to isolate troops in large pockets, if those pockets flanked the sea, evacuation by the German Navy was always possible. Because of this the Russians could not destroy the German troops 'en masse' as they often planned to do. That incompetence on the part of the Russian Navy continued to bring about bitter feelings between it and the Russian Army.

Throughout March and April 1945 Russian troops in the north maintained a stable line, while clearing pockets of resistance within East Prussia. In the south on the Hungarian Front Russian

forces continued to hold a favorable initiative by destroying Hitler's VI Panzer Army's counter-attack in the Danube Valley in March. That counter-attack was quite ridiculous in that the VI Panzers were poorly supplied and lacked enough fuel to exploit any opening they may have made. By the time that final attack was over 34,000 German and Hungarian soldiers were killed, wounded or taken prisoner, and the way was opened for Russian troops to move toward Austria. On 16 March Russian soldiers began an offensive against German and Hungarian troops within that same area. The attack was led by elements of the 4th and 9th Guard Armies and the 6th and 9th Guard Tank Armies. Within two days of the beginning of the attack sections of the 6th Tank Army reached the Austrian border. By the end of the month the 6th Army turned north heading toward Bratislava, while the 4th and 9th Guard Armies headed toward Vienna. German troops could no longer hold the line on any sector of that Front and forces of the 2nd and 3rd Ukrainian

Stalin expected the same 'tact' from the British when it came to Russian policy in their own areas of influence.

The most important conference of the war took place in February 1945 in Yalta. At that conference, although Churchill, Roosevelt and Stalin all attended, it was definitely a 'two man' discussion. Churchill was basically pushed aside by Roosevelt and Stalin and kept in semi-darkness as to the policies which were arranged between the United States and Russia. He seemed to realize that Britain would never again be able to approach the Soviet Union as a major world power. At Yalta Stalin seemed to confirm to all of Roosevelt's wishes. He promised to bring Russia into the war with Japan, and to support Chiang Kai-shek, not the Chinese Communists. He pledged Russia's participation in the United Nations Organization. It seemed at the time that Stalin expected to do as he pleased in Poland.

Through those compromise agreements between Roosevelt and Stalin the United States and Russia took the first steps forward in shaping the policies, and assuming the dominance, which would follow in the years ahead. Britain was relegated to a second-rate power behind the two new superpowers. Although Yalta was a moment of greatest optimism among the Allies, both Churchill and Roosevelt were severely criticized by their own parties and governments when they returned home. Contrary to any agreements, the large anti-Communist factions in both countries still held the fear of the 'Bolshevik peril' in even more apprehension than before, as it became apparent that Russia was emerging as a major dominant world power of the future.

To return to the conflicts at hand, with the beginning of April 1945 all the major Allied Powers knew that the German Reich had but a few weeks to survive. The leaders of Germany, including Hitler himself, knew that the war was ultimately lost. In the West American and British troops poured across the German landscape. German troops, although they put up initial resistance, were surrendering in large numbers. Many of the German people took to the roads in attempts to surrender to the Americans and British rather than face the reprisals which they knew the arrival of the conquering Russians would bring. The fear of the majority of German people in those final days was not concerned with the winning or losing of the war, but under whose thumb they were to live.

In the east, bordering the German lines of defense along the Oder River, lay three major Soviet Fronts. The 2nd Belorussian Front extended from the Baltic Sea to the area around Schwedt. From there to where the Oder River heads due east were the armies of Zhukov's 1st Belorussian Front. On that front alone Zhukov had at his disposal eleven crack Soviet armies which were poised, and whose mission it was, to take Berlin above all else. South of the Oder and into Czechoslovakia Koniev's 1st Ukrainian Front flanked Zhukov. Their object was to push west from their position in support of the 1st Belorussian forces. By comparison the remnants of the German Army at that time were a conglomeration of forces under the command of Heinrici, calling itself Army Group Vistula.

It was believed by the Russian Command that the 2nd Belorussian Front faced an area of very weak resistance. Zhukov and Koniev were given the bulk of the Russian reserve troops for the main battle in Berlin. Russian troops and equipment at the outset of the final campaign numbered at more than $2\frac{1}{2}$ million men and well over 6000 tanks. Forty thousand heavy artillery guns were brought forward in support, and the Soviet Air Force had no less than 7500 combat aircraft at their disposal. Against these numbers the Germans could muster no more than one million men, 10,000 heavy guns, slightly more than 1000 tanks, and approximately 3300 combat aircraft.

Although the Germans displayed stubborn resistance in those final days, the German Army was little more than young boys and old men, thrown together in makeshift units whose cohesion and determination stemmed from love of country and fear of Russia rather than military discipline. As for support, lack of armaments, tanks, artillery, aircraft and Germany's exhausted stocks of ammunition, petrol and regular supplies made the force assembled on that front almost totally ineffective. In those closing days only the SS combat units seemed to be receiving fuel for vehicles, and the majority of the 3300 aircraft considered available for the last defense were unable to fly for lack of parts and fuel. In contrast, under the Red Banners that unfurled before the German lines came the high caliber troops who marched forward to seal Germany's fate. This was the sweet victory for which Stalin had hoped and plotted; the victory toward which Zhukov and the others had led the Russian armies; and the revenge and victory for which the Soviet people and soldiers had sweated, bled and died.

Since February the Germans had been preparing defenses around the city of Berlin, organizing them in three interlocking belts $12\frac{1}{2}$ to 25 miles deep, and setting up the towns and villages in the area as points of key defensive positions. The Seelow Heights were considered as the major position for the defense of the city, by both the Germans and the Russians. These heights were taken early when on 16 April the first stage of the Russian offensive began. Elements of the 1st Belorussian Front broke through the Oder River defenses and pushed their forces to Prötzel and Seelow. The 1st Ukrainians were launched across the Neisse River at the same time and by 21 April had pushed to Spremberg. That combination of attacks from 16–21 April split the German armies into three main sectors.

Fighting in those opening days of the 'Berlin offensive' did not go exactly as the Russians had anticipated. Zhukov's forces managed to advance only seven or eight miles. The STAVKA became very concerned with Zhukov's slow moving armies and turned elements of the 1st Ukrainians north to help with the encirclement of Berlin. To accom-

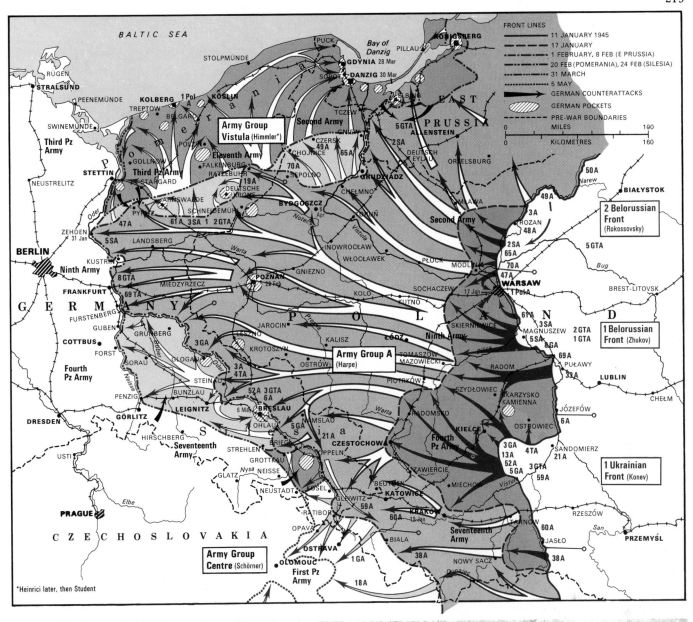

BELOW: German officers in a dejected mood are arrested by their Russian conquerors in Berlin.

RIGHT: Russian rockets fire their deadly salvo outside the German port of Stettin on the Baltic which fell to the Soviets shortly thereafter.

222

BELOW: Russian soldiers carry a wounded comrade through the streets of Berlin in early May 1945. The Soviets lost hundreds of thousands in the fight in and around the German capital.

BELOW RIGHT: Russian tanks and troops occupy western Berlin, which escaped some of the destruction which levelled much of the city.

RIGHT: Soviet rockets outside Berlin. The capital was devastated by aerial bombardment, rocket fire, artillery salvos and intense house-to-house fighting which left it almost totally in ruins.

plish that Koniev sent his 3rd and 4th Guard Tank Armies north, planning to attack Berlin from the south. The 2nd Belorussian Front was not due to commence its attack until 20 April, but with the advances moving so slowly the timetable for the encirclement of Berlin was thrown off. Thus by the end of the first four days of fighting, although Zhukov had managed to break up the German IX Army, the Russians had advanced only 19 miles from their original positions. In other areas the outlook seemed brighter for the Russians. Koniev's forces were maneuvering for an attack on the third and weakest sector of the German defense rings. During that time also, the Soviet Air Force inflicted heavy damage on the German VI Air Fleet, and effectively put the Luftwaffe out of action.

Although operations along the front were moving slowly, Russian superiority was taking its toll. After the 20th Zhukov took his troops to the outer defenses northwest of Berlin, and by that time Russian long-range artillery had begun to hammer the German capital. On 23 April the Russian armies commenced a breakthrough into the city limits, and by the evening of that same day the majority of German forces were encircled. Parts of the armies under Koniev and Zhukov were beginning to link. The 4th Guards from the south and the 47th Army were lying west of Berlin and only 25 miles apart. Zhukov's 8th Guard Army was less than ten miles from Koniev's 3rd Guard Tank Army southeast of the city. By 23 April Zhukov's forces were tightening the encirclement of Berlin when the STAVKA gave orders allowing him to bypass the city, link up with other Russian armies, and push west in order to grab as much German territory as possible before the arrival of the Anglo-American forces. The 25th, 65th, and 70th Russian Armies were given that immediate task and made very good progress.

By 25 April Berlin was completely encircled. Nearly half a million men converged on Berlin's defending forces. Within the city German troops numbered less than 200,000, with no more than 3000 guns and mortars and roughly 200 tanks for its defense. As important as the battle situation was the fact that on that same day the 5th Guards Army advanced across the Elbe River near the town of Torgaun, where Russian and American troops met, cutting the German forces in half.

The German High Command was in a desperate situation. A directive was issued, on the night of the 25th, in which the German Command ordered all troops to discontinue the fighting with the British/American forces and throw all their might against the Russian onslaught. The Command felt that their only salvation would come from an Anglo-American effort to gain more ground than the Russians.

Zhukov and Koniev, who cared little for the German change of tactics, stabilized their encirclement and decided that rather than push on they should eliminate the isolated German pockets southeast of Berlin. By 1 May, in the Frankfurt-Gubern area near Beelitz, more than 5000 German soldiers were killed and nearly 13,000 captured. Since the beginning tf the Russian offensive on 16 April, German losses numbered nearly 60,000 killed and more than 100,000 captured. Large

April the Germans within the city found themselves with no water supply. This meant that by the time the Russian attack came three days later, what water had been conserved and stored prior to the loss of supply was nearly if not totally exhausted. Marshal Zhukov knew of the plight within the city and offered surrender terms to the German Command on 23 April. They rejected the proposal. Hitler and his Staff for some reason believed that they could hold on until the Anglo-American forces would reach them. This seems to be a key point when viewing the Berlin situation. For unknown reasons in those final days the German Command lost sight of the war's 'total picture'. Instead of fighting the Allies to their West they seemed to have forgotten that the Anglo-American forces pushing across the heartland of Europe were also the enemy, and were not racing across to aid Hitler in the defeat of the Bolshevik hordes.

quantities of German artillery, light weapons and vehicles made up the victors' spoils. Only very small groups of German soldiers managed to escape the various entrapments, and the effective fighting strength of troops, except for those within the confines of Berlin, was neutralized.

The fortress of Berlin, though completely surrounded, had to be reduced, and the Soviets planned for a simultaneous attack by the forward attacking units all around the city on 26 April. Within Berlin itself every building and scrap of material available was used for the defense. Tanks were dug in as permanent pill-boxes, sewers were used in a trench-like manner to connect strong points from street to street, enabling the Germans to hold until the last minute, only to move underground to the next line of resistance, eluding the Russian fire. The fighting seen in the following days was unequalled by any operation seen on the Russian Front since Stalingrad.

The Germans had more problems than just defending the city and the Russians knew it. On top of being completely encircled, over two million German civilians were still trapped in Berlin. Many of these were the children and the old. Food was almost non-existent, and there were no public facilities to be found. In fact, the situation so degenerated that by 22

At daylight on 25 April the general assault by the surrounding Russian armies was preceded by heavy artillery

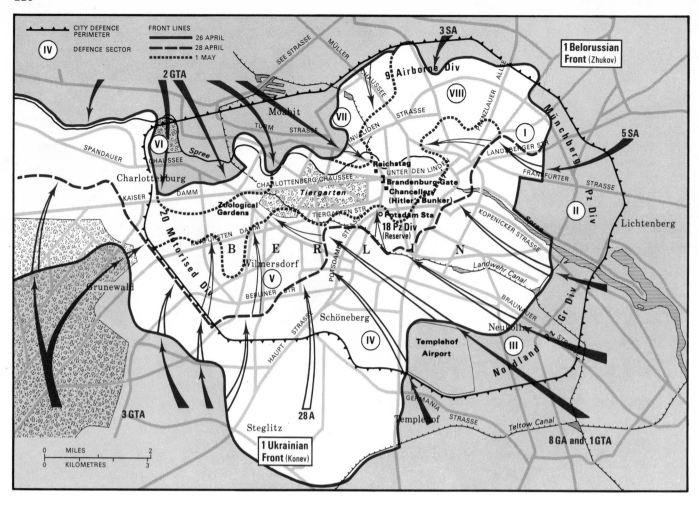

and air attacks. In every quarter the oncoming Russians found the German soldiers fighting fiercely, giving no ground. For many of the old veterans it must have brought back memories of those grim days at Stalingrad, as troops only made progress in inches, with each foot of ground bloodily contested. By the evening of 27 April the Soviet 47th Army had isolated Potsdam from Berlin. The 2nd Guards Tank and 3rd Shock Armies had crossed the River Spree and had established bridgeheads on the southern banks. The 5th Shock, 1st Guards Tank, and 8th Guards Armies were making the most progress in the east and southeast of Berlin, and late on the same evening managed to capture the Tempelhof Airfield. This was exhilarating news for the Soviet troops as it placed many of the Soviet forces near the city center on that flank. The result for the Germans meant that they were squeezed into a ten-mile long strip within the city, which in many places was only one to three miles wide. If it had been any other city but Berlin all resistance would have been broken, but the troops fought on.

Problems continued to mount for the isolated Germans. During the 26th and 27th the Luftwaffe attempted to fly supplies in to the beleaguered Berlin troops. This attempt was severely thwarted by the Soviet Air Force, and those few planes which did manage to get over the city were so terribly misin-

formed as to the whereabouts of the front that all the supplies they dropped fell into Russian hands.

Hitler continued to seek ways out of the situation. Strangely, he believed that the German IX and XII Armies could be used to lift the siege and save Berlin. What he failed to realize was that this whole concept was totally impossible. The IX Army was completely surrounded and the XII was falling back, trying to defend itself. Sporadic though often incorrect news and reports filtered through the Command, which informed Hitler that his idea was futile.

On the 28th the Soviet Army was pressing with increasing force on the Germans. Zhukov knew that it was only a matter of days, perhaps hours, until the battle was over. Hitler again used his 'answer' to alleviating the situation by sacking his generals. However, the case was so hopeless that he found himself in a position where no one would accept the responsibility of command of the crumbling German Army. On the following day General Weidling, who had commanded German forces, presented Hitler with a plan for a breakout and linking attempt with other German units. The plan included making their way west to either try to defend at another point, or to surrender to the Anglo-American units in that sector. Weidling made this proposal, not so much to save the

German war effort, but to end the senseless battle, the outcome of which was a foregone conclusion, and to put a stop to the suffering of the German civilians in the city. Hitler refused the plan, but on the following day, 29 April, approved a plan for a 30 April breakout. By that time it was too late, as German troops held only the central sector of Berlin and throughout the city Soviet troops were funneling forward in their assault.

In the meantime the STAVKA issued orders that it wanted all resistance in Berlin broken, and that the Red Flag was to be raised over the Reichstag. The 'honor' of this task was given to Major-General Perevertkin who commanded the 79th Rifle Corps of the 3rd Shock Army. The night of 28 April Russian troops seized the Moltke Bridge and fought their way toward the Reichstag. German troops constantly counterattacked as the lead elements crossed the bridge, but by the morning of the 29th not only was the bridge securely in Russian hands, but the building which housed the German Ministry of the Interior was being taken. The contest for that building, which the Russians called 'Himmler's House', was one of the heaviest seen in those last days. The battle raged all day between the Soviet soldiers and the hand-picked SS guards as they fought from floor to floor, giving way only when SS troops were killed or flames forced them to move.

The fighting was so severe that the actual attack on the Reichstag was held up and it was not until the morning of the 30th that their main objective could be assaulted.

Elements of the 380th, 574th and 756th Soviet Rifle Regiments hurled themselves at the Reichstag garrison, in what proved to be as desperate a confrontation as was seen throughout that city. In the corridors and rooms the German and Soviet soldiers fought with flame throwers, bazookas, grenades and with their bare hands when necessary. Fires broke out, and many of the wounded of both sides died in those flames. Despite German resistance the Soviet onslaught was overwhelming. By the morning of 1 May Sergeants M. A. Yegorov and M. V. Kontary had raised the Russian flag in victory on the Reichstag's dome. Even as this was taking place sporadic fighting still continued in several isolated corridors

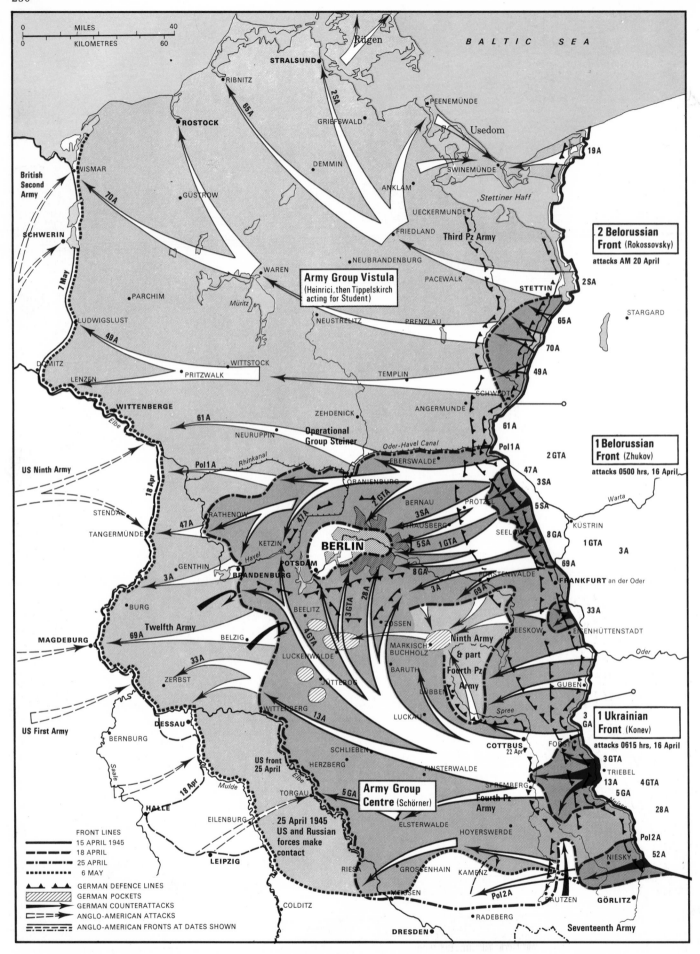

0 MILES 40
0 KILOMETRES 60

BALTIC SEA

Rügen

STRALSUND

RIBNITZ

PEENEMÜNDE

ROSTOCK

GRIEFSWALD

Usedom

19A

DEMMIN

ANKLAM

SWINEMÜNDE

Stettiner Haff

British Second Army

WISMAR

GÜSTROW

UECKERMUNDE

SCHWERIN

FRIEDLAND

Third Pz Army

2 Belorussian Front (Rokossovsky)
attacks AM 20 April

7 May

WAREN

NEUBRANDENBURG

Army Group Vistula
(Heinrici, then Tippelskirch acting for Student)

PACEWALK

STETTIN

2SA

STARGARD

PARCHIM

Müritz

NEUSTRELITZ

PRENZLAU

65A

70A

LUDWIGSLUST

49A

49A

SCHWEDT

DÖMITZ

WITTSTOCK

TEMPLIN

ANGERMUNDE

LENZEN

PRITZWALK

WITTENBERGE

ZEHDENICK

61A

61A

NEURUPPIN

Operational Group Steiner

Oder-Havel Canal

1 Belorussian Front (Zhukov)
attacks 0500 hrs, 16 April

US Ninth Army

Rhinkanal

Pol1A

EBERSWALDE

Pol1A

2 GTA

Warta

STENDAL

RATHENOW

47A

ORANIENBURG

47A

3 GTA

BERNAU

3SA

PRÖTZEL

5SA

47A

TANGERMÜNDE

KETZIN

3SA

STRAUSBERG

8 GA

KÜSTRIN

1 GTA

3A

BERLIN

POTSDAM

5SA

1 GTA

SEELOW

69A

GENTHIN

Havel

8 GA

FÜRSTENWALDE

FRANKFURT an der Oder

BRANDENBURG

3A

33A

BURG

3A

28A

3 GTA

BEELITZ

EISENHÜTTENSTADT

MAGDEBURG

Twelfth Army

69A

BELZIG

DÖSSEN

Ninth Army & part Fourth Pz Army

BEESKOW

Oder

LUCKENWALDE

MARKISCH-BUCHHOLZ

33A

ZERBST

JÜTERBOG

BARUTH

LÜBBEN

GUBEN

US First Army

WITTENBERG

13A

LUCKAU

Spree

3 GA

BERNBURG

Saale

DESSAU

US front 25 April

COTTBUS
22 Apr

FORST

1 Ukrainian Front (Konev)
attacks 0615 hrs, 16 April

18 Apr

Mulde

SCHLIEBEN

FINSTERWALDE

3 GTA

TRIEBEL

HALLE

EILENBURG

TORGAU

5 GA

Elbe

25 April 1945 US and Russian forces make contact

Army Group Centre (Schörner)

Fourth Pz Army

SPREMBERG

ELSTERWALDE

13A

4 GTA

5 GA

28A

LEIPZIG

HOYERSWERDE

Pol 2A

52A

RIESA

GROSSENHAIN

KAMENZ

NIESKY

MEISSEN

Pol 2A

BAUTZEN

GÖRLITZ

COLDITZ

RADEBERG

Seventeenth Army

DRESDEN

FRONT LINES
——— 15 APRIL 1945
– – – 18 APRIL
–·–·– 25 APRIL
····· 6 MAY
▲▲▲ GERMAN DEFENCE LINES
▨▨▨ GERMAN POCKETS
→→→ GERMAN COUNTERATTACKS
⇢⇢⇢ ANGLO-AMERICAN ATTACKS
═══ ANGLO-AMERICAN FRONTS AT DATES SHOWN

of the building. Finally the German soldiers still alive had been forced to the basement where they surrendered their hopeless cause. Of the 5000 German soldiers garrisoned at the Reichstag more than half were killed.

While all of this was happening Hitler had learned that Mussolini had been captured by angry crowds of Italians and murdered. Although Hitler was not surprised by this news, he knew that the same fate was in store for him if the

Soviets captured him alive. To save himself that fate, on midday 30 April, Hitler took his own life. A new government was to be formed with Grand Admiral Dönitz at its head.

From that point on sources become

LEFT: The final agony of the Third Reich: the fall of Berlin.

BELOW RIGHT: A Russian military policewoman directs traffic before the Brandenburg Gate in Berlin after its capitulation in May 1945.

RIGHT: General Koniev commanded the Northwest Front in 1943 and followed the retreating Germans to Berlin when he led 3rd and 4th Guard Tank Armies to the capital.

confused as to what actually happened in Berlin. Dönitz, who was in Flensburg, made a broadcast calling once again for German troops to stop fighting and resisting the Anglo-American forces and to concentrate their efforts against the Russians. In that statement he made it clear that he was not giving troops leave to surrender to the Western Allies, but to pull back and exert their strengths against the Russians. In spite of this, in Berlin Goebbels and Bormann set themselves up as the official heads of the government and late in the day of 30 April entered into negotiations with the Russians. These negotiations were handled between General Krebs of the German General Staff and Colonel General Chuikov. All the documents which passed hands at that time were signed by Goebbels and Bormann in their 'acting capacity' as heads of the new government. Krebs made it perfectly clear to the Soviet commander that Hitler had committed suicide, and that the Nazi leaders were willing to enter into negotiations if the Soviets would honor a temporary cease-fire. At that point Chuikov, who had been given the official task of representing the Soviet High Command at the meetings, stated that the Russian troops were willing to honor a cease-fire only when Germany had surrendered unconditionally, not only to the Russians but to all the Allies. This move on Chuikov's part seemed to display that the Russian Command still believed at that time in a solid Allied front, paying little attention to the German leaders' ideas for a united American-German fight against the Russians. General Chuikov warned that unless a surrender took place immediately the Russians would have no alternative but to continue the attack, causing greater casualties among the populace of Berlin. He also played on the mood of the situation and hoped to gain a quick surrender by promising Krebs that the Soviets would take no retaliations against, and would guarantee personally, the safety of the civilian population. Gestures as had occurred in Stalingrad were as 'noble' . . . Military awards and personal affects, and even the swords of officers, could be retained by the German soldiers.

After a five-hour meeting between the two, Krebs reported to Goebbels and Bormann and relayed the conditions outlined by the Russians. More than four hours passed before the two

LEFT: Russian tanks thunder into Berlin after Hitler's bunker was taken.

BELOW LEFT: Tank crews crouch behind the turrets of their T-34/85s outside Berlin in the face of heavy artillery fire from within the city.

BELOW LEFT: Marshal Georgi Zhukov, conqueror of Berlin and Russia's greatest general, sports his numerous decorations which he won during the war. Once the war was over this genuine hero of the Soviet Union was placed increasingly in the background by Stalin.

BELOW: A German mother and her child try to catch some sleep in the Berlin underground. Thousands of German civilians took shelter in subways hundreds of feet below the surface until Hitler decided to flood them; many Germans were trapped in the deluge.

Nazi leaders gave their answer. They rejected the proposals put forth by Chuikov and decided to continue the battle. When he received the rejection, not only Chuikov but the entire Soviet Command was shocked, and the Russians had no course but to continue their assault.

On the morning of 2 May, even as Goebbels and Bormann gave orders for the German soldiers to die heroically, the German troops decided that they had had enough. They knew that the battle was hopelessly lost and the end had come for Germany. As Zhukov threw troops in for the final attack, German troops began to surrender en masse. General Weidling had taken charge of the situation, overruled Goebbels and Bormann, and asked Zhukov for a cease-fire. Zhukov's orders were

explicit; Weidling was to disarm his entire Corps by 0700, 2 May. This condition was met by 0600 and for the most part at that point the whole of the Berlin garrison emerged from the rubble and surrendered.

The two Nazi leaders found themselves in a desperate situation of their own making, knowing that the Russians would come for them at any time. Goebbels decided to commit suicide, and after 'quietly murdering' his wife and children, took his own life. Bormann somehow managed to vanish into thin air. His whereabouts and the

versions of his escape from Berlin are many and varied.

Although Berlin had been captured, the 1st Ukrainians' Front broke off from the southern flank of Berlin and continued to press the XII German Army, who were fighting to reach the Americans for surrender. The 2nd Belorussian Front throughout the entire Berlin Offensive had fought their way across the front's northernmost flank, and by 2 May had destroyed all German resistance through the Baltic region to the Elbe River.

With the Berlin operation complete

the Second World War in Europe was effectively at an end. German military and administrative functions ceased, and except for a few scattered pockets and isolated fronts, the German Army no longer existed.

Overall, from 16 April to 8 May the great Soviet Army had smashed no less than 90 German Divisions, taken over half a million prisoners, and captured tens of thousands of guns, tanks, and aircraft. This victory cost the Russians no less than 300,000 dead for those few weeks of fighting, and a total Russian loss of 25 million military and civilian

FAR LEFT: Russian troops show British soldiers the spot where Mr. and Mrs. Hitler's bodies were burned outside the bunker after they committed suicide on 30 April 1945.

LEFT: Marshal Zhukov initials the surrender terms in Berlin on 9 May 1945 after General Carl Spaatz, Air Chief Marshal Arthur Tedder and General Jean de Lattre de Tassigny signed the document

which ratified and extended the surrender signed by Eisenhower in Reims on 7 May. Field Marshal Wilhelm Keitel, Admiral Hans Georg von Friedeburg and Colonel General Paul Stumpff signed for Germany.

BELOW: A Soviet band marches down the Unter den Linden in Berlin to celebrate V-E Day.

BOTTOM: Stretchers carrying both wounded civilians and combatants line a Berlin street after the surrender.

deaths during the entire course of the Second World War.

The war was finally over and the Russian War Machine which had crumbled so disastrously in those early days of 1941; which had fought so desperately in Stalingrad in 1942; which advanced, fought and conquered so heroically in the great offensives of 1943 and 1944; and which crushed the Reich in 1945, stood as a force welded together by blood, courage and determination with its feet in the heartland of Germany. Though we in the West have been taught the heroism and courage of our struggle in the European Theater, it was the Russian War Machine which broke the Nazi backbone in Europe. And it was between the mighty Nazi and Soviet nations that 'Total War' had been fought.

BELOW: Russian soldiers raise the Red Flag above the Brandenburg Gate as a symbol of victory.

BOTTOM: Major General Walter Robertson, Commander of the Second Division, Third US Army, and General Ivan Alexandrovich Gorbachov of the Red Army review Russian troops in Pilsen, Czechoslovakia on 18 May 1945. The Russians liberated Prague while General S. Patton's Third Army freed Pilsen some 50 miles away. Patton's forces withdrew after the surrender, allowing the Soviets to occupy the whole of Czechoslovakia.

BELOW: A German soldier sits in front of the ruins of the Reichstag after the fall of Berlin to the Red Army.

THE WAR AGAINST JAPAN

After the Armistice at Nomonhan in September 1939 there was a slight improvement in Japanese-Russian relations. A Soviet ambassador was appointed to Japan, and a Border Commission was set up to settle the Nomonhan dispute. But by the spring of 1940 this brief honeymoon was fast losing its charm; the Border Commission had come to a complete deadlock since neither side would accept the accuracy of the maps produced by the other; the fishery dispute had arisen once more, and an argument was arising over the ownership of Sakhalin. But the events in Europe during the summer of 1940 made the Japanese look more closely at the advantages of friendship with Russia, and, moreover, a friendly Russia on the borders of Manchuria would be a useful insurance for the 'Strike South' policy. So the Japanese finally agreed to the Russian demarcation of the border at Nomonhan and began preparing the ground for a Japanese-Soviet Mutual Assistance Treaty. Then came a change of Japanese government and a policy which favored an alliance with Germany. Eventually Japan ratified the 'Triple Alliance' agreement with Germany and Italy and signed a Non-Aggression Pact with Russia.

The net result of these agreements was to bring about a peculiar state of affairs in the Far East. Hitler had assured Japan that in the event of his going to war with Russia, Germany would be victorious within a matter of months and he would not require any assistance from the Japanese; and the Japanese, mindful of their bloody nose at Nomonhan and shocked when Operation Barbarossa was launched, made no moves when the German attack began. The Soviets, for their part, were careful to adhere strictly to the terms of their neutrality pact with Japan so that they could devote their energy to dealing with Hitler and not worry about the Far Eastern front. A watchful neutrality was observed on the Manchurian border.

By 1945 the outward appearance was the same, but there were powerful forces at work behind the scenes. After the collapse of Germany and their own severe losses in Burma and the Pacific, the Japanese began to extend peace feelers to the Allies via Moscow. But the Yalta Conference had given Stalin South Sakhalin, the Kuriles, and valuable harbor and railroad concessions in Manchuria as well as influence in Korea in return for his agreement to attack Japan once the European war was over. And Stalin, for his part, had every intention of seizing as much of the Far Eastern territories of Japan as he could, irrespective of what he had been promised. His only fear was the possibility of a Japanese surrender before he could make his attack, a move which could prevent the Red Army from 'liberating' Manchuria, North Korea, North China, Inner Mongolia and anywhere else they could set foot.

Japan's peace proposals to Moscow were therefore given a cool reception, while planning went on at great speed. The Far Eastern Armies in early 1945 comprised two 'Fronts', the Trans-Baikal and the Far East, together mustering about 20 infantry divisions, two armored divisions, two mechanized cavalry divisions, twelve rifle brigades and eight independent tank brigades, supported by about 1500 aircraft. The quality of these troops was not high; they were mostly local enlistments and few had any battle experience. On the Japanese side there were 40 infantry divisions, 7 cavalry divisions, 23 infantry brigades, two cavalry brigades and two armored brigades distributed throughout Manchuria, Korea, South Sakhalin and the Kuriles. The great majority of this force was, of course, in Manchuria; just over a million men, supported by 1155 tanks, 5360 guns, 1800 aircraft and a river flotilla of 25 gunboats on the Sungari River. The quality of these troops also was low; these were not the veterans of the Kwantung Army of the 1930s, most of whom had been drafted to other theaters of war. The Kwantung Army of 1945 was composed of reserve divisions and training brigades of indifferent quality; they had limited stocks of munitions and fuel, and their tanks and aircraft were mostly obsolete models. Their numbers had been greatly depleted, and the million-man army comprised not more than 250,000 troops.

Once the decision was taken to attack Japan, the Far Eastern Armies were strengthened from inside Russia: by May there were 47 divisions, and the area was re-organized into three 'Fronts', the Trans-Baikal based on Chita, the 1st Far East based on Vladivostok, and the 2nd Far East based on Khabarovsk. Although this combined force was superior to the Japanese in

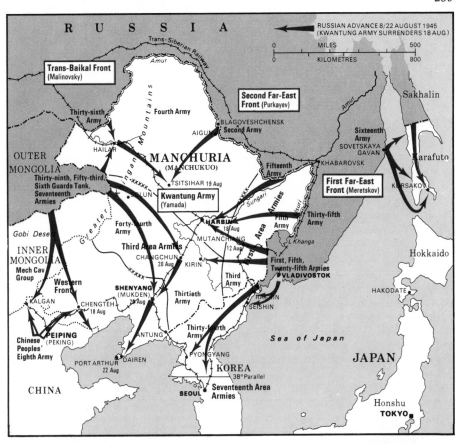

armor and aircraft and in the quality of its weapons, it was still inferior in numbers of men, so Stalin now ordered four of the most experienced and successful Soviet armies in the European theater to move to the Far East. The 5th and 39th Armies were withdrawn from East Prussia, and the 6th Guards Tank Army and 53rd Army were pulled out of Czechoslovakia. They were routed east over the Trans-Siberian railroad, a marathon of movement which occupied the line for three months. Meanwhile the tank factories east of the Urals were ordered to deliver their output directly to the Far East to await the arrival of the new formations. Had they taken their tanks with them, the move would probably have taken twice as long, and Stalin had told the British and Americans that he would be ready to attack in the latter half of August.

To control the operation an independent GHQ was set up under Marshal Vasilevsky, and Marshals Malinovsky and Meretskov were appointed to command the Trans-Baikal and 1st Far East Fronts respectively. The 2nd Far East Front was commanded by General Purkayev, who had, until then, been the Commander, Far East. There was a certain amount of discontent among the 'old Far East hands' when they found that most of the staffs and command positions were to be filled by men from the European zone, but Stalin was adamant; he wanted experienced combat commanders in all the vital places, because this operation had to go through on time.

The operational plan was extremely ambitious; the attack would be delivered in three principal directions so as to split the Japanese armies in Manchuria, isolate them one from the other, and then defeat them piecemeal. Malinovsky with the Trans-Baikal Front was to attack along the Chinese Eastern Railway line from Chita to Hailar, cross the Khingan Mountains and go for Tsitsihar and Harbin. Meretskov would attack from Vladivostok in the opposite direction, also heading for Harbin, with a subsidiary attack striking into North Korea to cut off the Japanese Army there. A third force, a component of the Trans-Baikal Front, would attack from Mongolia, across the center of Manchuria to Changchun, then turn south and secure Mukden and Port Arthur.

In addition to these principal thrusts,

a joint Soviet-Mongolian Mechanized Cavalry Group was to strike across the Gobi Desert to threaten Kalgan and Peking, while the 2nd Far East Front was to start from the northern border of Manchuria, at Blagoveschensk and Yermakovski, and strike south toward Tsitsihar and Harbin to link up with the main thrust. Thus the Japanese were to be chopped into little sections, contained and destroyed.

The Japanese, by this time, had few illusions about their chances of fighting the Soviet Army, at least with the kind of troops and equipment they had in Manchuria, and such operational plans as they had provided for a retreat from the northern and central areas to a prepared position in the mountains on the Korean border. Their principal hopes lay in the natural barrier of the Great Khingan Mountains which formed their western boundary with Mongolia and ran across the western end of northern Manchuria. This barren and rocky range, with peaks up to 5300 feet high, was crossed by three passes, the Shedyn which carried the Chinese Eastern Railway and the main road between Hailar and Tsitsihar, and the Tarshi and Zugan passes which carried secondary roads which were slightly better than farm tracks. North of the Shedyn Pass there was no way for any form of vehicle to cross the mountain range. Consequently the principal Japanese defenses were to the east of the mountains, with roadblocks in the passes, and little more than a frontier screening force on the western side.

The border with the Siberian Mari-

time Province, close to Vladivostok, was heavily fortified with concrete defensive works and was, apparently, a formidable line. Throughout the remainder of the country there were fortifications defending vulnerable points such as rail junctions and airfields, but there was no cohesive defended line between Tsitsihar in the north and the Muling-Hunchun line on the eastern boundary.

By the beginning of August all was ready. Some 76 Soviet and four Mongolian divisions, four tank corps, five independent infantry brigades, 24 independent tank brigades, 26,000 guns and mortars, 5500 tanks and assault guns, 3900 aircraft and a million and a half men, all ready to roll into Manchuria in the third week in August. Meanwhile the Soviet Government was pursuing some political maneuvers with the Chinese Nationalist Government in order to get them to accede to the forthcoming Soviet concessions in Manchuria and come to some agreement about postwar Soviet occupation of Port Arthur. Once agreement was secured on these matters, Stalin said, the Soviet Union would declare war on Japan and the armies would move.

But other events were in train which were not waiting for Stalin's approval. On 6 August the first atomic bomb was dropped on Hiroshima, and on 9 August the second was dropped on Nagasaki. After the first bomb Stalin realized that the Japanese were more than likely to surrender forthwith, which would cut the ground from under his feet and leave him with no excuse to attack and, more seriously, no spoils of war. Orders were sent post haste, and on the 8th the Red Army crossed the Manchurian border.

The speed of the Soviet advance temporarily paralyzed the Japanese. Malinovsky's tank armada roared for the Khingan passes, by-passing Hailar and leaving a blockading force to contain the Japanese garrison there. By the morning of the 11th the tank columns were at the passes, brushed aside the weak Japanese blocks, and rolled down the eastern slopes into the plain, driving the retreating Japanese before them. Their advance was so fast that they outran their fuel columns, and a hurried resupply was organized by air, thousands of gallons of diesel fuel being flown in to hastily prepared strips alongside the axis of the advance. Behind the tanks came the motorized infantry, mopping up isolated pockets of resistance and occupying the by-passed towns and villages.

When the Japanese finally pulled themselves together it was to react in a disorganized fashion. The General Staff in Tokyo, when they heard of the attack (for the Soviet Ambassador in Tokyo did not deliver a formal declaration of war until 1115 on the 10th), immediately ordered the armies in Manchuria to 'concentrate in order to defend the Japanese territory of Korea', but this aim was forestalled by the rapid advance of the Soviet 34th Army into northern Korea. Near Changchun the Japanese 44th Army Group began a counter-attack against the southern prong of the Trans-Baikal Army's attack, which was at first encouraged and stopped by the Kwantung Army Commander, a change of heart which confused his staff and hindered further operations.

On the Eastern border, the 1st Far East Front under Meretskov found the going harder than had Malinovsky, since the Soviets were attacking into the teeth of a prepared fortified line of considerable depth, and even indifferent troops can make a good defense when manning well-designed fortifications. Meretskov's initial assault was intended to be an intense artillery bombardment followed up by a night attack in which searchlights would be used to dazzle and blind the defenders. At this point the weather took a hand and the eastern sector vanished under a torrential rainstorm, ruining the idea of using searchlights. Meretskov therefore cancelled the whole plan and launched an infantry attack unsupported by artillery, relying on the rain to conceal his men and confuse the defenders. This attacking force was sent out in small groups to infiltrate through the defensive lines, avoiding strongpoints, to concentrate on attacking headquarters, communications and reserves. Fifteen divisions went in, and within 48 hours the defensive line was cut through. The 1st Far East Front was in possession of Muling, well behind the fortified line.

The advance continued on the planned lines but was checked by strong resistance by the 1st Japanese Army Group outside Moutankiang. While the main thrust was held there a secondary thrust bypassed the area and headed for Kirin. The following day saw an end to the rain and the Soviet Air Force mounted a series of heavy strikes on the 1st Japanese Army. Meretskov's armor now came up, Moutankiang fell, and, free of the mountainous defended zone the armored columns roared off for Kirin and Harbin and their meeting with Malinovsky's troops.

The 2nd Far East Front had moved at the same time as the others, but, as Stalin had foreseen, being less experienced troops their advance was slow and cautious. Nevertheless, they crossed the Amur River, contained the Japanese border garrisons and pushed down to the main axis. Meanwhile the second element of the Trans-Baikal Front had crossed the Khingan mountains at its southern end—having left Mongolian soil not far from the Nomonhan sector—and, splitting into two thrusts, had swooped across the plain aiming to take Changchun and Mukden. The most remarkable maneuver of all was also proceeding well; General Pliev was leading the Soviet-Mongolian Cavalry Army across the featureless waste of the Gobi Desert toward North China.

On 14 August the Japanese government announced its formal surrender. The staff of 3rd Japanese Army, the principal force in Manchuria, ordered a general cease-fire forthwith, but the Kwantung Army HQ rescinded it, a sequence which caused more confusion. The Commanding General in Manchuria, Yamada, refused to order a surrender until he had written instructions, which eventually arrived on the 17th. On the 18th Yamada's Chief of Staff flew to Marshal Vasilevsky's HQ and a surrender was quickly negotiated and signed.

During this period of indecision and confusion on the Japanese side there was absolutely no indecision or confusion in the Soviet ranks. Vasilevsky had rounded up all the transport aircraft he could find, loaded them with reserve troops (mainly engineers) and a leavening of paratroops, and ordered them off to the main centers of Manchuria. The paratroops dropped and secured landing grounds, whereupon the aircraft landed and disembarked the troops to occupy airfields and other important targets in Mukden, Changchun, Dairen, Port Arthur, Fushun and Antung. Having done this the transports returned to Russian airfields, loaded up with drums of diesel fuel, and once again resupplied Malinovsky's tanks ready for their run south. By 20 August Mukden was taken, and by the 22nd Port Arthur was once more in Russian hands. General Pliev's cavalry force appeared from the Gobi Desert and moved north to link up with the Trans-Baikal force and with the Chinese Communist 8th Route Army, while General Chistyakov's 34th Army occupied Korea down to the 38th Parallel. Soviet forces were also occupying Southern Sakhalin and the Kuriles.

On 23 August Stalin issued an Order of the Day which marked the official end of operations in Manchuria. He also delivered a stirring piece of rhetoric; 'For forty years we, the men of the old generation, have waited for this day and now the day has finally come'. Coming from a man who had hailed the Tsar's defeat at Port Arthur in 1904 as a victory for the revolutionary movement, this sounded a trifle meretricious. Times had changed.

Although the Order of the Day ended the fighting, it didn't help the Kwantung Army very much; nor did it help the people of Manchuria. For the Soviets now began the most blatant act of exploitation ever seen in history. In the first place the entire Japanese Army in Manchuria, Korea, North China, Sakhalin and the Kuriles was rounded up, disarmed, and marched off to forced labor camps in Siberia, from which few ever returned. Then the country was systematically stripped bare of all factories, workshops and industrial plant, trainloads of booty being transported into Siberia until little was left of the commercial, agricultural and industrial complex the Japanese had

built up in the 1930s. Officially the Soviets were supposed to leave Manchuria by 2 December 1945, but on one pretext or another they remained there until 31 May 1946, by which time the Chinese Communist Army had infiltrated some of the territory.

All in all the Manchurian Campaign was less a feat of arms than a masterpiece of organization which belied the prevailing Western belief that the Red Army was strong in the arm and weak in the head. Vasilevsky's control of such widely dispersed forces was faultless. Malinovsky displayed a splendid aptitude for improvization to meet changing circumstances, when he hastily organized air supply of tank fuel and equally quickly deployed airborne troops to take advantage of the Japanese indecision. Pliev's march across the Gobi is a little-known triumph of organization when one contemplates the nature of the obstacle. The Far Eastern Armies conquered an area of 600,000 square miles, an area bigger than France, Spain, Germany and the Low Countries put together, in just 24 days. It was an operation which made Hitler's Blitzkrieg look like a horse-and-cart operation.

CONCLUSION

The war in Europe was over and with the last of the German troops surrendering in Czechoslovakia Russia heaved a sigh of relief knowing that the great struggle was at an end. Since June 1941 Total War had existed between the two countries. It was not merely a war of soldiers, tanks, and aeroplanes, nor of battles won and lost, but a conflict between two ideologies—Fascism and Communism—which could not co-exist.

Although Russia had turned the tide and was on the road to victory by 1943, what had that victory cost? Over 70,000 towns and villages were completely laid waste. Tens of thousands of new industrial projects were totally and irrecoverably destroyed. It can only be estimated how many Russians, soldiers and civilians as well, died on that Eastern Front. It is fairly certain that at least 25 million were killed. All documents point to the fact that nearly 12 percent of the total Soviet population

was eliminated. Where agricultural goods were concerned, Russia survived through the food supplies sent by the United States. Even after Soviet troops had liberated the Ukraine, millions upon millions of acres of farmland destroyed in the war would take years to return to profitability. The war had drained Russian manpower of its vital working force. To free men for the front, women had taken their places in the factories at a staggering figure of 51 percent of the work force. The other 49 percent of the working class was made up primarily of the elderly and the young, a labor force which remained relatively unchanged for several years after the war.

Total War had brought other wounds to the Russian people in its wake. The partisans, who had given so much to the war effort became, in many cases, enemies of the State, and as such suffered the penalties of death and imprisonment. Liberated areas, having

survived the purges of the Nazi invaders, were forced to pay retribution in the face of what the Soviets deemed collusion with the enemy. In the wake of wholesale slaughter the question of prisoners demanded attention. Well over five million Russians had been captured by the Germans, but after liberation only a few hundred thousand were repatriated. As if the torture, deprivation and execution at the hands of the Germans were not enough to have been endured by those troops captured in the early days of 1941 and 1942, they faced new suffering upon returning to the Soviet Union. The NKVD, the Soviet Secret Police, screened all prisoners as they were returned, and many were found guilty of treason for failing to fight to the death in 1941. Various other crimes, usually grouped under the heading of treason, sent a vast majority of the returning prisoners to slave labor camps throughout Russia, most notably those

in Siberia. As for the German prisoners, Stalin looked upon the German soldiers as an immense supplement to his manpower shortage, and used many of the Russian-held prisoners as slave labor for the giant reconstruction needs of the Soviet Union. Of those soldiers, hundreds of thousands never saw their homelands, and those few who were released returned after more than ten years imprisonment.

The Soviet Union did not fail to strip Germany of what food and cattle could be found, and under the heading of 'war booty' even went so far as to disassemble complete German factories, shipping them back to Russia. Stalin still found time in late June 1945 to hold a spectacular military parade in Moscow. Units from each of the Army Fronts, with their Generals and Marshals, paraded across Red Square, in front of Stalin and his Deputy Supreme Commander Marshal Zhukov. In that bizarre parade not only were the Rus-

sian troops turned out draped in their medals and ceremonial swords, but they carried the symbols and standards of the defeated Wehrmacht. In a display of triumph they threw these 'momentos' at Stalin's feet. For Stalin this not only symbolized his victory over Germany, but Russia's dominance as the leading power of Europe.

Although Stalin's power was to be seen by all, the actual might of the Russian Army was indeed a question in those closing days. It must be remembered that it was the Soviet Army which felled the death blow on Nazi Germany, and that although the Allies fought their way across Europe into Germany, they never faced the same onslaught of all-out destruction experienced on that Eastern Front. However, by those first days of May 1945 Russian troops were finding themselves at the end of their tether. The Soviet Union had had enormous resources and were able to evacuate many of their industries at the

BELOW: Marshal Koniev, commander of Russian forces in the Ukraine and subsequently one of the conquerors of Berlin, welcomes US General Omar Bradley in a postwar victory party held at Koniev's headquarters.

beginning of the war, but they found themselves unable to support their armies. At the Battle of Berlin Russian troops were burdened with useless vehicles as petrol became scarce at the front. Several incidents occurred where triumphant Russian soldiers entered Berlin on tanks drawn by horses. Supplies destined for the troops were constantly delayed as the vehicles in convoy heading for the front broke down through fatigue and lack of fuel. When Roosevelt died in April 1945 and was succeeded by Truman, Lend-Lease deliveries to all recipient nations, including those headed for the Soviet Union and Britain, were halted. This not only put the Soviets, whose whole economy had been eaten away by the war, in bad straits, but made a clear statement to the Allied Powers: although Japan still had to be defeated, America considered her wartime alliances at an end. Any type of support or assistance given to any country in the

future would be handled by the new American leaders in a businesslike and efficient manner, not on the sympathetic basis of destruction of the common enemy.

With the ending of the war in Europe not only Germany but all of Europe found itself at the mercy of the two Super-Powers. The United States and Russia slowly reached a settlement, one which would bring a conclusion to the war in the traditional sense of demanding satisfaction from the vanquished. In Soviet opinion it had to be a settlement which secured its borders and its economic and political interests in Europe from that day forward. In spite of the crushing defeat levied against Germany, Stalin still greatly feared German potential. He felt that he had to keep Germany in a decimated state so that another war would never again recur. It was decided at Yalta and Potsdam the course which would be taken in Germany. But it was clearly

seen by Churchill, at least, that in 1944 when Russia had begun its offensive sweep into the Baltic and Eastern Europe, wherever Russian troops would be able to hold territory, the Soviet sphere of influence would follow.

Toward that end the Soviet Union had to accomplish several things. First, they wanted to secure their boundaries. Secondly and most importantly, the war had been the flame that tempered and shaped the Russian people and Army into one of the greatest forces ever seen. This feeling needed to be kindled and rekindled in the Soviet peoples. Through that unity the Soviets would be able to spread their spheres of influence over the states of Eastern Europe.

Eastern Europe, under the so-called liberation by the Soviet Army, was open for the Communist Party to forge ahead rapidly. With the aid of sympathizers within those countries, Russia was able to turn those states into satellite nations whose economic and political basis would be linked to Mother Russia.

Every war leaves a legacy. The conclusion of the First World War and the Treaty of Versailles left Europe in a position whereby the defeated nations, the Central Powers, mainly Germany, would, when given the chance, right the wrongs done against them by the Allies. The mishandling of the conclusion of 'the war to end all wars' was merely another example of how war breeds war. The culmination of the Second World War produced an analogous situation, caused not by major treaty arrangements, but through agreements reached during the war. The primary result of those agreements was the division of Germany into equal sectors among the three Allies. What originally was to be a division for administrative purposes only evolved into a divided Germany whose beliefs and economic and political aims are as different as night and day and whose soil is the confrontation ground between East and West.

In the sectioning of the country the Allies went so far as to segment Berlin itself, dividing it among the same Allied Powers for the same purpose. Today of course, it is not only divided by differences of belief but by the Wall, which stands as an infamous memorial to the distrust and failures of the postwar reconstruction era. Similarly Austria was divided, and although reunified, her neutrality is a pawn to the whims of Moscow.

East Germany was not the only country to fall under the Soviet thumb after the war: Poland, Czechoslovakia, Hungary, Rumania, Bulgaria, Albania and Yugoslavia succumbed to the postwar dependency on the Soviet Union. Today, except for Yugoslavia and Albania, who broke their dependency upon Russia, these nations of the Warsaw Pact—or Iron Curtain Nations as they are known in the West—bear witness to the Soviet power, domination and influence which has been maintained since the end of the war. A new legacy of war, the Cold War, had come into being.

The Cold War doctrine is quite simple to define. In opposite camps are the pro-Western Capitalist bloc, opposed by nations in the Communist or Soviet Bloc. The Cold War is and has been nothing more than the reaction to imperialistic advances made by the Soviet Union to establish a domain of economic and political influence, something that the Western Powers had done for nearly 300 years prior to the 20th century. Unlike Russia at the end of World War II, the Western nations found themselves at the end of their expansionist period.

The Cold War between the West and Russia over the past thirty years has brought the Russian War Machine to a level of parity in terms of Western technology on the battlefield if not economic strength. Ironically the West has found itself like the elephant stamping on ants. Although it can stop thousands, there are thousands more. Instead of carrying its role as the protector of democracy, America has been cunningly maneuvered out of the good graces of many people of the world by a versatile opponent whose policies have expanded her influence.

In the light of the 'post-1970' Russian activity, a look at the Soviet Armed Forces of today must be taken to decide the strength, weaknesses, potential, and direction of the modern Russian War Machine. The Soviet armed forces at the end of the Second World War, although they were immense, had learned their military lessons well from the Germans. Although they must be credited with the defeat of Germany and the winning of the war in Europe, they were not the fearsome giants which many believed at the time. True, the Russian Army was probably the largest and most experienced by the end of the war, but

Total War with Germany had stripped the Russian War Machine of the natural wealth and resources which would have allowed it to carry out war further. The Soviets knew that it would take many years to put themselves back on their feet on a military basis. Consideration also had to be given to the natural resources and food production means of their country, for although there was no longer a war, the Russians were developing an 'empire' which rapidly drained those resources.

The Russian Air Force, when compared to the United States at the conclusion of the war, was basically its equal in terms of size. The quality of that Air Force fell behind that of the Western World. The Russian Navy was still traditionally locked in the Baltic and Black Seas, and throughout the war had not managed to show much initiative or give the Soviets much support. The major problem within the Russian Army at the end of the war was its inability to continue due to the economic exhaustion of the Soviet Union. The expansionist process which alarmed the West immediately after the war was largely impossible for Russia to carry out.

From 1945 to the 1970s Russia was committed to a policy of strengthening her economic power and political influence, not actively involving her army in a conflict. However, she supplied the necessities of war to others—for a 'price' —and reaped the technical and military lessons gained through watching others wage war. The equipment of the Soviet Army during that time was basically Second World War matériel which had been updated. One of the examples of this is the 120mm mortar used by Russia throughout its campaign against Germany. This mortar is today a standard weapon, and a very effective one. Another weapon commonly used through the Second World War was the rocket. Those surface-to-surface, multi-round rockets and launchers have not only been the backbone of many guerrilla campaigns but are still found as integral parts of the Army's battlefield bombardment arsenal.

Tank development over the years has continued, but ever since the construction of the T-34, Soviet armor has been designed for simplicity and reliability, a trait which has remained up to the present generation of tanks.

Aircraft have also kept to this theme,

and though the technology is not as far advanced in the West, as in the Phantom, Jaguar and Mirage models, Soviet fighters, when placed in the hands of skilled pilots, are equally effective.

Although the quality may not always have been in the Soviets' favor, numbers have. Assuming that the quality of the Soviet forces and equipment had not been drastically different from the Western Powers, what has stopped the confrontation which so many believed was always just around the corner? The Russian economy until recently would not have been capable of supporting such open confrontation. Equally important has been the fact that the West has always maintained a superiority, until the 1970s, in the ability to deliver nuclear weapons. Although the nuclear arms race was fearsome, since the limitation talks the arsenals for both countries since 1970 have been relatively equalized. Open conflict involving those weapons had deterred both sides from pushing the other into a situation where this type of war became imminent.

Therefore, for a number of years the Russian War Machine found itself in a position where it played minor countries off against the West, yet avoided actual armed conflict with its major opponent, the United States.

As the 1970s rolled around a change of opinion has led many to believe that we have entered into a new era for the Soviet Army. Through the various conflicts which have been fought between clients of both East and West, the Russians have managed to catch up with the Western Powers' technology, ironically through the capture of US weapons. The wide range of Russian weaponry has for the most part taken on a new identity, and the Soviet Army now leads the West in several fields, rather than lagging behind as they had done for so many years. Simplicity has always been the key to Soviet weapons development, and they can now boast of an armed force where simplicity and effectiveness are its major assets. Numbers have always been the Soviet strong point, and over the years through a strong pro-military budgeting and non-involvement in open combat, Russia has been able to evolve its Army into a giant fighting force which has rarely been equalled.

Another factor, and perhaps the most important, is that Russia has been

able to create a navy which rivals that of all the Western nations. Their development in surface-to-air missiles and surface-to-surface missiles is considered a force to be reckoned with. In all major aspects Russia now sits in a position where it no longer need play second fiddle to the West. She is a main contender for the top world position.

Laying aside the emotional and psychological effects of the new Russian War Machine, the actual statistics of the strength of the Soviet forces is tremendous. A study conducted by the Institute for Strategic Studies in London for the 1975–76 period showed that of the total Russian population of more than 250 million, its armed forces numbered more than 3.5 million. From a Gross National Product of 469 billion roubles in 1974, the Soviet defense expenditures were 238 billion roubles Through such budgeting in 1974–75 the Soviets increased their ICBM force by at least 40 over the previous year, in both single and multi-warhead models. The power of its submarine fleet was increased by the combined power of some 784 ballistic missiles. Several new nuclear ballistic missile carrying submarines have gone into production; and construction of a new, longer version D class submarine has been started, which can carry 16 5000-mile range submarine-launched ballistic missiles. During that same time a new supersonic bomber was deployed, and a new surface-to-surface air missile was under development. This missile is reported to have an 800 km stand-off range. The 1974–75 period also brought the continued production of a new tank model, new APCs, a self-propelled howitzer, a new tactical SAM system.

In addition to all of this the Soviets still maintained a long-range air force of 800 combat aircraft; an interceptor force of 2500; and no less than 12,000 missile and aircraft launching site in approximately 1600 different areas throughout their air defense zones.

The Army itself, which consists of no less than three million men, is deployed in 49 Tank Divisions, 110 Rifle Divisions, and 7 Airborne Divisions. These troops are located in the areas of Central and Eastern Europe, which have no less than 31 Divisions; European Russia with 63 Divisions; Central and Southern Russia with 29 Divisions; and the Sino-Soviet border forces number roughly 43 Divisions. The Navy now possesses 236 major surface combat ships and 265 attack and cruise submarines. Of those subs, at least 75 are nuclear-powered. These forces are divided among the four Soviet Fleets: The Northern Fleet, the Baltic Fleet, the Black Sea Fleet, and the Pacific Fleet. The Air Force with its 5000 combat aircraft, divided into classes of long-range, interceptors and air transport, are stationed with its 16 Air Armies, four in Eastern Europe and one each in the military districts of Russia.

With the new Russian War Machine being developed and disunity rife among the Western nations, Russia has entered into an era where its policies no longer need take place under the guise of fomenting revolution against capitalist imperialism through the smaller nations in limited confrontations with the West. It has reached the proportions where East and West must agree to decide policies concerning the future of world peace. There was a time when Russian policy could not be dictated by its war machine, but this is no longer so. Through appeasement, détente, division, the Western World is finding itself in a position where it must struggle to maintain its strength to counter that of the Soviet Union. It is to this end that the Russian War Machine, frail and weak in its creation as the Red Army during the Revolution, has been molded, built and strengthened throughout the period since the end of World War II.

Although détente and such agreements as the SALT talks have relieved the minds of many Western people and lent evidence to the opinion that the Russian War Machine is being brought under control of the non-Communist world, it should not be forgotten that it stands more awesome than ever on the frontier of Western Europe. Soviet areas of influence continue to spread, and as the Russian War Machine becomes as technologically capable as any Western Power or combination of Powers, a time of reckoning becomes more inevitable. The Russian War Machine, born in Revolution and Civil War, and forged in World War II as a force as hard as steel, has continued to expand since 1945. Its dynamism, growing in confidence through hard-won victories and grievous sacrifice, continues to reach out for new worlds to conquer. Its self-confidence has never faltered. The world waits to see if the modern Russian War Machine will be tested in the frightening and awesome context of the atomic age.

BELOW: Early 1945
Soviet poster, showing
the Red juggernaut in
defiance against the
forces of capitalism. Note
the caricatures of
Churchill, Franco and
Roosevelt. Elements of
Cold War propaganda
were already in evidence
even before the Axis was
defeated.

OVERLEAF: Sorrow.
Russian peasant women
mourn their dead. The
Soviet Union lost some
25 million soldiers and
civilians in World War
II, the greatest human
sacrifice of any nation
which participated in
the war.

ACKNOWLEDGEMENTS

The editor would like to thank the following people for their help in preparing this book: Helen Downton for her technical illustrations; Jinbo Terushi for his two illustrations which appear on page 156; Masami Tokoi for allowing us to use photographic material from his private collection; Ian Hogg for providing additional illustrative material; and Arlene Pataky for her design assistance. Richard Natkiel of *The Economist* prepared all the maps. David Eldred designed this book.

Robert Hunt Library: 1, 2–3, 7 (all 3), 8, 9 (both), 10, 11, 13 (both) 14 (both), 16, 17, 18 (right), 19 (bottom), 24 (top left), 32 (right), 33, 34 (left), 35 37, 38–9, 39, 40, 41 (both), 42–3, 45, 52–3, 65 (both), 66, 67 (top), 68–9, 71, 72, 73 (both), 75, 76, 76–7, 79, 80–81, 81 (right), 84–5, 85 (both), 86, 88, 89 (both), 91, 91–2, 92, 94 (left), 96 (right), 99, 102 (both), 102–3, 103 (below), 104 (bottom), 105 (all 3), 106, 107 (both), 108 110–11, 111 (both), 112 (bottom), 114 (both), 114–15, 115 (both), 116, 117 (both), 118 (2), 118–19, 120 (bottom), 122 (3), 123 (both), 124 (bottom), 125 (below left), 126 (3), 127 (both),

128 (both), 129 (top), 130, 130–31, 131, 132, 133 (all 5), 154–5, 155 (both), 156, 158 (2), 158–9, 160, 166, 176, 178–9, 182 (2), 183 (top), 184 (both), 185 (both), 186, 191, 192–3, 193, 194, 195 (bottom), 196, 196–7, 197 (center), 199, 201 (top 2), 202, 202–3, 203, 204–5, 205 (2), 206, 207 (3), 210 (top), 212 (both), 214, 214–15, 215 (left), 217 (all 3), 218 (both), 220 (top), 222, 222–3 (below), 227 (bottom), 231 (top), 232, 233 (left), 234 (both), 236, 243, 245, 248, 251, back jacket.

Novosti Press Agency: 4–5, 12, 14–15, 18 (left), 19 (top), 20–21, 26 (bottom), 44 (top), 50

(bottom), 59 (bottom), 67 (bottom), 106–7, 112 (top), 129 (bottom), 135 (top), 140, 141 (center), 142, 142–3, 143 (both), 144 (both), 148, 149, 150 (top), 151 (2), 162, 165, 167 (top), 174, 175 (top 2), 179, 181, 183 (bottom), 187, 195 (top), 197 (top), 198, 201 (bottom), 204, 211 (bottom), 213, 215 (right), 216 (top), 219, 220–21, 221, 222–3 (top), 224 (bottom), 227 (bottom), 231 (bottom), 232–3, 234–5, 235, 237, 242–3, 246–7, 252–3, front jacket.

Imperial War Museum: 15, 113, 134–5, 137 (both), 138–9, 141 (bottom), 145, 147 (both), 148, 148–9, 151 (top), 152 (2), 153 (top), 156–7, 167 (bottom), 175 (bottom), 205 (top), 209 (bottom), 210 (bottom), 236–7, 244, 250

Bison Picture Library: 6–7, 22 (both), 23 (both), 24 (3), 25 (all 3), 28 (both), 29 (all 3), 30–31, 31, 32 (left), 34 (right), 36, 82 (both), 83, 86–7 (both), 87, 90 (both), 91, 94 (3), 95, 120 (2), 121

(both). 124 (top), 125 (3), 161, 173 (both), 176, 209 (top), 211 (top), 220 (below), 224 (top), 225, 228–9, 233 (right).

Radio Times Hulton Picture Library: 26 (top), 26–7, 27, 69.

Bundesarchiv: 30–31 (bottom), 42 (both), 43 (bottom), 81 (left), 82–3, 84, 86–7 (bottom), 88–9, 90 (top), 90–91, 92 (top), 96 (left), 96–7, 97 (both), 98 (both), 100, 100–101 (both), 101 (all 3), 103 (top), 104 (top), 108–9, 122 (top right), 126 (center left), 135 (center), 162–3, 168 (both), 169, 171, 172–3, 181 (center), 184–5.

Courtesy of Ian V. Hogg: 43 (top 2), 44 (center), 46 (2), 47 (top), 51 (both), 55 (2), 57 (all 3), 58, 59 (top), 60–61, 62–3 (2), 118 (left), 177, 216 (bottom), 241, 242.

Courtesy of Masami Tokoi: 44 (top center, bottom 3), 46–7, 47, 48 (all 6), 49, 50 (top), 54–5, 55 (2), 59 (center), 178, 188 (2), 188–9, 189, 190.

Mainichi Newspaper Company: 69 (top right), 70